Dynamics of Media Politics

Broadcast and Electronic Media in Western Europe

edited by
Karen Siune and Wolfgang Truetzschler
for the
EUROMEDIA RESEARCH GROUP

SAGE Publications
London · Newbury Park · New Delhi

First published 1992

 SAGE Publications Ltd
6 Bonhill Street
London EC2A 4PU

SAGE Publications Inc
2455 Teller Road
Newbury Park, California 91320

SAGE Publications India Pvt Ltd
32, M-Block Market
Greater Kailash – I
New Delhi 110 048

British Library Cataloguing in Publication data

Dynamics of media politics. – (Communications in
society)
  I. Siune, Karen II. Truetzschler, Wolfgang
III. Series
302.23094

  ISBN 0–8039–8573–8
  ISBN 0–8039–8574–6 pbk

Library of Congress catalog card number 91–50842

Typeset by Photoprint, Torquay
Printed in Great Britain by Biddles Ltd, Guildford, Surrey

Contents

Foreword

This book and its companion volume *The Media in Western Europe* constitute two further results of the attempt by the Euromedia Research Group (ERG) to reach an understanding of current developments in relation to policy for the electronic and broadcast media in Western Europe. These publications follow on from the two 1986 books by the ERG: *New Media Politics* and *Electronic Media Policy in Western Europe*.

The Euromedia Research Group is a network of media social scientists from seventeen Western European countries who have been engaged, since 1982, in the review and analysis of policy and structure developments relating to electronic and broadcast mass media. We meet on a regular basis in working conferences in different European countries under the convenorship of Karen Siune. Our research does not receive any central funding and relies primarily on the resources of the individual members and their employing institutions. However, over the last few years we have received support from national institutions and public and private broadcasting companies, as well as other sectors of the communications industry in general. We would like to take this opportunity to convey our group's gratitude to all the numerous organizations who have supported our meetings in the past.

All chapters in this book were discussed at meetings of our group, some more than others and some over a period of a few years. While the division of responsibility for the different parts of the book is reflected in the authorship listed for the various chapters, all members of the group have contributed towards this book. Without representatives from all the countries we include in our analysis, the book would not have been the same.

In the book we have endeavoured to provide a comparative and integrative analysis of the processes of change in European media in the early 1990s, rather than a country-by-country assessment of events in individual countries. The latter can be found in our companion volume. Although specific details in individual countries may change from month to month, the information contained in the book should be correct, unless otherwise indicated, as of June 1991.

Editing manuscripts from all over Europe is not the easiest of tasks and would not have been possible without the help of all contributors and those members of the group who provided the necessary information for this book, often at very short notice. Thanks are also due to the University of Aarhus and the Dublin Institute of Technology (College of Commerce), which provided us with the facilities to complete the editing of this book. Finally we would like to express our gratitude to Denis McQuail, whose ideas and comments were invaluable and instrumental in bringing this project to a successful realization.

Karen Siune and Wolfgang Truetzschler
on behalf of the Euromedia Research Group

References

Euromedia Research Group (edited by Denis McQuail and Karen Siune) (1986) *New Media Politics: Comparative Perspectives in Western Europe*. London: Sage Publications.

Euromedia Research Group (1992) *The Media in Western Europe: The Euromedia Handbook*. London: Sage Publications.

Kleinsteuber, H., McQuail, D. and Siune, K. (eds) (1986) *Electronic Media and Politics in Western Europe: Euromedia Research Group Handbook of National Systems*. Frankfurt/New York: Campus Verlag.

Members of the Euromedia Research Group

- Marit Bakke, researcher with the Audience Research Department of the Norwegian Broadcasting Corporation (NRK).

Kees Brants, lecturer at the Department of Communications, University of Amsterdam, Netherlands.

Els De Bens, professor at the Department of Communications, University of Gent, Belgium.

Panayote Dimitras, assistant professor of political science at the Department of Economics, Athens University of Economics and Business (ASOEE), Greece.

Hans Fabris, professor and head of the Department of Communications, University of Salzburg, Austria.

Mario Hirsch, journalist, teacher and researcher on economic and policy aspects of mass media, Luxembourg.

- Olof Hultén, lecturer in communications at the University of Gothenburg and member of the strategic planning group in the Swedish Television Company.

Mary Kelly, lecturer in the Department of Sociology, University College Dublin, Ireland.

Hans J. Kleinsteuber, professor at the Institute of Political Science, University of Hamburg, Germany.

Denis McQuail, professor of mass communication, University of Amsterdam, the Netherlands.

Rosario de Mateo, lecturer at the Facultat de Ciences de la Informacio, Universitat Autonoma, Barcelona, Spain.

Gianpietro Mazzoleni, professor of the sociology of communications, University of Salerno, Italy.

Werner A. Meier, media consultant and lecturer, Seminar für Pubizistikwissenschaft der Universität Zürich, Switzerland.

- Helge Østbye, senior lecturer, University of Bergen, Norway.
- Bernt Stubbe Østergaard, managing director of Telsam Gruppen, Copenhagen, Denmark.

Michael Palmer, professor of communications, Sorbonne University III, Paris, France.

Vibeke G. Petersen, head of section, General Directorate of the P&T, Copenhagen, Denmark.

Ulrich Saxer, professor, Seminar für Publizistikwissenschaft der Universität Zürich, Switzerland.

Karen Siune, professor at the Institute of Political Science, University of Aarhus, Denmark.

Claude Sorbets, research director at the University of Bordeaux, France.

Helena Tapper, researcher and lecturer at the Department of Communications, University of Helsinki, Finland.

Josef Trappel, researcher and lecturer in the Department of Communications, University of Salzburg, Austria.

Wolfgang Truetzschler, lecturer at the Department of Communications, Dublin Institute of Technology (College of Commerce), Ireland.

Jeremy Tunstall, professor of sociology, City University, London, UK.

Abbreviations

A3R	Antena 3 de Radio (Spain)
A2	Antenne 2 (France)
ACT	Association for Commercial Television
AEA	American Electronics Association
ARD	Arbeitsgemeinschaft der öffentlich-rechtlichten Rundfunkanstalten der Bundesrepublik Deutschland (Germany)
BBC	British Broadcasting Corporation (UK)
BRT	Belgische Radio en Televisie – Nederlandse Uitzendingen (Belgium)
BSB	British Satellite Broadcasting
BT	British Telecom (UK)
CCIR	International Radio Consultative Committee
CCITT	International Telegraph and Telephone Consultative Committee
CEPT	Conference of European Post and Telecommunications Administrations
CLT	Compagnie Luxembourgeoise de Télédiffusion (Luxembourg)
CNN	Cable News Network (US)
CoE	Council of Europe
CPF	Canal Plus (France)
CSA	Conseil Supérieur de l'Audiovisuel
DBS	Direct broadcasting by satellite
DR	Danmarks Radio (Denmark)
EAT	European Advertising Tripartite
EBC	European Business Channel
EBU	European Broadcasting Union
EC	European Community
ECS	European Communication Satellite
ERT	Ellinki Radiophonia Tileorassi (Greece)
ESA	European Space Agency
Eutelsat	European Telecommunications Satellite Organization
FCC	Federal Communications Commission (USA)
HDTV	High definition television
IBA	Independent Broadcasting Authority (UK)
IFRB	International Frequency Registration Board
ILR	Independent Local Radio (UK)
INR	Independent National Radio (UK)
ITC	Independent Television Commission (UK)
ITU	International Telecommunication Union
ISDN	Integrated Services Digital Network
ITV	Independent Television (UK)
MAC	Multiple Analogue Component
MUSE	Multiple Sub-Nyqvist Sample Encoding
MTV	Music Television

NOS	Nederlandse Omroepprogramma Stichting (Netherlands)
NRK	Norsk Rikskringkasting (Norway)
NTSC	National Television System Committee (USA) (colour television norm)
ORF	Österreichischer Rundfunk (Austria)
PAL	Phase alternation by line (colour television norm)
PC	Personal computer
PSB	Public service broadcasting/broadcaster
PTT	Post Telephone and Telegraph administration
RAI	Radiotelevisione Italiana (Italy)
RDP	Radiodifusão Portuguesa (Portugal)
RTBF	Radio-Télévision Belge de la Communauté Française (Belgium)
RTE	Radio Telefis Eireann (Ireland)
RTL	Radio-Tele-Luxembourg (Luxembourg)
RTVE	Radiotelevisión Española (Spain)
SECAM	Séquentielle couleur à mémoire (colour television norm)
SER	Sociedad Española de Radiodifusión (Spain)
SES	Société Européenne des Satellites (operator of ASTRA satellites)
SR	Sveriges Radio (Sweden)
SRF	Radio France (France)
SRG	Schweizerische Radio und Fernsehgesellschaft (Switzerland)
SSR	Société Suisse de Radiodiffusion et Télévision (Switzerland)
TF 1	Télévision Française 1 (France)
TDF	Télédiffusion de France (France)
TVRO	TV (receive only) (satellite TV earth station)
TVWF	Television Without Frontiers
UNESCO	United Nations Educational, Scientific and Cultural Organization
VCR	Video Cassette Recorder
VTM	Vlaamse Televisie Maatschappij (Belgium)
WARC	World Administrative Radio Conference
WDR	Westdeutscher Rundfunk (Germany)
YLE	Oy Yleisradio AB (Finland)
ZDF	Zweites Deutsches Fernsehen (Germany)

PART I

SETTING THE SCENE

1

From Structure to Dynamics

*Karen Siune, Denis McQuail and
Wolfgang Truetzschler*

Technological challenges

In the 1980s technological developments were perceived as the major challenge to the established national media structures, and policy reactions to the technological challenge were the main object of study for the Euromedia Research Group in *New Media Politics* (McQuail and Siune 1986). Changes in the media structures which were seen as a result of different kinds of new communication technology headed the agenda in the 1980s.

The dominant challenges were the availability of cheaper communication technologies, which made decentralization and privatization possible, and the increase in the number of communication satellites, which with their intended or unintended 'overspill' put an end to the idea of a coherent national media policy. What were the political reactions to these challenges? And were policy-makers aware of the coming changes?

Actors and logics

In *New Media Politics* we established a framework of analysis for the study of media policy, in which the chief elements were actors and the logics which they pursued in reacting to events and in following innovatory strategies. We also found it useful to distinguish different levels at which different actors operated, and at which different issues arose and had to be dealt with. The choice of actors for our attention was relatively straightforward. These represented the main interests at stake in either defending the 'old order' or in promoting change. We described policy-making as 'a reaction to a challenge, a reaction . . . intended to find a reasonable balance between "forces of change" and "forces of preservation"'. We referred to actors in media policy-making as 'being intentional in their behaviour', having 'a specific set of purposes they want to fulfil'. In our views 'wishes, goals and the associated interest are the elements in what can be termed the "logic" of an actor'. We expected different actors to have a different logic guiding their respective behaviour and their initiatives in relation to mass media.

The most significant actors at the *national* level were held to be government, ministries, political parties, some social institutions (including trade unions) together with existing media organizations and other media-related actors (such as the PTT and the advertising industry). At the *supranational* (or transnational) level, we identified specifically European bodies such as the EC, CEPT and the EBU and others such as ITU and UNESCO. At *local* and *regional* level, there were also relevant political and media interests. In addition, we observed the interested activity of industry and commerce, with its own distinctive logic, at work *at all levels*, from transnational to local.

We have approached the present study with essentially the same basic conceptual elements. Five years later, the relevant categories of actors have not changed significantly, nor have their basic logics in approaching issues of policy. The balance of power between actors has probably changed, however, as the forces at work have developed. In general, it seems that the relative power of transnational over national actors has increased somewhat, and along with this the force of their particular logics. This applies most obviously to the increased significance of the European Community, because it has an immediate impact on member states and exercises a wider influence by example. Its logic of 'harmonization' has gained momentum and it has given weight to the logic of technology. The second main gainers at the transnational level have probably been different categories of industry actor, but especially those associated with developing and selling new technology. Despite these changes, the framework of analysis can still serve its original purpose of locating issues for enquiry and helping to plot and record change. An innovation in this book is that we have given more attention than previously to actors at the local level. While these are not major 'players' in European terms, developments of local media can have a significant impact, for better or worse, on the quality of everyday social life.

Dynamic processes

In *New Media Politics* we concluded that there were signs of commercialization, internationalization, decentralization and industrialization. Breaking monopolies was on the agenda and 'culture at stake' was one of the issues. In *Dynamics of Media Politics* we pursue these issues further. In this book we emphasize the processes, the dynamics of the changes to a much greater extent than the details of the process. Details of national changes are described in our companion volume to this book, *The Media in Western Europe*.

New trends can be seen: there is clear fragmentation as against coherence, and a multiplication of regulations at a time when everyone talks about the spirit of deregulation. Diversification is visible – many more channels, more choice for consumers, new and alternative market opportunities for investment and exploitation, new kinds of communication employment, growth of independents, corresponding segmentation of audiences into smaller, more homogeneous cultural and economic categories. Denis McQuail asks in Chapter 2 of this book whether this will necessarily lead to a 'new order', one that is less unitary in structure than the old one. The answer to this will depend on how the competition develops, nationally and internationally, and on who succeeds. The ways in which competition develops in the form of national and transnational dynamic changes in media offers and the analysis of national and transnational policy reactions are the topic of this book.

Throughout this book it is demonstrated in various contexts that in country after country in Western Europe the old order is being swept away. A shift, slow-moving in the early 1980s and increasingly faster towards the end of the decade, has raised a challenge to the traditional balances in media domains. Public service broadcasting institutions are still to be found in all European countries, but the definition of the concept has somewhat changed. And the PSB organizations are in a period of transition, fighting for survival. What takes their place will be the result of several simultaneous power struggles, political, economic and technological. Media structures change, and some of these changes come about as a result of changes in media politics. Media politics is to some extent a field in itself, with its own dynamics. But media politics also follows some general policy tends. This is essentially what this book is about. The process of change itself, rather than the component details, is the object of our study.

National media systems are challenged by the forest of television and local radio stations, and by the increasing number of transnational offers. In fact local broadcasting could have been chosen as the dominant issue of a book on European media developments. As described by Hans Kleinsteuber in Chapter 10, during the 1980s local media were a topic of increasing importance and relevance in Europe.

Technology was the basic factor that facilitated the 'explosion' of the simple nation-bound media structure, and thus the power of technology should not be forgotten. It has played a role, and it will still play a role in the future. Whereas in the mid-1980s we were concerned primarily with the power of the technological forces leading to changes in media structures, nowadays it is much more the power of economic forces that is of interest. The impact of technological change has been more to shake the foundations of the existing broadcast media institutions than to change the essence of the means of communication or even the balance of what is being communicated. Economy puts its limitations on what is possible, and on what is worth pursuing. And market forces to a great extent dominate numerous formerly totally regulated areas.

Political regulation

In between the technological factors and the economic factors are the political factors. Throughout Europe the national regulatory environments are becoming weaker, although national political systems still play a very important role in the regulation and the steering of national and subnational broadcast and electronic media. Differences between the Western European countries in their development of local media as discussed by Els De Bens and Vibeke Petersen in Chapter 11, and differences in the evolution of former national monopolies in the broadcast media as shown by Kees Brants and Karen Siune in Chapter 7, indicate the variety of European media models. The variation in political regulation of media at the local level is presented by Wolfgang Truetzschler and Denis McQuail in Chapter 12.

What has frequently been referred to as deregulation has turned out to be regulation in another form, and the concept of 're-regulation' is much more appropriate. In this regard fragmentation shows itself clearly, in that detailed rules are created, concerning minor aspects of the media structure, contrary to an expected overall framework that provides only vague guidelines. This is the situation for most of the broadcast media as well as for other forms of electronic media in Europe.

Three issues are at stake: firstly, the relative importance of the market versus regulatory bodies in shaping the new order; secondly, striking an appropriate balance between the public and the private sectors; and thirdly, the type of conditions that can be imposed by regulators on the private sector.

These developments in the national, centrally controlled media systems have weakened the regulatory power of traditional politically oriented policy-makers. In this regard small states have particular problems, as is argued by Werner Meier and Josef Trappel in Chapter 9. Combined actions from within nationally based institutions and those of transnational institutions seem to work together in removing some of the crumbling walls protecting the media, and increasingly emphasizing the significance of a commercial outlook.

External forces

External pressures on public broadcasting (and on the whole idea of a national media system) were the general rule in Western Europe at the end of the 1980s, and will remain so for the 1990s. The ways in which public service broadcasting institutions are reacting to the competition are outlined by Olof Hultén and Kees Brants in Chapter 8.

Transnational forces in the form of European institutions such as the EC and the Council of Europe, are attempting to re-regulate the whole area. Although this is undertaken in a spirit of liberalization, according to Vibeke Petersen and Mario Hirsch in Chapter 4 of the book, nevertheless the end result is regulation.

The transnational multimedia actors, labelled the media tycoons or media magnates, are the great challengers of the regulatory systems. The media magnates are themselves the 'new' actors bearing 'new logic' for media development. The media tycoonery is both a consequence of and one of the forces causing disruption of the media structure in individual European countries, according to Gianpietro Mazzoleni and Michael Palmer in Chapter 3. What has been called (in Chapter 2) 'a vogue for market solutions and deregulation' has affected the general mood of media consumers and has changed the outlook of political and government forces, who seem to have been converted to the idea of 'going commercial'.

Commercialization is one of the ongoing processes, its input is to be found everywhere, but the concept is vague and diverse. It has had a heavy normative weight. In positive terms commercialism is seen as a symbol of freedom of expression, in negative ones as a symbol of vulgarization and destruction of traditional qualities. Central to commercialization is the dimension of competition, the struggle for limited resources. Both time and money are limited. As argued by Olof Hultén and Kees Brants in Chapter 8, there are different stages of competition, and these can be applied to public service broadcasters fighting back in order to survive in a changed environment.

Reactions by the media

An analysis of the ways in which European actors define their goals and how they interact with European politicians is particularly important for a discussion of Europe's place in the international media world. How national actors such as, for example, public service broadcasters define their business and how they devise their strategies is crucial for determining their choice of response to changes in their environments.

The content of television programmes provided to Europeans is one strong example of a trend which has attracted some attention and which needs to be given even more. The situation here can again be analysed with reference to logic. What kind of logic is behind the observable reactions of the media? And what kind of logic is behind reactions to changes in media content, reactions by individuals and by institutions, both national and transnational? What policies can be pursued, if any, in the form of initiatives, support programmes, regulations, etc., in response to the situation as described by Els De Bens, Mary Kelly and Marit Bakke in Chapter 6?

Shift of power

Apart from the logics, the forces behind the actors' initiatives are also of concern, irrespective of whether we are dealing with public or private broadcasters, national politicians or transnational actors.

The industrial logic and its problems are described by Bernt Stubbe Østergaard and Hans Kleinsteuber in Chapter 5. They argue that little is left of the democratic and participatory visions of the 1970s, when the introduction of cable was discussed in Europe. They argue that, while cable systems are part of the local structure and as such provide an opportunity to strengthen local communications, linked to satellites they turn into networks for centrally fed programmes. Satellites themselves are the most global and as such the most centralistic technology that is currently available and conceivable.

The technological/industrial situation is characterized by a basic shift of power between actors and between the different fora of decision-making. New actors have entered the arena over the last ten years, mainly large international media companies that feel no allegiance to any of the existing actors, or are even openly hostile to them. Their successes are mainly a result of the trend toward liberalization of markets in Europe.

The discussion of dynamic processes in this book does not show a clear picture of the future media structure of Europe, but rather a future situation characterized by a high level of uncertainty, increasing commercial influence, increasing insecurity in planning, and a mixed impact on the process of European unification.

Europe has gone through a process of loosening national ties during the 1980s, but the question remains as to whether or not the next tie will be European or international? A fragmentation in politics, into specialized fora with a narrower focus and involving a smaller number of actors, is evident. In this situation the EC is increasing its influence on media policy because of its close ties with the commercial interests involved, and because of its influence on the media policies of member governments. If the decision-making process results in action and not just in statements of intent, then the strongest influence may emanate from the European fora. It is for this reason that we have entitled the conclusion: Wake up, Europe!

References

Euromedia Research Group (1992) *The Media in Western Europe: The Euromedia Handbook*. London: Sage Publications.

McQuail, D. and Siune, K. (eds) (1986) *New Media Politics: Comparative Perspectives in Western Europe*. London: Sage Publications.

2

A Framework for Analysis of Media Change in Europe in the 1990s

Denis McQuail, Rosario de Mateo and Helena Tapper

The established 'order' of one major sector of Western European mass media – that of broadcasting – is undergoing substantial change. The *process* of change itself, rather than the component details, is our object of study, more so than when, in an earlier study, we focused on the new technologies of communication, which were thought likely to give rise to new forms of 'telematic' mass communication such as electronic mail, teletext and home banking (McQuail and Siune 1986). It is hard to avoid the conclusion that the impact of technological change has been more to shake the foundations of the existing electronic media institutions than to change the essence of the means of communication or even the balance of what is being communicated. While this might have been anticipated, we were largely unprepared for the task of analysing institutional change on the scale which has been occurring.

No comparable shift has occurred in the media of Western Europe within the lifetime of communication science or in the modern (postwar) political economy of Western European media. Until now the most historic media institutional events have been the addition of television to the spectrum of mass media and its rise to great prominence, plus the wave of concentration which affected the newspaper press in the 1950s and 1960s. The first change was largely accomplished within the framework of radio broadcasting, the second came to a halt before the more apocalyptic warnings had been fulfilled. As a result, neither political science nor communication science has been very well equipped conceptually for handling the processes of change now under way. This chapter tries to put in place a provisional model of media change as it has occurred during the 1980s, which might also be able to contain the most significant developments to be expected during the 1990s.

The task is complicated by the very broad range of issues which are involved, having to do with commercial and financial changes, new cultural politics and also industrial/economic policy. These three have become intertwined and, to complicate matters, the nation-state no longer provides a self-contained location for the unfolding and management of events, as it once seemed to do. As well as losing many of the familiar institutional certainties, the terrain of research has been much enlarged and the theoretical guideposts have often been removed or obscured. Much of the story of what has been happening is now well known. Many data have been collected and issues aired in a climate of almost constant public debate in each country about future developments of the media and under the spotlight of commercial attention. This too is a feature of the current moment which might have surprised the visitor from the not-so-distant past, used to more gradual, less visible and less openly political institutional change.

In place of a history of the changes which form the essential background to this account, we offer a summary typification of the 'old order' of broadcasting in Europe which has been so shaken at its foundations.

The 'old order' of European electronic media

Despite great inter-country differences, we can broadly identify the main features of the typical broadcasting system in Western Europe before the current changes began to be felt, beginning approximately at the start of the 1980s.

Firstly, broadcasting was subordinated to *public service* goals and to public accountability, especially in the sphere of culture and information and with particular reference to minority claims and interests, according to varying national circumstances.

Secondly, typical of systems was their *national* character, designed, as they were, to serve audiences and social institutions within the national territory, centre–peripheral in form of organization, expected to protect national language and culture and (however implicitly) to represent the national interest. As an aspect of their national character, broadcasting institutions were also usually monopolistic or quasi-monopolistic in their form of control, often in the hands of a single competent public authority.

Thirdly, broadcasting was *politicized* in various ways, either by way of enforced political neutralization or through balanced representation, or access, for different political views. Broadcasting structures were a creation of the political and cultural (rather than the economic) system, established by law and sensitive to the prevailing political and social climate.

Fourthly, broadcasting was generally *non-commercial* in principle, here and there by way of the total exclusion of all forms of commercial revenue, but nearly everywhere in the sense that the purposes of broadcasting were not to be primarily commercial or economic, but cultural and political. Commercial elements in the system were closely regulated. An important result of this and other features of the typical system was regulation of the amount of television transmission time, leading, in many countries, to a very limited output by the standards of North America and more commercial systems generally.

Destabilization

The recognition of crisis conditions for the institutional 'order' described above was rather slow to develop and, in many countries, the potential for crisis seems hardly yet to have been recognized. Instead, the obvious changes in technology (especially in the means of distribution via satellite and cable) were seen by policy-makers and by the main institutional actors as requiring adaptation and adjustment of regulations and wider European cooperation, and also as offering opportunities for new services to consumers and beneficial economic effects for national economies.

The main components of what has eventually developed into a serious challenge to several key features of the 'old order', as characterized above, can be summarized as follows:

- A decline in the legitimacy of the monopolistic arrangements which support public broadcasting systems, leading in turn to a reduced willingness to finance new developments in the media from public sources and, in several cases, to an effective end to the national monopoly of broadcasting.
- A vogue for market solutions and deregulation in communication matters, coupled with a measure of consumer dissatisfaction with a restricted supply of television. The presence of entrepreneurs with both the will and deep enough pockets to develop alternative services, using the new means of distribution, has led to the logical consequence of accelerating commercial competition both for the television audience and for advertising revenue that once flowed to quasi-public bodies.
- Moves to harmonize rules for broadcasting within the EC and the wider Europe, reinforced by the declining real possibility of holding national frontiers against foreign media intrusion by cable, satellite and over the air.

- The widespread desire to gain national and European profit from developing hardware and software industries associated with new technologies.
- Popular dissatisfaction with the old 'official' cultural regulation and national 'establishment' control. At the same time, the forces of the established cultural order have not usually been willing to surrender without a struggle.

The effect on the 'old order' of these factors at work, often mutually reinforcing, can be seen in many examples of change – more channels, new services, relaxed rules, more advertising, more competition, etc. – although the results so far are sometimes exaggerated.

The decay, if not breakdown, of the old order can also be described in terms of new fears and uncertainties which surfaced in public debate. Public broadcasters have become less confident and more uncertain about their role. There has been talk of dangers from new kinds of private monopoly, especially where ownership can cross media, as well as national, boundaries. Defenders of cultural quality are alarmed, and the supply of impartial information to service the political system and feed democratic participation and opinion-forming is thought to be in danger.

A new fear has been added to older anxieties about cultural decline, by the increase in transnationalization (for some, equated simply with an older fear of 'Americanization') and the possible decline of national cultural identity (Sepstrup 1989; Thomsen 1989). The problem has been compounded by a new pragmatism and insouciance, on the part of many politicians, about the coming of commercial or private broadcasting. Even the old alliance, formed out of the socialist politics, cultural elitism and appeal to national interest which supported public broadcasting, cannot be depended on any longer to save the system. The new politics of a more integrated Europe seems to work against, rather than for, the protection of culture at national (or regional) level. In general, economic objectives have gained primacy, creating uncertainty about *which* or *whose* culture should be protected, how and by whom (European Cultural Foundation 1988).

In search of a model

For reasons indicated, most media researchers, ourselves included, have been not well prepared for tackling changes of the kind and scale which are, rather suddenly, in prospect. The unusual mixture of technological, economic, political and cultural issues has been difficult to deal with in any comprehensive way, especially since the forces at work and the phenomena to be studied transcend national frontiers and particular national experience.

We can identify three or four alternative (although divergent and not interchangeable) kinds of model, or of conceptual frameworks, within which the current changes can be contained for description and analysis: a technological determinist model; the critical, political economic perspective; the free market, deregulatory perspective; the 'information society' framework.

The first of these indicates an interpretation of change as a more or less inevitable and logical consequence of the technological innovations in communication which undercut arguments for control based on scarcity and high cost. Low-cost media abundance is seen as inevitable in response to the application of new technologies for more efficient production and distribution of information and communication. Institutional arrangements have in the end to yield to this logic.

The next two perspectives mentioned have a normative basis and both refer to the logic of capitalist market systems, albeit from different value positions. The critical perspective foresees the inevitable destruction of those elements of the old order which gave protection to vulnerable cultural and political communication values, should the new technologies be developed and exploited primarily as economic and market opportunities. The longstanding critique of commercialism, manipulation and class dominance via private media monopoly can be applied to the circumstances now being allowed to unfold. It is hard to deploy such a framework to current change without turning against change and generally deploring what is happening.

The free market perspective, on the other hand, both welcomes the commercial exploitation of the new communication technologies and sees no logical alternative path that can be followed in liberal societies. The inevitable conclusion is deregulation and consumer abundance. A model based on this point of view would involve little more than a celebration of the decline of the public sector and public control.

The 'information society' perspective is less clear in its origins and implications, but the theory of an information society posits a condition of maximum exploitation of opportunities provided by developments of computation and electronic communication. Communications destroy old constraints of time and space, change the basis of economic reality and dissolve old conflicts in society of the kind which underlie the political–economic critique or its free enterprise alternative. A social–economic as well as a technological logic indicates a path towards communication abundance, which spells the end of the very restricting and heavily controlled 'old order'. However, change is likely to be a more or less planned response to informational imperatives.

Between them, these perspectives certainly offer ways of handling the facts of change so far and the trends that are clearly observable in relation to mass media in Western Europe. However, for different reasons, none of the options is very satisfactory. Technological determinism offers no analytic edge and is not very helpful in accounting for variations between countries. The critical perspective tends to entail a restrictive kind of cultural as well as material politics and another kind of determinism. The free market model is prescriptive in a different direction. It also presumes as a driving force a degree of individual consumer demand and of dissatisfaction with the 'old order' for which there is not enough evidence. The 'information society' model is vague and empty of predictive content. There is something more immediate happening which needs to be captured.

A choice of perspective

We have tried to formulate a more specific and made-to-measure analytic mode or framework which can better capture the essence of the institutional changes which are taking place and which might provide a guide to problem formulation, data collection and interpretation. This has involved making assumptions about what really are the most salient general features of the current situation of media change. The chosen perspective highlights three such features.

First, we examine the degree to which change is being *externally* driven (external to existing national media and political systems and also external in the sense that change is a result of new possibilities for supply – essentially a technological intervention – rather than increased demand). Second, there is an element of *conflict* between old and new players in the game, over the establishment of a 'new order' which incorporates technological and socio-political changes. Third, we emphasize the *fragmentation* which is occurring and which can be observed in the diversification of regulations and legal arrangements as well as in the institutional structures and the conduct of the industry.

The first of these principles, that of 'externality', helps to identify the main protagonists and interests which have to be taken into account – mainly of four kinds:

1   commercial operators seeking profit from a branch of economic
     activity which has largely been shut off until now from the free
     market;
2   would-be communicators (performers, writers, producers, film-
     makers) who may have been excluded or restricted by monopoly
     arrangements or simply by scarcity of access possibilities;
3   transnational media wanting access to particular national
     'markets';
4   governments who want to shake up, open up or use the system
     for new (mainly industrial and economic) goals.

The ways in which external pressure to change is being exerted
are similarly multiple in kind, including: the exploitation of new
distribution systems, especially by way of cable/satellite; investments by (often foreign) media entrepreneurs in existing national
media companies; legal and political pressures by way of EC
regulations; pressures for technical development and standardization from large manufacturers and standard-setting bodies;
increased independence and ambition of telecommunications
bodies; *de facto* cross-frontier competition for audiences and advertising revenue; a wide range of would-be independent producers of
services and products looking for a share of the expanding national
and international communication sector.

These external pressures clearly operate at different levels, in
different ways and on different kinds of issue. It is hard to say which
of the agencies named is the most important, but it looks as if the
major international media companies have the most power to
realize change in their own and neighbouring countries, even if they
do so by way of national systems. They have adopted the logic of
expansion and they have capital reserves and expertise to carry out
their plans.

The second main principle mentioned, that of *conflict*, draws
attention to the considerable value of the economic and social goods
at stake, the inevitable politicization of such a struggle and the fact
that conflict has to take place between specific agents, in specific
locations, over specific issues. Not surprisingly, the resistance on the
part of those who have had a measure of privileged access,
guaranteed by public monopoly, locates and defines a large element
of the conflict which can be observed. There is often a basic conflict
between traditional, possibly elitist, cultural and political values and
the 'new commercialism', with its own ideologues as well as its self-
interested actors.

In general, the many different actors end up as aligned either with
the defence of the status quo or as supporters of externally driven

change. The most prominent defenders of the old order (a somewhat heterogeneous crew) have been: public broadcasting bodies; established cultural (sometimes religious) institutions; consumer organizations; political parties of the left. On the side of change are usually to be found: would-be suppliers of hardware and software; political parties of the right; investors; advertisers and advertising agencies. Some agents and interests are less predictable in their alignment. These include: media and related trade unions and media workers (the producers of 'software'); governments, which have more at stake than just a political ideology; non-broadcasting media, which may lose more than they can gain by change; the public, in its capacity as consumers, often having conflicting requirements amongst the potentially available good things of more choice and lower prices. In many countries, a fissure has opened up between abundant potential supply and effective consumer demand for new channels and more television (Britain is a prime example). The slow response and relative failure of several new commercial ventures has provided government and other interested parties with either excuses or time to slow down radical policy changes.

The principle of *fragmentation* reminds us to look for the ways in which the elements might be *re-integrated* at the end of a process of break-up and diversification (as well as simply at the break-up of a unitary system). The elements of fragmentation are very obvious. Most countries now have more complex legal and regulatory arrangements in order to cope with the appearance of new media channels and possibilities (such as cable, video, satellite, videotex, pay TV), alternative forms of ownership and control, increase of local radio and television, requirements of international agreements, realities of cross-border transmission, legal claims for copyright, greater autonomy and wider functions for telecommunications, etc. This contrasts with the typical 'old order' case, where virtually all formal regulation concerning broadcasting could be found in the basic laws of the national broadcasting body or in wireless and telegraph law. This multiplication of regulation is in sharp contrast to the spirit of deregulation which is widely said to characterize the new communication era.

The signs of fragmentation and diversification are also very obvious 'on the ground and in the air': many more channels, more choice for consumers; new and alternative market opportunities for investment and exploitation; new kinds of communication employment; growth of independents; more profiling and specialization of channels; corresponding segmentation of audiences into smaller, more homogeneous cultural and economic categories. The days of the regular mass television audience viewing the main national channel are over, even if certain events and spectacles still draw mass attention. Even family viewing becomes more fragmented as choice and reception opportunities diversify.

The changes leave open, nevertheless, the possibility of an ultimate 'new order', which might be not much less unitary in structure than the old order, even if based on market forces rather than on public monopoly and national political control. This will largely depend on how competition develops nationally and internationally and who succeeds. So far the national audience, rather than the transnational, remains the main target for programme suppliers and advertisers and, in the larger countries, one or two channels still claim the majority of the audience at any one time.

Models of policy change in Europe

The general dynamics and sequence of events indicated can be represented by the model in Figure 2.1, which summarizes key elements of the process described. The existing orders of broadcasting, under various forms of public monopoly, are first destabilized by technological and other changes. New commercial operators

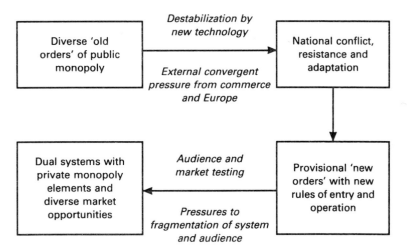

Figure 2.1 *Sequential model of system change*

seek to take advantage of conditions of breakdown and national media policy vacuum and also of the opportunities created by supranational (European level) pressures. Their possible admission to the system, or freedom to operate, stimulates conflict as well as a degree of organized opposition within the framework of the old order, and new rules for access are forged as a provisional outcome of conflict. At the same time, pressures towards convergence of systems, as between nations, are experienced (especially as a result of technology and European policy), but also through shared experience and definitions. The provisional 'new order' is tested in practice and some tendencies towards fragmentation (or diversification) are likely to be experienced. This stage is followed by further adaptation of system rules and operator strategies, depending on several factors, but especially the success or otherwise of the new commercial or independent operators. In theory, a more stable version of the 'new order' in each national society should develop. Because of the similarity of external pressure and tendencies to harmonization and internationalization, the various 'new orders' are likely to be more similar to each other than the much more culturally idiosyncratic arrangements of the past. They are at least likely to be similar in having both public and private (commercial) elements. The latter are likely to be characterized by ownership concentration (mainly because of high entry costs, the operation of existing multimedia conglomerates and the nature of the television audience market).

This hypothetical sequence has nowhere yet been fulfilled in Europe and there is a good deal of variation as to the stage currently reached by each country. In the case of Italy, a rapid and early transition from old to a seemingly stable new order occurred without the central stages having been gone through at all. Spain was unusual at the outset in having an 'old order' which was both statist and commercialized. In the other larger states, Britain, France and Germany, the commercial challenge has also been largely of domestic origin, even if from agencies which were excluded from the previous system and with a transnational character (Murdoch, Berlusconi, etc.). Unlike the case of Italy, however, in Britain, France and Germany it was the national governments which chose, for different reasons, to encourage a new private sector alongside the old. A common element in the motivation of each was, nevertheless, to reap economic benefits from an enlarging information economy.

In Britain, the process was initially advanced by way of new cable franchises, but when this apparently failed the initial test of the market, government and private investor policy looked to another technology, that of direct broadcast satellite, to achieve a breakthrough (as to other policy options). In France, a series of fundamental changes, also implemented as government policy, established a new, much more 'mixed' order, which is only now receiving a market test. In Germany, privatization of television, by way of cable and satellite initially, but now terrestrially, has advanced steadily along the sequence indicated, without much obstacle except in initial consumer resistance, which is now giving way. Because the Spanish public television system was already financed entirely by advertising, there were both fewer pressures and fewer obstacles to change. An alternative, commercial television sector is now beginning to challenge the old order.

In the smaller, more densely cabled, countries of Holland, Belgium, Denmark, Switzerland and Austria, the 'external' (foreign) commercial challenge for audiences and advertising has generally been more direct and the model works much as indicated up to the point of market testing, where difference of national circumstances is leading to divergent outcomes, but certainly to a new share-out between commercial and public operators. Ireland has a much longer history of 'external' media influence and is a long way along the path indicated by the model. In those smaller countries which are less accessible to outside penetration and have strong cultural traditions, like Sweden and Norway, the phases of potential destabilization and commercial challenge have been experienced without, as yet, any major structural changes in the established order. However, the stage of conflict and adaptation has certainly been reached and system change will not be resisted for long.

This single model works in some degree for different countries because of the similarity of starting points (much the same kind of 'old order', as sketched) and because the pressures described have been widely experienced. A more elaborate version of the model is required to deal with typical conflicts which have arisen and with the 'new politics' of the media landscape. There are too many variants to present in one simple form but, essentially, account has to be taken of five different variable elements in the general dynamics and sequence sketched above. These are:

1   the level at which action occurs;
2   the kind of actor involved;
3   the terrain of decision-making or action;
4   the forum in which decisions are taken; and
5   the type of decision taken.

It is the outcome in terms of actual decisions which moves the process outlined in Figure 2.1 along and reshapes the broadcasting order. While the reality of change is much less neat, this way of

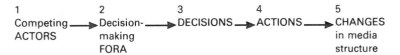

1 ... different *actors* [especially: private media companies/operators; public broadcasters; financial investors; governments; hardware and software industries; advertisers; PTTs; public administrators] ...

2 ... compete in various *fora* [as determined by level (global, European ...), terrain and type of actor] ...

3 ... over *decisions* [relating to matters of: culture; technology; technical standards; economics] ...

4 ... leading to various *actions* [law-making; de- or re-regulation; investments; new and adapted media operations] ...

5 ... leading to *changes* [in media structures, forms of ownership, market opportunities, contents on offer, audience behaviours, etc.].

Figure 2.2   *Elements of media policy decision-making*

thinking helps to identify problems for analysis. The process can be graphically represented as a verbal statement as in Figure 2.2.

Obviously, more distinctions could be introduced and there is much variability in the strength and predictability of links between decisions, actions and effects. Much of this variability depends on the power resources of the actors involved, the nature of fora and the kind of decisions made. On the last point, we have to distinguish between decisions which are binding (say, European law), those which are indicative (technical standards) and those which are only recommendations (the European 'share' of content).

There are also distinctions between decisions or actions (for instance, laws and regulations) which are tested in the political arena and those which are tested in the market (such as investment decisions). Amongst commercial decisions we can distinguish in general between large investments made for expected profit (such as the SES Astra satellite enterprise or the British Sky and BSB direct broadcasting ventures) and those with the character of 'staking' – laying limited claims for various reasons: to test the climate, the market or the regulations; or to keep an option open for the future.

Perhaps the 'terrain' of decision-making and action which is most in need of more detailed specification and research is that of 'economics' (and commerce). There are new trends of ownership and new markets which can be opened up or exploited as a result of the decline of the old, non-commercial, order. In the next section we discuss some of these economic trends which have already been influential in causing changes and which are likely to shape the emerging and future audiovisual landscape much more than the old kind of national media politics.

Changes in forms of ownership structure

The changes which took place in the mass media sector during the 1980s have led to the emergence of relatively new types of ownership structure for electronic media. These forms supplement or replace the previously dominant public ownership model. Before the recent changes, only Italy, Luxembourg and the United Kingdom offered significant models of privately owned broadcast media in Europe. Despite the pressures from different lobbies, technological developments and new consumer demands, the structural changes are not yet very radical. At the start of the 1990s, the traditional forms of ownership are still largely in place, alongside some of the newly organized media businesses which have been set up to exploit the possibilities of new technologies and new investment opportunities. In general, new private organizations have simply emerged as competitors to the older national public monopolies, which have not been replaced. The intervention of new businesses is most evident in the field of satellite broadcasting, where infrastructure could be bought or rented and used to transmit to new markets. This has often been facilitated by the absence or weakness of domestic regulation.

Another factor which has influenced the dynamic of change has been the new limitations which have been applied to the ownership of radio or television services, especially by foreign companies. Although the aim of such regulations is to limit concentrations of ownership in national markets, one result has been to produce complex relations of interlocking capital between companies from different countries. The general aim is to distribute much the same service in different markets with little cost or economic risk, but keeping overall control for the parent company.

The case of Canal Plus provides an example of a company with little capital participating in the media enterprises of several countries and offering the same service. This has allowed the development of a genuinely transnational television organization which has attracted wide participation on the part of different media. Alongside this we can observe the operation of multimedia strategies by some agencies of the printed press. The latter have taken advantage of the liberalization of access to ownership and to management of radio and television services, and have gone as far in this direction as the law allows. In Spain, for example, the PRISA enterprise, originally the publisher of *El País* and other titles, has moved to gain control of the main private radio network (SER) in order to achieve a 25 per cent share (the maximum permitted) of the Spanish Canal Plus company. The same has happened in the case of other press enterprises and the broadcast media networks of Antena 3 Radio and Antena 3 Television. Before the coming of privately owned electronic media businesses, virtually the only form of ownership in Spain (as in most of Western Europe) was the public corporation, which could not itself participate in print media activities.

Another factor leading to change in ownership structures is an increasing functional separation within the radio and television sector. The many technological developments in communication systems, plus the multiplication of terrestrial channels and expansion of cable and satellite, have brought into question the whole established relation between the different functions of programme production, ownership and management of channels and programming itself. Under the public monopoly regime, a single organization took care of all these activities, but current conditions of private operation call for separate technical and economic solutions for each function.

In addition, there is now a widespread tendency to make room within the public sector for independent audiovisual productions, as a matter of policy as well as for reasons of efficiency. In respect of audiovisual production, television is now likely to cooperate with the established film industry (by way of shared investment or commercial agreements), as well as with independent television producers. Nevertheless, governments still try to establish the lines between different kinds of publisher in order to avoid monopoly and ensure the proper working of the market, in the public interest. For this reason, limits are often set to cross-media ownership and especially to the relationship between the print and the audiovisual sectors.

There remains a role for governments in technical and infrastructural regulation, for instance in the allocation of audiovisual channels or cable franchises, where conditions of scarcity or natural monopoly often still apply. There are also often advantages to all parties concerned in separating the distribution function (whether over the air, by cable or satellite), from that of programme provision. Some European countries have established structures specifically to take care of distribution. In some cases, this is a joint effort between state and PTT or it is allocated to some other public body (Retevisión in Spain, TDF in France). In some cases, a concession has been established allowing telecommunication structures to be used for radio and television transmission. The case of

cable is clearest, where the local natural monopoly obliges government to lay down rules allowing private companies to participate (or
to have concessions) in the installation and management of
networks.

In short, future organizational structures for communication are
likely to be much more diverse than hitherto and we can distinguish
the following main types:

- Co-existence between public service corporations and private
  enterprises in the radio and television field. This is now a
  widespread phenomenon in nearly all West European countries, although ten years ago it was rare.
- Private television enterprises which manage to escape from
  national regulation and control, by taking advantage of the still
  unfinished forms of international regulation. This is the case, for
  instance, with the operations of Murdoch, using the Luxembourg Astra satellite. It also applies to the successful RTL4
  venture in Holland and to the unsuccessful Canal Plus operation
  in Spain, which used British facilities to broadcast private
  satellite television.
- Transnational corporations which organize networks in several
  countries, keeping operative control and exploiting their 'know-
  how' and their global communication business activities and
  connections. Canal Plus is one example, participating in national
  companies in France, Germany and Spain. Berlusconi is
  another case, with operations in Spain and France as well as in
  Italy.
- Multimedia activity, whether national or transnational, with
  interests in print as well as audiovisual media. PRISA (publisher of *El País* as well as owner of the SER radio channel) has
  been mentioned. Bertelsmann is another major example. The
  multimedia firms can sometimes be primarily media companies
  (such as Maxwell or Bertelsmann), but can also be primarily
  industrial (for instance Fiat) or service companies (such as
  Berlusconi's Fininvest).
- Increasing separation of functions in the audiovisual process. In
  the cable and satellite business there is an increasing differen-
  tiation between the programme providers and the channel
  managements. Television companies are entrusting programme
  production to independents or are setting up separate production companies (for instance, RTVE in Spain) or participation
  in the film industry (Canal Plus).
- Increasing regulation by the state of transmission and distribution facilities, in order to unify technical infrastructures or to

regulate local cable monopolies and other natural monopolies. This state activity is illustrated by the Spanish case, where a single semi-public company is in charge of television distribution of all channels.

General dynamic of media market developments

The main relevant changes already noted have been: the breakdown of the monopolistic public service model; the expansion of local media possibilities; the increase of multimedia and cross-national activities (now also observable in Eastern Europe). One source of pressure for change has been the fact that print media (especially newspaper) advertising markets were saturated and both print media companies and advertisers were interested in expanding into the electronic media (especially local radio, cable TV and satellite television). On the audience side, there have also been incentives towards change on the part of the media. Media consumption has tended to polarize either into segmented audiences based on specific needs or into large audiences for standardized mass media content. The addition of new television channels and of local commercial broadcasting offers more differentiated opportunities for advertising.

In general, the large media companies in Europe, such as Berlusconi or Maxwell, have tended to operate mainly in their original countries, but with gradual geographic expansion into adjoining markets. The dynamics of the media field can be understood according to the 'map' in Figure 2.3. The arrows indicate the main directions of current changes of market expansion and integration.

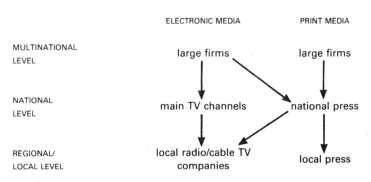

Figure 2.3   *Media market dynamics*

At the multinational level, the electronic media are expanding geographically, but not into other kinds of media. The print media seem to follow the same general pattern of transborder expansion, but they also tend to expand to some extent into the electronic media. One new market for both types of media is in Eastern Europe. Language still sets up major barriers and to some extent determines the area of media operation. Advertising also exerts a limiting influence on patterns of expansion, partly the result of specific aspects of advertising markets, partly because national advertising regulations can limit the use of commercials in multinational media.

At the national level, the print media have, in many countries, reached the limits of their potential income from advertising and are seeking to expand into the electronic sector, especially at local or regional level. There are new electronic media operators in many countries which are often partnerships between the press and older electronic media companies. The larger national media companies, both electronic and print, expand into other media fields, becoming small or medium operators there. At the local level, the electronic media have expanded rapidly, especially cable television and local radio. This is the domain in which there are the largest number of new operators, especially because of the attraction of opportunities for local advertising. For this reason in particular, local radio and TV operations and the new information services are often partly owned by national print media.

Concentration of ownership leads to economies of scale and the possibility of distributing similar media contents across Europe, as far as language and culture permits. There are also economies of scope, with opportunities for new companies to diversify products and enter new media fields. Because of the trends outlined, it is possible that it will be left to local and regional media to provide the most culturally characteristic media contents. The terrain described seems characterized by polarization between large media companies and small or medium-sized operators. Privatization leads to more intense competition at each level because of the large number of companies and the declining role of the state as regulator.

References

Dyson, K. and Humphries, P. (eds) (1986) *The Politics of the Communications Revolution in Western Europe*. London: Frank Cass.

European Cultural Foundation (1988) *Europe 2000: What Kind of Television?* Manchester: The European Institute for the Media.

Ferguson, M. (ed.) (1990) *Public Communication: the New Imperatives*. London: Sage Publications.

McQuail, D. (1989) 'Commercial imperialism and cultural cost', in C.W. Thomsen (ed.), *Cultural Transfer or Electronic Imperialism?* Heidelberg: Carl Winter Universitätsverlag. pp. 207–17.

McQuail, D. (1990) 'Communication research past, present and future: American roots and European branches', in M. Ferguson (ed.), *Public Communication: the New Imperatives.* London: Sage Publications. pp. 135–51.

McQuail, D. and Siune, K. (eds) (1986) *New Media Politics: Comparative Perspectives in Western Europe.* London: Sage Publications.

Michael, J. (1989) 'Regulating communications media', in M. Ferguson (ed.), *Public Communication: the New Imperatives.* London: Sage Publications. pp. 40–60.

Sepstrup, P. (1989) 'Transnationalization of Television in Western Europe', in C.W. Thomsen (ed.), *Cultural Transfer or Electronic Imperialism?* Heidelberg: Carl Winter Universitätsverlag. pp. 99–135.

Thomsen, C.W. (ed.) (1989) *Cultural Transfer or Electronic Imperialism?* Heidelberg: Carl Winter Universitätsverlag.

PART II

CROSSING BORDERS

3

The Building of Media Empires

Gianpietro Mazzoleni and Michael Palmer

Europe: concentration and change

In the Europe of the 1990s, many leading communications media groups have, on the one hand, both strong domestic roots in one of (Western) Europe's many nation-states and a significant presence in other national markets. On the other hand, these groups adopt an international, if not global, development strategy. Transnational media companies, whether involved in one, more, or all the industries concerned in the production, packaging and distribution of media and their content, often have a long tradition of operating internationally. In Europe during the 1980s, the move towards economic integration and the testing of the commercial prospects of new communications technologies and (sometimes revamped) media outlets saw groups expand and diversify, while attending, as ever, to the requisite level of horizontal and vertical integration. Some dominant European media groups of the 1990s have been leading actors in the communications industry for over 150 years: the French Havas and Hachette groups, and Germany's Bertelsmann, trace their origins to the 1830s. Others – like Silvio Berlusconi's Fininvest – are more recent reactions, whose expansion is linked to one of the major developments of the past twenty years, namely that of commercial television across Western Europe.

Leading private sector groups – and, indeed, many of their public sector counterparts – have both a predominantly commercial outlook and a proven expertise in circumventing rules and regulations, laws, directives and judgements, all of them aimed at limiting their growth to that which is politically acceptable. In the 1980s the relative weakness of national legislation became increasingly apparent, as the concentration of ownership intensified in certain market sectors such as commercial television in Italy, the national daily and Sunday newspaper press in Britain, the national and regional daily press in France, etc. As leading groups pursued their expansion and diversification strategies across Europe, some politicians argued in national parliaments that groups flying the flag (France's Havas, Hersant and Hachette groups, for instance) should not be weakened by tight national anti-concentration controls. Other politicians pressed for the regulation of cross-media ownership at the European level.

This chapter will attempt to monitor some of these developments. The sands are shifting: across Europe, such controls as exist at the national level have often proved weak and inoperative; there is increasing pressure for action at the European level, with the EC Commission making proposals on television, telecommunications and advertising. But it will be argued here that at the European level, as previously at the national level, there are many indications that communications media groups often appear more successful than public policy-makers in fashioning and interpreting such rules as exist.

Some of these groups are present in local and regional, national, European and international markets, some are active across a wide range of media – for example, from newspaper publishing to direct-to-home satellite television broadcasting, etc. They may themselves be part of conglomerates with interests outside the communications and leisure service industries. Whether (formally) based in London, Luxembourg or Liechtenstein, in Rome, Paris or Hamburg, leading European media groups argue that the nature of the industry and of the patterns of media production, distribution and consumption force them to have a global outlook. They press for the least possible regulation.

Rivals in many markets, Rupert Murdoch, Robert Maxwell, Silvio Berlusconi and the like are at one in resisting attempts at Euro-regulation, just as they have often successfully ridden roughshod over such ownership controls as exist at the national level. They reinforce the lobbying activities of the various communications trade associations – such as the European Advertising Tripartite (EAT, set up circa 1980), or the European Council of Newspaper Publishers and Proprietors (set up in 1991). Just as, during the 1980s, communications policy – centred primarily on the debate over television without frontiers (1983–9) – assumed an increasingly high profile within both the European Community and the Council of Europe, so the European lobbying activities of major media groups and trade associations intensified.

Media combines: think big, act local

The US–Europe connection and the trend toward the concentration of multimedia ownership shape much of the debate about the communications industry in Europe. The dangers perceived in the chain ownership of newspapers were already the subject of controversy before 1914, in the days of Britain's Alfred Harmsworth, Viscount Northcliffe (1865–1922), and America's W.R. Hearst (1863–1952). Indeed, the self-same Northcliffe, who founded the popular *Daily Mail* and acquired the prestigious newspaper, *The Times*, already envisaged in 1900 a single organization or combine that would own, produce and operate multiple editions of the same publications world-wide; based in Britain, he owned forests in Canada to provide the wood pulp needed for the countless publications of a group controlling its own news and features services and its own distribution organization.

Northcliffe, like many a later European media tycoon, was fascinated by America – the birthplace of the mass information and entertainment industry, the richest media market in the world and the testing ground of communications developments that would subsequently affect Europe. Decades later, the Australian Rupert Murdoch (1931–), already heading an empire which straddled Australia, the United Kingdom and the United States, became a US citizen, and thus got round the law barring a foreigner from directly owning more than 20 per cent of a TV station, and more than 25 per cent through indirect ownership. The same year he acquired the film and entertainment company Twentieth Century Fox and the TV stations of the Metromedia company. He subsequently transformed these into a serious rival to the three traditionally dominant networks of American television, ABC, CBS and NBC.

The reasoning adduced by international multimedia groups such as Murdoch's runs thus: the communications industry involves the provision of news, information and entertainment by whatever means possible – including print and (increasingly) broadcast media. The distinction between film and television is obsolete, and a company producing and controlling audiovisual material can transmit and distribute it world-wide, to, say, the Murdoch Fox TV network in the United States and to his satellite-beamed Sky TV channels in Europe.

European media empires, such as Germany's Bertelsmann or France's Hachette, expanding from a strong domestic base, likewise see the American market, which accounts for a little under 50 per cent of total world advertising expenditure, as the testing ground for their international pretensions. Even Italy's Silvio Berlusconi, the European commercial broadcasting tycoon *par excellence*, derived much of his strength in European TV from bulk purchase of the European rights to Hollywood TV productions and films. In 1991, his Fininvest company had a film library of about 6,000 titles and operated a chain of about 300 cinemas in Italy. On the other hand, Berlusconi stressed his commitment to co-funding European productions when he applied for TV franchises in France, Spain and other national markets in Europe.

Nation-states versus media combines: anti-trust legislation

In 1991, the overwhelming majority of the media within Europe remain rooted in the context of the nation-state. The European Community has twelve member-states; the Council of Europe twenty-four; Europe in total, following the demise of the Soviet bloc in the East, comprises over thirty nation-states. The expansionist logic of European media groups therefore operates within the context of a geographically small and culturally mosaic-like continent. Its population – EC alone or Europe *in toto* – may be significantly higher than that of the United States, but its linguistic, socio-demographic and, above all, political diversity complicates the task of those pressing for the least possible media regulation.

Whether its political structure is relatively centralized or federal, the nation-state imposes constraints on the operations of a media combine. Generally based in one of the larger or more affluent of Europe's national markets – Germany, France, Britain, Italy, Spain – successful media groups seek to expand both into a wide range of commercial media and beyond their domestic market. But, within most, if not all, nation-states, public opinion – parliamentary, journalistic and other – expresses concern at the threat posed to pluralism by the concentration of ownership and the diversification strategies of such mega-groups.

But public opinion and those who make and implement media policy are, in the main, *re*active: media tycoons are, as business entrepreneurs, *pro*active. In many European parliamentary democracies, the lengthy process of consultation prior to legislation or executive action (and regulatory implementation) sometimes results in attempting to close the stable door after the horse has bolted. Mega-media groups often succeed, through their staying power, economic muscle, political connections and lobbying skills, in circumventing the legislative and regulatory barriers placed in their path.

There are at least six EC member-states where there is no anti-trust legislation specifically concerning multimedia groups: Belgium, Greece, Ireland, Luxembourg, the Netherlands and Portugal. Among the democracies of southern Europe which joined the Community in the 1980s – Greece, Portugal and Spain – Spain is the member state with possibly the most extensive legislation concerning multimedia ownership. Spain's law of 5 May 1988 stipulates that no shareholder may control more than 25 per cent of a private commercial TV company; no individual or company may own more than 15 per cent, if he or it has a similar-sized stake in a daily general interest newspaper, a national weekly, a radio station or a news agency.

Not dissimilar provisions exist in national legislation elsewhere: Italy and France are the two EC member-states with the most recent and complex anti-media trust and cross-ownership legislation. In France, provisions of laws enacted in 1982, 1984 and 1986 concerned the ownership of broadcasting and the press, with the 1986 law specifically addressing the issue of multimedia groups. In Italy, the anti-trust provisions of the media law enacted in 1990 are to take effect in 1992.

Of course, there had long been provisions in the national legislation of various EC member-states – Denmark and the UK, for instance – to ensure that newspaper publishers and print media companies did not acquire a majority stake in private sector radio or television companies. But, by and large, leading media groups often proved adept both at increasing their interests in and share of a given media market sector, and at diversifying into other sectors. In Italy, the August 1981 press law failed to halt the trend towards further concentration of newspaper ownership; nine years later, the law courts had still not pronounced definitely on whether or not the Fiat RCS group had exceeded the authorized limit for the ownership of national titles – 20 per cent of the circulation of all national dailies.

In France, between 1983 and 1984, the socialist-led government battled for a press bill intended to clip the wings of the Hersant group, whose dailies accounted for some 30 per cent of the total circulation of national newspaper titles and approaching 20 per cent of that of provincial titles – to little, or rather to no, avail. After the promulgation of the 1984 press law, the Hersant group did not divest itself of a single publication. Indeed, in January 1986, with the cynical comment – 'I am merely anticipating the next law' – Hersant acquired a further major regional newspaper company, *Le Progrès de Lyon*, despite protests by government ministers and the press ownership commission set up by the 1984 law. He was proved correct: the conservative government, appointed following the general elections of March 1986, both raised the limits governing the concentration of newspaper ownership (to 30 per cent of the total circulation of general interest newspapers) and obtained parliamentary approval for new multimedia legislation. As a result of this latter, Hersant, with a 25 per cent stake, was able to lead the consortium which successfully bid for the franchise to operate France's fifth TV channel, La Cinq (1987).

In 1990–1, with a moderate socialist government in office, financial rather than political or regulatory pressures led Hersant to reduce his stake in the loss-making channel. But he continued his expansion in the newspaper press, acquiring a 24 per cent stake in the company which publishes the regional daily *L'Est républicain* (1991). In Britain, likewise, the Murdoch group expanded its interests in the print and broadcasting media (controlling, for example, some 35 per cent of the circulation of national paid-for daily and Sunday titles), irrespective of all talk of referral to the Monopolies and Mergers Commission and other regulatory bodies.

In 1991, the expansion of multinational media groups appeared to be conditioned less by regulatory and ownership constraints than by financial considerations. Admittedly Berlusconi's Fininvest was obliged by the 1990 Italian media law to dispose of one of its three TV networks, but the main consideration curbing its expansion appeared to be its heavy debt burden and the need to reschedule debts at a time of economic downturn, when banks and other shareholders were less inclined to support it than in the more prosperous 1980s.

Governments in France and elsewhere in continental Europe periodically invoke the spectre of American 'cultural imperialism', of US dominance of Europe's information, entertainment and cultural industries and output, especially in the audiovisual sector. Such arguments were used by France's liberal communications minister in 1986 to plead for minimalist anti-trust legislation. Its provisions should not threaten the strong domestic base of France's leading multimedia groups – such as Hersant, Havas and Hachette – which have been striving to develop their European and international operations despite the competition of other, more powerful, European and American media empires.

Another lesson can be drawn from the experience of the Hersant group. When left-wing governments fail to curb the expansion of mega-groups with a differing political philosophy, right-wing governments find it all the easier to invoke the need for such strong domestic groups in the competition against American and other European groups.

Have anti-trust laws, rules and regulations forced media empires in Europe to expand outside their prime national market because they have reached the limit of the degree of concentration permitted in law or – which is not the same thing – which is acceptable politically? There is some evidence to suggest this is the case. In a report commissioned by the French government, Pierre Todorov argues thus:

> Regulations limiting the concentration of the ownership of newspaper publishing companies play a not insignificant role in encouraging their expansion abroad. Thus, the existence of long-established and relatively draconian anti-trust legislation has led both the German periodical press and British national popular dailies to develop European strategies aimed at the search for new markets. In France, it is possible that the recent international expansion (Spain, Belgium and elsewhere) of the Hersant group is due, in part, to the limits on its expansion within France imposed by the 1986 law.[1] (Todorov 1990: 14)

The case of the Hersant group, however, is by no means proven. In the press sector, Hersant acquired substantial minority stakes in newspaper publishing companies outside France (such as the Belgian quality title, *Le Soir*) both before and after the enactment of the anti-trust provisions of the French press law of 1984 and the communications law of 1986. In France, the total circulation of his group's general daily newspapers appeared to exceed the authorized limits: in 1990, his titles accounted for 35 per cent of the circulation of the national daily press and for 18 per cent of that of the regional daily press; and he controlled significant minority stakes in companies publishing regional dailies (*Midi libre, L'Est républicain*, etc.) other than those of his own group. For all the group's expansion into Eastern Europe following the collapse of various communist regimes in the 1980s, Hersant remains the least international of the world's leading press groups.

Analysts of the German situation, by contrast, claim that anti-trust regulations have indeed hastened the international diversification strategies of major media companies. In 1976, special provisions were introduced into the existing cartel law. These required that proposed mergers of media companies obtain the approval of the Federal Cartel Office. This was withheld if the merger, or even a mere joint agreement, promised to give the resultant company a dominant position in a given market. The federal economics minister had the power to override Cartel Office decisions.

These decisions, however, were often applied. Thus, in 1981, limits were placed on the acquisition of a shareholding in Axel Springer by another large German group, Burda. Likewise, the Cartel Office refused to authorize the Springer group to increase its stake in a Munich daily newspaper and thereby secure effective control of the Munich newspaper market. In Germany, however, partial concentration remains possible through the partial acquisition by the major groups of minority shareholdings (under 25 per cent) in other media companies. In short, the anti-trust provisions of the cartel law may have encouraged German print media groups such as Bertelsmann in their international expansion strategy.

To recapitulate: in 1990, in six EC member-states – Belgium, Denmark, Greece, Luxembourg, the Netherlands and Spain – there was no legislative provision to limit trends to the concentration of ownership of the press. In six member-states – Belgium, Greece, Luxembourg, Ireland, the Netherlands and Portugal – there were no laws limiting the concentration of multi- or cross-media ownership. Such legislation as did exist stemmed largely, from the 1950s onwards, from a concern to prevent print media groups dominating broadcast media.

In subsequent decades, and especially following the expansion in the number of TV channels in the 1980s, three factors highlighted the fallibility of such national cross-ownership limits as existed: the development of TV channels delivered by technologies (cable and satellite, as well as the conventional terrestrial mode) whose *modus operandi* completely disregarded existing national rules and regulations; political, economic and other pressures for the emergence of a Europe that was more than the sum of its national parts; and the rise of global communications groups, chafing at regulatory constraints and anti-trust provisions in their domestic, and other national, markets, and with international strategies and media synergy ambitions in which Europe played an important, but by no means isolated, part.

Multinational multimedia empires expand and adjust like the proverbial amoeba. Often presented as the archetypal modern communications group, Rupert Murdoch's News Corporation grew by a factor of six between 1984 and 1989. By 1988, the USA had overtaken Australia and the UK, and accounted for the lion's share of News Corporation's total revenue (42 per cent) compared to Australia's 30 per cent and Britain's 28 per cent. The much vaunted synergy between Murdoch's US Fox film library, studios and TV network, with the provision of video material for his European Sky/BSkyB (cable and satellite) TV interests, was a strategy that had a semblance of logic. Murdoch, like Italy's Silvio Berlusconi and Germany's Leo Kirch, controlled American-made film properties and their distribution rights at a time of increasing demand: according to some industry estimates (Carat International), the number of commercial terrestrial TV channels in Europe rose from twenty-seven in 1980 to seventy-three in 1990.

The shortage of home-grown European audiovisual material led the larger communications media groups to build up their US assets and (like France's subscription TV company, Canal Plus, for instance) to diversify into film production. In 1991, its film library –

some 6,000 titles – was reckoned to be the most valuable asset of Berlusconi's Fininvest company. The need for European programme material even led traditional rivals, such as Italy's public service RAI and private sector Fininvest, to co-produce, with an American partner, tele-films (thereby heightening fears, within Italy, of cartel practices by the dominant duopoly). The increase in cross-media ownership and multimedia synergies goes hand in hand with international expansion strategies. Thus, based primarily in the print media, but with growing broadcast media interests, France's Hachette and Germany's Bertelsmann acquired major US assets in the 1980s: Bertelsmann acquired Radio Corporation of America and the publishing group, Doubleday; Hachette in 1988 became the majority shareholder of the seventh biggest US press group, Diamandis, and of one of the top ten US publishers of directories, Grolier.

Jean-Luc Lagardère, Hachette's chief executive, argued: 'if you're involved in advanced technologies, you have no choice but to diversify – and to internationalize'. Like other continental European media groups, Hachette claimed that, in order to overcome the advantages of language and market penetration enjoyed by Anglo-American groups, it was imperative both to have a US R&D and market presence, and to tap the other major language markets – in the case of Hachette, book publishing (and, later, broadcast media) in Spain and Latin America.

European audiovisual media policy, networks and lobbies

In a celebrated phrase concerning Latin America, the early nineteenth-century British politician, George Canning, spoke of calling 'the New World into existence, to redress the balance of the Old'. In the late twentieth century, European audiovisual producers and policy-makers strive to redress the imbalance in programme material, and lament the US products and genres that flood Europe's TV screens. In countries such as Britain, quota provisions governing the import of foreign material were traditionally respected. But, throughout the 1980s, the increase in the transmission time, and number, of TV channels led to increased demand for programme material and for a relaxation of quotas.

Many of Europe's media tycoons enjoy relatively favourable relations with the political and financial establishment of the main countries in which they operate. Behind the imagery and hype (often assiduously cultivated) of 'buccaneers', 'mavericks', 'outsiders', and 'condottieri', media tycoons, whose companies may themselves be part of a financial and industrial conglomerate, include figures who are well versed in political skills. They may, on occasion, openly flout the law – as did Robert Hersant in France. More often, they bend it and exploit the loopholes in media legislation and regulation – as did Silvio Berlusconi in Italy, from the mid-1970s to 1990. Innumerable examples can be cited of the violation of national laws and regulations governing the ownership, control, programme content, transmission and distribution arrangements of commercial broadcasting channels.

Media tycoons curry favour with prominent national politicians and carry political clout. Some of the more celebrated friendships include those between Rupert Murdoch and America's Ronald Reagan and Britain's Margaret Thatcher. The courtship of Robert Hersant by various right-wing leaders in France is well attested: in the 1986–8 Chamber of Deputies, over ten MPs had been or were in his employment. In Italy, the friendship between Silvio Berlusconi and Bettino Craxi (leader of the socialist party and prime minister, 1983–7) helped the tycoon in the manoeuvres and debates that ultimately led to the 1990 audiovisual law. These friendships transcend the frontiers of the nation-state: the Craxi–Berlusconi connection brought the Italian tycoon a reward of sorts in France. It appears that it was Craxi who first introduced Berlusconi to the socialist president of France, François Mitterrand; months later Berlusconi was presented as the 'experienced professional broadcaster' of the consortium to which the French government awarded the franchise for the new commercial channel, La Cinq.

The shortcomings of national laws, regulations and practices were one factor behind pressure for action at a European level. This intensified during the 1980s. As far back as the 1970s, the (then 21-strong) Council of Europe (CoE) and, in the early 1980s, the EC Commission approached – albeit from different perspectives – what came to be known as the issue of 'television without frontiers' (TVWF). This concerned the various implications of technologies that were coming on-stream: the transmission and distribution of electronic signals that may deliver not only computer data and telephone traffic but also radio and, above all, television programmes across Europe and beyond. Existing broadcasting regulatory practices – founded, as often as not, on the argument of the scarcity of available frequencies – collapsed. Private sector media tycoons – either long-established in the print media (Murdoch, Springer, Hersant, etc.) or recently established in commercial broadcasting (Berlusconi) – sought to tap the possibilities that emerged as the monopolies of state-owned or public service systems – or, in Britain's case, the BBC–ITV 'duopoly' – appeared threatened. In 1989, after much lobbying and many compromises, the EC adopted its (TVWF) broadcasting Directive and the CoE declared its (non-binding) transfrontier broadcasting Convention open for signature.

Burgeoning TV channels attract commercial broadcasters who seek to deliver audiences to advertisers by attractive programming. But there has been many a slip – technological, political, regulatory and economic – between cup and lip. Several gambles – Murdoch, a poker player, likes to present himself as a gambler – did not pay off. Staying power, through the resources of the cash cows and revenue generators – the *Sun*, for example, in Murdoch's case – bank loans and credit lines, is very important. Media groups are at the cutting edge. Murdoch, Maxwell, Berlusconi and Hersant – to name but four – all lost heavily on many of their European broadcasting investments.

This proved a further reason for the pooling of resources within a media empire and, indeed, between media empires. Transmitting to the British Isles and north-western Europe, channels of the Murdoch-controlled BSkyB broadcasting company (1990) frequently show films initially produced by the Hollywood major, Twentieth Century Fox. In 1985, Murdoch acquired control of the Fox studios, film library and distribution rights. He therefore controls programming material for transmission via his media outlets in the USA, Europe and elsewhere.

Other media empires, while they may be rivals in some market sectors in Europe, increasingly team up in others. In France, for example, in late 1990, the major shareholders in the consortium operating the franchise for La Cinq included the French print media rivals, Hachette and Hersant, and Italy's Berlusconi. Berlusconi also had a small stake in TF1, France's leading commercial TV channel, whose operating consortium numbered (until 1991) the British-based Robert Maxwell among its major shareholders (alongside the lead operator, the Bouygues construction group). Cross-holdings, and the control of assets or stock, may be prompted by speculative and financial motives rather than by specific strategies aiming at vertical and horizontal integration. But there was growing evidence by 1989 that some sectors of the broadcasting and communications industry in Europe were experiencing a period of consolidation, and that existing conglomerates were buying up assets in different countries and various sectors.

While they generally succeed in circumventing attempts at the level of the nation-state to circumscribe their expansion, European media groups express increasing concern at 'Brussels activism'. One outcome of the TVWF debate in the 1980s, according to the EC Commission, was that it had succeeded in proving that broadcasting policy – insofar as broadcasting is a service industry – fell within its remit (as defined by the Treaty of Rome of 1956). In a related move, the Commission moved to prepare a directive on advertising (1991).

Various media, advertising and communications industry actors strengthened the organization of the trade associations concerned with the defence of their interests and lobbied hard in Brussels, Strasbourg and elsewhere. Representing advertisers, advertising agencies and the media, the European Advertising Tripartite (EAT) lobbied successfully, by and large, during the TVWF debate. Europe's commercial TV moguls likewise felt they must make their collective voice heard: in June 1989, Silvio Berlusconi became the chairman of the (new) Association for Commercial Television (ACT), set up to defend the cause of free competition in broadcasting. Its members included Berlusconi's Fininvest, Britain's ITV companies, SAT-1 of West Germany, France's TF1, and the grandfather of Europe's commercial broadcasters, Luxembourg's CLT. They argued that at a time of increasing numbers of policy bodies and initiatives their interests were insufficiently represented in the main organization of European broadcasters, the European Broadcasting Union (EBU).

In 1991, for example, the ACT lobbied for EC aid if its members were to accept the D2-MAC European satellite transmission standard favoured by the EC Commission. Similarly, in 1991, fears prompted by the proposed EC Directive on advertising prompted leading European newspaper publishers and proprietors (including the Murdoch and Springer groups) to create a further media lobby, aimed at preventing, or weakening, EC intervention.

Brussels 'activism', as is outlined in the next chapter, proceeds regardless. In February 1990, the EC Commissioner Jean Dondel-inger presented a Commission communication on audiovisual policy. This contained much to disturb Europe's media tycoons. It pointed out that national anti-trust legislation was often ineffective and that the EC regulation on mergers of December 1989 was insufficient to cover the threat to pluralism posed by cases of multimedia ownership. A new Directive, to harmonize certain aspects of national legislation, might well be necessary . . . (Dondel-inger 1990).

The many 'logics' of media empires [2]

The question raised in the introductory chapters to this book, as to whether there are any new issues on the agenda for European media policies, finds a further answer in the rise and establishment of transnational media empires in the late 1980s. The media magnates are themselves the 'new' actors bearing a 'new logic' for media development. The media tycoonery is at the same time a consequence of and one of the forces causing the disruption of the media structure in individual European countries. It is a consequence because the last decade has seen what has been called in the previous chapter, the 'vogue for market solutions and deregulation'. This vogue has affected the general mood of media consumers (who want more entertainment, more choice) and the outlook of political and government forces who seem converted to the idea of 'going commercial'.

Such a shift, slow-moving in the early 1980s and increasingly faster towards the end of the decade, has raised a challenge to the traditional balances in media domains, where broadcasting was generally regulated as a public service, the press seen as an 'old' medium, managed by well-established small and medium-sized publishers, and the 'new media' were considered a marginal territory where ectoplasmic entities would wander in a foggy landscape. The ensuing crisis of the national, centrally controlled media systems has weakened the regulatory power of traditional, politically oriented policy-makers, thus allowing internally and externally driven forces to aim at the heart of the system.

The 'new' interest groups are also independent variables of the transformation in the media structures. The media barons are both domestically rooted and trans/multinationally based. The nature of today's media production, distribution and consumption markets is such that the protagonists cannot help holding a global outlook and expansionist policies. Accordingly, the magnates urge domestic policy-makers at home to open up the national market, arguing that it cannot be protected and self-contained any more vis-à-vis the world-wide flow of media products. Outside, the media barons act as pressure agencies on governments and local markets, which are still unwilling to join the global trend, and toward the new EC policy-makers who are working on regulations of media matters.

These combined actions from within and from without on the part of nationally based but internationally projected media companies and transnational media providers – with an exclusively commercial outlook – seem to be succeeding in shaking the already crumbling walls of monopolistic and protectionist media precincts.

There are several independent variables that account for the rise and the consolidation of the media empires in Europe. Some have already been hinted at or illustrated, some others are to be found in the domain of macroeconomics, where financial forces are pointed to as crucial factors. A few additional ones can be detected by means of the 'media politics' key that characterizes the outlook of this book.

These latter variables can also be labelled in terms of 'logics' that underlie the phenomenon:

- the logic of the *fait accompli*;
- the logic of the gap between global processes and localistic policy-making;
- the logic of the market place;
- the interplay between the political logic and the industrial logic.

In the first part of this chapter we have given detailed examples of the tensions that arose in the European countries in the 1980s between policy-makers and communications media groups in relation to the regulatory policies in the media field. These examples reveal that the power balance in the game was leaning towards one corner, i.e. the groups, to a point where the winning forces were almost legitimized, not as counterparts, but as partners in the policy-making process.

The intense interventionism of the various lobbies of the multimedia magnates at all political levels in different countries and in Brussels, vis-à-vis the low-key legislative and government actions in the electronic media and anti-trust domains, in fact leads to a reconsideration of the very definition of 'policy-makers'. Since it appears that, in general, the media groups succeeded in getting what they demanded in the domestic and in the international market place, or in preventing restrictive measures and even in invalidating the regulations that were eventually worked out, it may be a matter of course, perhaps more from a sociologist's than a political scientist's point of view, to include these 'actors' amongst policy-makers. Together with the classic policy-makers, that is, the legislators, the magnates and many other commercial and industrial agencies have contributed to creating a situation in Europe in which the *fait accompli* seems to constitute, in certain countries, a regulatory framework in itself. No high authority (but, as was shown above, nothing of this nature exists in the EC) is so strong as to threaten the existence of or to put a stop to the media conglomerates. The few fences erected by national authorities have in some cases, pushed domestically based groups to expand beyond their frontiers, and consequently to take on a multinational outlook and to pursue multimedia interests.

A further explanation of the phenomenon of multimedia empires can be found in the divide between an unstoppable drive of businesses world-wide toward mergers and acquisitions, and the provincial outlook of several domestic policy-makers. In line with the futile attempts to defend national frontiers against the intrusion of foreign television programmes, the potential impact of domestic media conglomerates both within and beyond national boundaries, on the media system has often been underestimated.

Certainly, the logic of expansion of many global groups could not be resisted effectively by hypothetical supranational bodies; even less so by national authorities. Even so, this acknowledgement by decision-makers in individual countries does not account for their weak policies. They have tended to ignore the world-wide scope of the phenomenon, hoping to succeed in checking it by short-sighted measures. It has been easy for the merging businesses to flout domestic checks and to pursue their plans elsewhere, and even, in many cases, at home. Even the EC competition law, as outlined above, has shown itself unfit to govern the process of media concentration.

This apparent invincibility of multinational multimedia tycoons or conglomerates hardly constitutes deviant behaviour, as it finds its rationale in the logic of market place dynamics. If the global trend demands large concentrations of ownership in order to develop synergies, and to make investments profitable in defined sectors of the media industry, any action aimed at obstructing the compliance of businesses with the laws of the market place is in principle, and in practice, objectionable. The US anti-trust legislation itself has succeeded in channelling mergers rather than in preventing them. The Time–Warner case is just one example to back this argument. After all, it cannot be otherwise unless the free market order is questioned. One of the dividing forces of the market place in post-industrial society is the drive toward a global commercialization of the media domain. The changes that public broadcasting systems are undergoing in Europe lead to a greater emphasis on commercial factors in production. Public and private channels compete for larger audiences and fight each other for significant slices of the advertising cake.

In the field of news publishing (undoubtedly one of the key businesses in the 'global village'), information has gradually lost its romantic aura and taken on the more secular stamp of a commodity, to be manufactured and sold purely for profit. With a few minor differences, the same can be stated for the press, book publishing and the audiovisual industry. The tycoons, betting their capital in these and connected fields, first look at the 'commercial personality' of such assets, and then pursue their financial policies accordingly.

Finally, the tycoons' story can also be interpreted in terms of the interplay between two of the above logics: the political logic and the market logic. Often industrial interests clash with political concerns, as argued above, but can also come to terms with each other, and even cooperate for the attainment of their respective goals. It is a general assumption, firmly rooted in repeated empirical evidence, that the economy, the media and politics are closely interlinked. For their part entrepreneurs and industrialists maintain the kind of relations with the political establishment that allow them to pursue their goals with the least possible risk, or with the maximum possible benefit, either in financial terms or in policy terms. Governments and political parties, on their own, are traditionally quite sensitive on communication issues, as witnessed by the control, usually indirect but often direct (even in liberal democracies), over the domestic media systems. Moreover, the media, be they the press or the broadcast media, are at the same time the object of intense attention from financial or political interests, and the subject of actions liable to have an impact in the economic and political arenas.

The media tycoons epitomize such a triangle of interests and mutual relations. They are very much part of the entrepreneurial class and pursue the specific logic of the industrial establishment. But the peculiar nature of the commodity they trade in, communication, singles them out as 'political' actors. All of them, in fact, in their home countries as well as on the international stage, inevitably establish close ties with law-makers and politicians. They make deals or engage in tugs of war with them, and it is from them that they receive the green light to pursue their interests. So there is a one-to-one relationship between the economic power and the political power for the control of the resource of communication: the tycoons flatter the politicians, and the political circles favour the tycoons' inroads into the media strongholds. The results are the weakening of the public media structures and the fortification of the private media combines in Europe as well as in the rest of the Western world.

Notes

1   Author's translation.
2   This section was written by Gianpietro Mazzoleni.

References

Dondelinger, J. (EC Commission) (1990) 'Communication from the Commission to the Council and Parliament on audiovisual policy.' Brussels: COM (90) 78 final.

Hott, T. (1990) 'European Commission plans single market for film and television', *Screen Finance*, 7 March.

Todorov, P. (1990) *La presse française à l'heure de l'Europe*. Paris: la Documentation Française.

Tunstall, J. and Palmer, M. (1991) *Media Moguls*. London: Routledge.

4

Regulation of Media at the European Level

Mario Hirsch and Vibeke G. Petersen

Towards Television without Frontiers

During 1989 European regulators adopted rules to permit the free circulation of television programmes across borders. This happened – after a lengthy gestation period – with a rapidly increasing number of television channels as backdrop and the single European market only a few years away. The Council of Europe Convention on Transfrontier Television, opened for signature on 5 May, and the EC Directive 'Television without Frontiers' of 3 October are different instruments, the former only binding those countries that choose to ratify the Convention and the latter becoming binding for the 12 EC member-states from October 1991. They also differ in their point of departure, the Convention primarily aiming at a free flow of information in all of (Western) Europe and the Directive more concerned with securing the free flow of services in the internal market.

These differences notwithstanding, the two sets of regulations are basically identical, because they respond to the same external pressures arising from technological change bringing many more channels, and increasing privatization and commercialization of television bringing new operators with economic power of their own to alter the media landscape. It should not be overlooked, of course, that the governments of the EC member-states, shuttling between Brussels and Strasbourg, had an obvious interest in avoiding contradictory instruments in the two fora.

Regulatory efforts at the European level were preceded by significant and gradual changes in the broadcasting landscape. The emphasis on the economic dimensions of broadcasting took some time to come about and imperceptibly superseded the conventional approach that viewed broadcasting as a prominent vehicle of culture, national identity, education and information (the so-called public service philosophy).

The advent of new delivery technologies such as cable and satellite, which gained momentum in the second half of the 1980s, put under strain the comfortable position of broadcasting monopolies. The expansion of these technologies also gave a new international dimension to broadcasting, enabling the establishment of new cross-border services.

The growing commercialization and internationalization of broadcasting forced governments to loosen the monopolistic outlook of their broadcasting policies. Deregulation became the name of the game, and it led to the emergence of a dual sector. The advent of a private, market-oriented sector alongside the public one brought corporate actors and entrepreneurial figures to the fore and led to an increased involvement of banks and financiers in broadcasting.

These new actors were encouraged by prospects of terrestrial frequencies being put out to tender and by a general relaxation of controls on advertising and programming. Well before policy was enacted at the European level, the European Court of Justice had already paved the way for the business-oriented approach in the early 1980s by developing case law on transborder broadcasting, stipulating that broadcasts were to be considered 'services' falling under the free circulation provisions of the EC Treaty.

The European-level efforts to regulate transfrontier television entered the public debate through the publication of the EC Commission's Green Paper 'Television without Frontiers' in 1984 and the First European Ministerial Conference on Mass Media Policy held in Vienna in December 1986. During the subsequent elaboration of the two initiatives into draft regulations a certain element of competition between the responsible agencies was discernible – with the Council of Europe pointing to its natural role in cultural affairs and its inclusion of all the Western European countries (and potentially also those of the Eastern bloc) and the EC claiming to have the only effective regulatory power.

It was, however, over the content of the rules that battles in this competition were won and lost. As could be expected, opinions on the measures appropriate to ensuring the free flow of television differed a great deal between the parties involved. The most important areas to be regulated were advertising, protection of minors, moral standards, European programming (the quotas) and the exceptional right to refuse re-transmission of a cross-border programme (the issue of copyright was included originally in both instruments, but eventually had to be dropped because of insurmountable disagreements). In each case, national interests diverged, and compromises had to be found.

As a consequence of these instruments coming into force EC member-states or parties to the Convention may receive and retransmit broadcasts without fear of government interference. Channels which are authorized by the country of origin and comply with the minimum standards laid out in these documents cannot be blocked for ownership, content or commercial reasons.

Article 2 of the Directive (Article 24 of the Convention) sets conditions under which a government can suspend the re-transmission of a broadcast coming from another country. These conditions are very strict and in favour of the broadcaster. Thus, the repeated, manifest, serious and grave infringement of the rules on violence, racism and pornography is considered to be a violation, enabling the receiving country to suspend re-transmission of a broadcast. Suspension can take place only after warnings have been issued and negotiations have taken place and is liable to cancellation by the EC Commission or by the arbitration procedure of the Convention.

Articles 3, 8 and 19 of the Directive (Article 28 of the Convention) allow for countries to apply stricter or more detailed rules to broadcasters within their jurisdiction than those provided for in both the Directive and the Convention. These provisions enable a country like France to retain a stricter quota system for its national broadcasters, namely one based on linguistic considerations.

Article 7 of the Directive (Article 10 of the Convention) establishes that a two-year period has to elapse between the time a cinematographic work is shown in cinemas and its screening on TV.

Both documents are very precise regarding the minimum guidelines applicable to advertising (Articles 10–18 in the Directive, 11–16 in the Convention). Advertisements are limited to 15 per cent of total airtime and a maximum of 20 per cent of any given hour. Movies may have one advertising break for each complete period of 45 minutes. A further interruption is allowed if their duration is at least 20 minutes longer than two or more complete periods of 45 minutes. Other programmes can be broken for advertisements every 20 minutes except for news, current affairs, religious and children's programmes, which have to exceed a duration of 30 minutes before a break is allowed. Advertisements should not discriminate on the grounds of race, religion or sex, nor should they incite to hatred. Advertisements for tobacco products are banned as are those for medical products or for medical treatment. Advertising for alcoholic drinks is restricted in as much as it may not be aimed at minors, nor depict minors drinking.

For all the controversy and debate over the minimum guidelines, it should be pointed out that nearly all the provisions except for those dealing with advertising are rather 'woolly' and open to interpretation by individual regulatory authorities. The Directive is neither restrictive nor exclusive, but liberally worded. In effect, the need for a compromise reduced it to a skeleton of its original, which had been much more protectionist. It would seem that Europe has successfully avoided the threat posed by a misguided approach to television market regulation, despite the fears of the Association of Commercial Television in Europe (ACT), which believed that the EC and the Council of Europe were unwise to regulate a field which is currently undergoing fundamental transformations. ACT argued that this may 'set undue restrictions for the future. If regulation is too heavy handed and guided by political rather than economic criteria, there is indeed a danger that the industry will remain fragmented and inefficient. Viewers would suffer because they would have access to less television at a higher cost'. It remains to be seen, however, whether Europe will escape the many pitfalls of too loose a regulatory framework. If regulation is too weak and insufficiently concerned with promoting competitive markets, then there will indeed be a dangerous increase in market concentration, with the industry controlled by a small number of multimedia multinationals.

The breakthrough (for both sets of rules, as it turned out) came at the 2nd European Ministerial Conference on Mass Media Policy in Stockholm, in late November 1988, when a consensus was arrived at with respect to the insertion of advertising and the Council of Europe was able to present a near-finished Convention. A week later, the EC Council of Ministers at a meeting in Rhodes agreed to proceed with the work on the Directive 'in the light of the Council of Europe Convention' – another way of saying that what had been agreed on in the Convention more or less constituted the highest common denominator that anyone could hope for at that moment. One such 'light' to be followed was the formulation of the quota article which later caused a large number of problems.

The battle over quotas

During the first half of 1989 the Council of Europe and the EC both became aware of the extent of internal opposition within member-states. Regional authorities, opposition parties, commercial interests, multinational broadcasters and professional organizations all put pressure on their governments in an attempt to minimize the damage to their own interests. In West Germany the federal government was attacked by the Länder governments for usurping their monopoly on cultural policies, including broadcasting. Hence the last-minute declaration by the EC Commission and the member-states that the quota article was politically rather than legally binding. This interpretative declaration was obviously made in order to calm American fears and to weaken the legal teeth of the Directive. Spokesmen for the Commission made it clear that failure to reach the quota goals would not be sufficient for the Commission to bring member-states to court for breaching the Directive. In France the government ran into massive protests from film-makers, who branded the Directive 'an audiovisual Munich' and 'a hole in the audiovisual ozone layer'.

The fact that it was the quota issue which aroused most controversy can be explained by the dual purpose of the Directive as a remover of barriers to the cross-border flow of programmes *and* as an encouragement to European audiovisual production. (This dual purpose is also inherent in the Convention, but here it is perhaps less controversial because of the Council of Europe's role in cultural policy and the optional character of a Convention.)

Following the Commission's proposal for a broadcasting Directive in 1986, it was calculated that the demand for TV programming material would double by the mid-1990s. It became apparent that European productions could not satisfy this demand. European film producers – mainly the French – reacted, expressing their concern that the gap would be filled with US programmes. In France, artists and producers put pressure on the government to protect French culture from American 'cultural imperialism'. French parliamentarians were the driving force in the European Parliament for a 60 per cent local content provision.

At the beginning of 1988, and as a result of this pressure, the Commission introduced the 60 per cent quota in the Directive proposal. Several countries, however, rejected the proposal. The Directive's final wording, 'Member States shall ensure, where practicable and by appropriate means, that broadcasters reserve for European works . . . a majority proportion of their transmission time . . .', combined with the declaration that this article of the Directive is only politically binding, is the result of a process in which several parties exerted different influences and pursued different objectives.

European dependence on imported American films has grown dramatically in recent years. American feature films have more than a 40 per cent share of the feature film market in Europe. However, the total American share of European TV programming is only 23 per cent. American media groups dominate distribution by owning some 60 per cent of the distribution networks in Europe. So US film producers are directly concerned with the Directive's economic implications. Their interests have been represented for many years by the Motion Pictures Association of America (MPAA) which is said to be one of the most effective lobbying groups in Washington.

The United States government's opposition to the Directive is based on the view that it is an economic measure designed to protect the European industry from external competition. In the light of the US trade deficit, the trade surplus generated by the motion picture industry is a motivating factor for Congress to take action. Furthermore, TV film production for Europe is a growth area which could help diminish the trade deficit even more.

The American entertainment industry is a consistent net exporter. In 1988, the US production industry earned over $2.5 billion in surplus balance of trade, of which some $1.8 billion are reported from TV and home video sales in the EC member-states. In 1988, Europe bought some $700 million worth of American TV productions. This figure was expected to have reached 1 billion in 1989. The administration and the MPAA both vigorously opposed the Directive by lobbying all European parties, claiming that 'the implementation of the Directive would be blatantly discriminatory, patently unjustifiable, and would almost certainly have a disastrous effect on the US industry's substantial European earnings'. The government and Congress are against any quotas in the European single market, fearing that protectionist measures will create a 'Fortress Europe'. Against this background the US government has used the quota sections in the Directive as an additional bargaining element in the overall trade negotiations with the EC. The US envisaged several retaliatory measures at various stages. Among the more serious threats was the Intellectual Property Rights Provision of the 1988 US Trade Act, which allows the US government to establish import quotas in retaliation for import restrictions on US goods. The USA maintained that the 'local content' (= quota) provisions in the Directive violate the most-favoured nation provisions of GATT article I by according preferential treatment to works from European non-EC member-countries, as well as article III's national treatment provision which requires GATT contracting parties to extend to the products of other contracting parties treatment 'no less favourable than that accorded to like products of national origin.' This lingering transatlantic conflict over broadcasting policy certainly contributed to the deterioration of trade relations between the US and the EC which escalated into the failure to conclude the so-called GATT Uruguay round at the end of 1990.

The European political actors had different rationales. For the EC Commission the Directive was the much-needed legal basis for allowing it to start a European audiovisual policy. The fixed quota provision was put in at a rather late stage because of pressure from the French government and the European Parliament, and taken out again because of rejection by several member-states and the American protests.

The French insistence on a high, fixed quota is primarily a reflection of domestic policy in this area, but also of the importance given in France to cultural policies in general – official animosity against American imports, be they new words or movies, goes back much further than the Directive. In the end the French government had to back down, not only because it was isolated, but also because even the vague quota formulation that was eventually adopted was too restrictive for some other governments to be accepted as legally binding.

During the summer of 1989, when the final compromise was hammered out, for a while it looked as if the whole project would collapse. Denmark and Belgium, which early on had announced that they would vote against the Directive, were joined by West Germany, the Netherlands, France and Greece, and the suspense was kept up until the very end when, on 3 October, the Directive was adopted by a qualified majority. Only Denmark and Belgium voted against, the Danes because they have consistently objected to EC competence in cultural affairs, and the Belgians because they wanted more protection for their audiovisual industry.

Because of its geographical location and its extensive cable systems, Belgium is one of the most accessible countries for foreign television. As a consequence, it has seen its own broadcasters lose audiences on a large scale. Attempts to protect its national programme industry, for instance, through licence requirements for foreign commercial channels, quotas for cultural productions and exclusion of foreign advertising, have brought it into conflict with EC rules and policies.

The German resistance to the Directive came, as mentioned above, from the Länder, jealously guarding their constitutional right to decide in cultural matters, including broadcasting. It is, however, the federal government in Bonn that determines German policies in relation to the EC. In order to arrive at a decision on the Länder/federal government controversy in this area, Bavaria has brought the issue before the Constitutional Court in Karlsruhe, and other Länder have joined in action. A decision is expected some time in 1991.

Most of the other member-states had little objection to the Directive. In the UK, advertisers and commercial broadcasters were unhappy about the stricter advertising regulations, but otherwise the spirit of 'Television without Frontiers' was broadly in line with government policies of more competition and liberalization. Italy, which at the time of the EC negotiations was still working on a new broadcasting law, was generally positive, among other things because the Directive would be helpful in 'levelling the playing field' between public and private broadcasters at home. The Italians succeeded in exempting from the quota clauses 'local television broadcasts not forming part of a national network' – known as 'the Berlusconi article'.

It should be added that the European Parliament was throughout strongly in favour of the introduction of tough quota provisions. Its somewhat frustrated role in the EC decision-making hierarchy was underlined when the Commission – in the light of political reality – refused to incorporate the Parliament's main suggestions in the final draft of the Directive.

At present it is impossible to set up European TV networks, for political reasons (ownership limitations) and because of compartmentalization of the market and a national broadcasting structure. One of the quotas' main objectives is to avoid devitalizing the existing industry in Europe. European Community films seldom enjoy the necessary economies of scale and penetrate only with difficulty into other member-states. The Commission has calculated that 80 per cent of European films never leave the country in which they were made, and that intra-European audiovisual transactions represent only 8 per cent of total European transactions.

By the time American series go on sale in Europe, the bulk of their production costs have been written off in the home market. The economic reality is such that American programmes are always a better bargain for broadcasters in Europe than European programmes. The local content provision in the Directive is designed to favour the emergence of a European film and television programme production industry that can compete with the US industry.

The USA claims that a programming quota which requires a majority of television entertainment programmes to originate from within Europe could cost American firms hundreds of millions of dollars over a period of time. Realistically, however, there will be no reduction in terms of dollars because the European market will expand. Furthermore, the USA can increase its current market share of 40 per cent to 50 per cent. Finally, it can be argued that the American entertainment industry would have risked losing a bigger portion of the European broadcasting market if the quota provision had not been agreed on. National legislation was pending in a number of European countries to protect their culture against imports, and the 'soft' quotas in the Directive may have pre-empted the call for stiffer compulsory measures.

The circle of potential beneficiaries of the Directive extends well beyond the film production industry – American broadcasters, advertising agencies, manufacturers and investors all have an interest in the development of a unified European market. One unintended effect of the quota provision is that holders of existing European film rights will benefit greatly. In the short term not enough financial resources can be generated to produce the volume of film required to fill the quota. This will lead to re-transmission of old movies and provide large additional revenues to the owners of film libraries.

The MPAA lobbying in the USA proved to be very successful. It seems to have spurred the Bush administration to toughen its stance on the Directive. But US lobbying in Europe has to some extent been counterproductive. European officials claim that the pressure from across the Atlantic was too much, too late, and too un-informed. Lobbyists for Hollywood were dealt a lesson in the perils of overkill. No European government wished to be seen to be giving in to such overt American pressure, even if they themselves had no particular enthusiasm for the Directive. So, in the end, US trade representative Carla Hills' tour of the European capitals in the summer of 1989 to warn against the adoption of the Directive may have been more helpful to the Commission's efforts than to her own purpose.

Boosting the industry

Disagreements aside, it is evident that there is a strong and justified fear in European political and professional circles that the benefits of a single market will be reaped entirely by the American industry, unless a boost is given to European audiovisual production. The issue is not just economic, however, but also cultural: the danger that small countries will lose their cultural identity increases in an 'invaded' market and can only be averted through a deliberate European policy. The task, thus, is to replace 'wall-to-wall' Dallas – not with its imitation, 'Europudding' – but with a diversified product capable of attracting a wide audience.

A number of initiatives to that effect were taken in the late 1980s. The EC Commission launched the Media 92 programme in 1987. (In December of 1990 it got the go-ahead from the Council of Ministers to graduate from the pilot phase to become a fully fledged community programme under the name Media 95.)

Media 92 consisted of several separate projects which, in collab-oration with professionals, provided seed money to support train-ing, research and development, script-writing, independent production, distribution of cinema films and video cassettes, multi-lingualism, new technology and cartoon production. The pro-gramme gives priority to small and medium-sized enterprises and is thus primarily geared towards assisting the audiovisual industry in the smaller community countries.

Eurimages was set up by the Council of Europe in 1988 as a fund designed to support cross-border co-production and distribution of films and TV programmes. As of late 1990, 18 countries participate in this project (among them Hungary).

It can be said for both of these programmes that they are fairly modest in financial terms and that they are not in themselves capable of solving the complex problems of the audiovisual indus-try. A much more comprehensive effort, Audiovisual Eureka, was set in motion by the French president Mitterrand in conjunction with the EC Commission at the European Council meeting in Rhodes in December 1988. The name Eureka is borrowed from the European technological cooperation programme and denotes the character of the plan: a mobilization of industry, professionals and governments 'with a view to providing a flexible, pragmatic res-ponse to the challenge facing Europe' – in this case the insufficiency of audiovisual production, the growing imbalance in the flow of programmes between Europe and the United States and between European countries, and the paucity of resources available for European initiatives. It is also inherent in the scheme that it is not reserved for EC member-states, but encompasses in principle the whole of Europe.

The key words in this context are greater transparency in the market, co-production and co-distribution and promotion of Euro-pean technologies, especially in the area of HDTV. It is perhaps worth noting that Audiovisual Eureka is not richly funded to help along the transition from a fragmented, uncompetitive industry to a unified and booming one.

There is no doubt, however, that the project was launched at a most opportune moment and with political skill. At the Rhodes summit it was clear, as mentioned previously, that the European regulatory framework under elaboration in the EC and the Council of Europe had reached a conclusive stage – with a quota provision that aroused protests for diametrically opposite reasons. But what-ever individual countries had against the instruments, they were all in favour of strengthening the audiovisual industry, and the Eureka plan acquired a role as an acceptable substitute for the perceived shortcomings of the regulatory compromise. It did so mainly through the strong backing given to it by Mitterrand, who, in early October 1989, gathered together professionals and experts for a two-day discussion and planning session, 'les Assises de l'audio-visuel'. The conference resulted in a joint declaration by ministers from 26 participating countries and the president of the EC Commission, officially establishing Audiovisual Eureka. It was no coincidence that the following day the French government made official its acceptance of the Directive on Television without Frontiers.

The joint declaration lists the measures to be taken within the Eureka framework. Among the most important are the establishment of a Coordinators' Committee, composed of government representatives, which is to act as a board of directors, a secretariat, and plans for an observatory which will function as a databank for the industry. Among the tasks of the Committee will be to give official Eureka approval to cross-border cooperative projects.

In the end, of course, it is up to the industry itself to give substance to the venture. It will have to use its own resources and will receive little more than political good-will and moral support from the Eureka management. It would be a mistake, however, to underestimate the potential of this favourable attention to the audiovisual field. Not being confined to the EC member-states, Eureka can be a means of practical cooperation among all European countries, not least those of Central Europe (thereby appeasing those member-states that take a dim view of the EC's role in cultural affairs), and it can provide the Commission with a platform for new initiatives.

The EC momentum

Commissioner Jean Dondelinger presented, in February 1990, the EC Commission's audiovisual policy in a Communication to the Council and the European Parliament. With the aim of securing a single market for film and television, this policy is greatly inspired by the results of the Eureka conference, and it proposes specific actions to be taken in each of the three sections of what is called the audiovisual 'triptych': the rules of the game, the programme industries, and new technologies.

The first item on the list of areas to be regulated is copyright. As mentioned earlier, the Directive contained copyright clauses in its draft edition, but they had to be dropped because of strong opposition from several states. The Commission now promises to take a new approach by avoiding the controversial issue of statutory licences and by opting for the contractual solution which is more widely acceptable in the Community.

In November 1990 the EC Commission published a discussion paper on copyright questions concerning cable and satellite broadcasts. This paper outlines its new views on the matter with the hope of translating them into a Directive in 1991. The Commission proposes to introduce supporting measures in order to safeguard and supplement the acquisition of rights to simultaneous, unaltered and unabridged re-transmission of programmes via cable (secondary broadcasting), which in practice has been up to now largely organized through collective agreements. To achieve this, the Commission intends to bring national legislation more closely into line in two respects. Firstly, cross-border re-transmission should no longer be at risk from individual rights invoked by outsiders not represented when the collective contracts were concluded. Secondly, cross-border cable re-transmission should be further promoted by providing a minimum level of certainty that the cable operators can in practice acquire the necessary rights. The Commission wants to make sure that an outsider is no longer free to exercise his right individually against the actual user of the work, but is confined to a claim for remuneration against the collecting society or organization of rights owners. Measures to facilitate rights acquisition, such as arbitration and supervision, are also envisaged.

Copyright aspects of satellite transmissions will also be dealt with. A major uncertainty in this respect concerns the question of whether satellite transmissions which can be received directly in more than one country are subject only to the copyright laws of the country of origin, or whether they are subject at one and the same time to the law of all those states in which the transmissions can be received. In order to overcome this problem the Commission proposes that the relevant copyright law should be the law of one state only. The relevant state would be the state in which the broadcaster carries on business in a real and substantial manner. This simplification, of course, raises the problem of how to confer an appropriate level of protection on rights owners. The Commission considers it necessary that the authors' satellite broadcasting rights should not be restricted by a system of statutory or compulsory licences but rather that the rights owners should be left free to exercise their rights on a contractual basis, either through individual contracts, through collective contracts, or through an extension of collective agreements to non-represented rights owners.

Another important part of the policy proposal concerns the nurturing of independent productions. A first step was taken in Article 5 of the Directive, which reserves 10 per cent of transmission time or of the programming budget to independent productions.

New steps to be taken will include the promotion of a secondary market structure that allows for the establishment of new channels that are not bound by content rules. Regulations on competition, media concentration and subsidies are also on the agenda, as are measures designed to assist the media industries in smaller countries.

The Media 92 programme has been moved from its pilot phase to full-scale operation and has been given substantially increased resources. In the proposals for production-oriented measures the Eureka programme plays a major role as a complement to Media 95.

As far as technology is concerned, the policy proposal concentrates on extending the existing MAC packet Directive to low- and medium-power satellites and promoting HDTV, which the Commission wishes to be widely available by 1995. The attempts to impose MAC as the compulsory route to high definition television appear, however, to be ill-fated. Many observers see in this a 'blind alley' approach or a straitjacket that prevents Europe from exploring other, more promising technologies leading to HDTV, such as, for instance, a digital HDTV standard. The biggest liability of MAC-based systems appears to be the fact that they are dependent on delivery by DBS satellites, all of which have been plagued by problems, the latest casualty being the absorption of BSB by Sky Television. The domination of the Astra satellite system as the preferred satellite delivery system has turned the PAL standard (to be upgraded to PAL Plus) into the *de facto* standard for satellite broadcasting in Europe. PAL, as well as its enhanced version, is much better suited to serve consumer needs and to deal with the problem of 'backward compatibility' (compatibility with existing television standards and hence existing television sets) than is MAC, which occupies wide bandwidths not suited for cable networks and imposes significantly greater cost and complexity.

Neither the Convention nor the Directive addresses the problem of cross-media or multiple ownership. In view of the fact that large, and frequently multimedia, groups with extensive market shares have gained ascendancy in Europe, regulation of these issues would have to pursue three conflicting objectives: viability of the broadcasting system as a whole, localism and diversity/pluralism. Experience from outside Europe indicates, however, that the achievement of these conflicting goals becomes problematic as soon as commercial operators dominate the broadcasting environment to the detriment of operators devoted to the public service concept.

The EC Commission now seems to be aware of the need for appropriate anti-trust legislation designed to deal specifically with European media giants such as the Berlusconi group, the German conglomerate Bertelsmann or the French Hachette group, not to mention, of course, Rupert Murdoch's News Corporation. In the early stages of the process leading to the EC Directive, cross-ownership was considered, but along with many other issues it was dropped on the way to the eventual 'soft' policy document we have described.

The EC Commission has at its disposal a whole array of competition policy instruments which enable it to intervene against restrictive practices and abuses of a dominant position. So far, it has made sparse use of these instruments in the case of media enterprises, primarily because such enterprises typically involve hot political issues, but also because, as the media tycoons would argue, 'before you can dominate the industry you have to create it'.

The EC Commission has promised a television industry without frontiers. It is obvious that the boundaries have been torn open to a large extent for the media tycoons and entrepreneurs just as it can hardly be disputed that the position of media conglomerates has been greatly improved in view of the completion of the internal market by the end of 1992. Yet, these developments contain the danger of contravening the ideals enshrined in the Directive and its philosophy. Without any adequate and consistent countervailing powers European broadcasting will make the big jump from a system based on public monopoly to one where private monopoly is king, destroying in the process all that has made Europe's broadcasting tradition so distinguished and exceptional.

European-level regulation is significant as much for its momentum as for its content. Facilitating the free flow of programmes across European borders and the co-production of audiovisual works cannot of itself create a thriving and competitive industry. It remains to be seen whether European audiences will prefer European programmes to their American counterparts – the popularity of national programmes notwithstanding. It could also prove difficult to reconcile the goal of encouraging economies of scale with that of preserving the cultural diversity of Europe. But the very visible internationalization of broadcasting, combined with increasing private ownership of television channels in all European countries, seems to be fertile soil for a continued drive towards a shift in regulatory power over broadcasting away from the national towards the international arena.

References

Council of Europe (1989) 'European Convention on Transfrontier Television.'
Dondelinger, J. (EC Commission) (1990) 'Communication from the Commission to the Council and Parliament on audiovisual policy.' Brussels: COM (90) 78 final.
EC (1989) Council Directive of 3 October 1989 on the co-ordination of certain provisions laid down by law, regulation or administrative action in Member States concerning the pursuit of television broadcasting activities (Television without Frontiers).

5

The Technology Factor

Bernt Stubbe Østergaard and Hans J. Kleinsteuber

Dreams

Over the last hundred years, since Jules Verne imagined a global wireless picture transmission system, many have dreamt and speculated about the possibilities of all-pervasive information systems freeing us from constraints of time and place. The ability to be 'present' anywhere at any time touches some of our deepest feelings of the oneness of humanity. The mass media that offer us some of these possibilities – radio and television – have come to dominate our daily lives to such an extent that some social scientists point to this as the single most important social aspect of this century. The dreams, however, combine technical fantasies with ideal usage patterns. Technical possibilities rarely become social reality.

The penetration of television, video recorders (VCR) and cable/satellite in Western Europe is discussed in detail in the companion volume to this book, *The Media in Western Europe*. Television is found in 90–99 per cent of all European homes. VCR ownership is more unevenly distributed, with Italy showing a particularly low penetration due to the large number of television channels available and to a very high tax rate on VCR equipment. In most countries VCR penetration is between 35 and 50 per cent of TV households, but in the UK it exceeded 66 per cent in 1989. Cable TV penetration is very high in the Netherlands (80 per cent), and in Belgium (93 per cent); Luxembourg (66 per cent) and Switzerland (64 per cent) are the two countries with the next highest cable TV penetration rate. Most other countries have a penetration rate of between 20 and 40 per cent. The corresponding cable TV figures for Italy, Portugal, Spain and the UK are minimal. Finally, the figures for ownership of satellite TV receivers are highest in the UK, but practically negligible in Belgium, Greece and Luxembourg.

According to the fourth consecutive Petar (Pan-European Television Research) survey, in 1990 106 television channels were available in eleven Western European countries – 46 of these were broadcast by satellite. In one year alone (from 1989 to 1990), the study claims, the audience share of commercial satellite television in cable households (24 million) increased from 20 to 39 per cent, while that of terrestrial channels fell to 60 per cent (*Cable and Satellite*, October 1990, p. 10).

This chapter analyses the forces that will shape the next generation of electronic sound and picture systems, known as high definition television (HDTV), and the developments in cable and satellite transmission technology.

Looking at broadband cable developments in the last decade, very few of the 'promises' that these held came true. Nowhere have cable systems been provided with the interactive capabilities that are technologically possible; and local programme origination, intended exclusively for cable, is still the exception in Europe. Such dreams are costly to maintain and attract only very little consumer interest.

Based on their technological potential, cable and satellite – perhaps together with the VCR – are sometimes seen as not just a new and improved technology, but as the technology of 'consumer choice', one that threatens the formerly closed systems of Eastern Europe as well as the state responsibility systems of Western Europe. The American author George H. Quester argues:

> . . . the net trend of technology will be supportive of choice in at least two ways. More and more channels for the transmission of television signals are becoming available, including various forms of terrestrial television transmission, broadcasts from satellites orbiting the earth, and the extensive use of VCRs. And more and more countries have become active in the transmitting of television programming, with their signals crossing the international boundaries, inadvertently or by design allowing the decisions of one state regime to frustrate the restrictions of any other . . . (Quester 1990: 2)

The pace of technical development in recent decades has left the consumer with the task of choosing between many new alternatives specified by the industry, whereas needs voiced by 'concerned citizens', such as the democratization of media access, have had little response from the industry. Public media regulations previously based on monopolies are being circumvented in many different ways, forcing policy-makers constantly to redesign the media landscapes.

Relating dreams to ongoing technological developments in society has led to concepts such as the 'post-industrial society' (Bell 1973), where developments in information technology are seen as changing the way we work and ultimately the material basis of Western society. However, several intervening factors seem to delay the societal transition to this global village, as Marshall McLuhan calls it. New complex technological developments seem to create new complex social problems, and often solutions to these emerging social problems are met with technological solutions or 'technological fixes' that provide no solution in themselves.

In this chapter we view technological development as a strategy used by the involved actors in order to strengthen their position in the media field (or to weaken the position of opponents). The natural barriers limiting the number of available frequencies for television transmission over the air, the high cost of setting up and running a television channel and the close cooperation between industry, public broadcasters and PTTs have all broken down due to technological developments in transmission systems and video equipment which are controlled by new actors in the media field. This has changed the balance of power and to a certain extent also the rules of the game.

Actors and fora

In order to analyse media developments we begin by introducing the various forces shaping technological developments. This is achieved by considering first of all the actors involved and then the fora in which decisions are made regarding the development, implementation and standardization of information technology. Finally, we analyse the decisions emanating from the fora, and the ways in which these commit the actors involved.

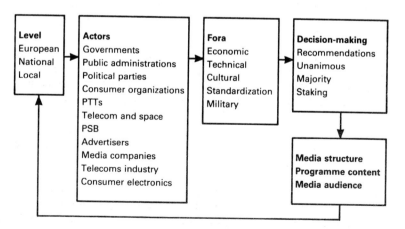

Figure 5.1 *Analytical feedback scheme*

The analytical scheme used in this text is illustrated in Figure 5.1. Decision-making leads to actions that affect media structure, programme content and ultimately media audiences, which in turn supply actors with feedback and in this way affect the relative positions and influence of the actors.

Governments, political parties and public administrations have the overall responsibility for making and implementing broadcast mass media policy – integrating cultural, industrial and consumer demands for entertainment with existing state institutions and tight national budgets. Often legislation is simply a realization that control or monopoly positions are impossible to enforce, and is overtaken by technological developments and general consumer demand for more programming. Organized consumer interests have little or no influence, but are often used to legitimize the interests of other more powerful actors.

The Post, Telephone and Telegraph administrations (PTTs) are the state controlled or licensed public telecommunications service providers, either nationally or regionally. Most are organized as private shareholding companies with the state having a controlling interest. Typical examples are British Telecom and Deutsche Bundespost. The PTTs own the cable networks and have monopoly rights to deliver telephone services. The national PTT monoliths are now being dismantled; competition from private telecommunications companies is being introduced in specific service areas and limits are being set on their pricing policy which hitherto has not been cost-related but a combination of cost-pricing and cross-subsidization.

The PSBs, public service broadcasters, are licensed by the state and have public service programming obligations, such as news, cultural and regional programmes, as well as obligations related to democratic rights (the right to reply, etc.). As discussed in Part III of this book, the PSBs are currently being challenged by private media companies often with international and multimedia activities. From a position of national monopolies 20 years ago with little competition from abroad, today they face national competition from private channels and international competition from multinational broadcasters. Their primary source of revenue, the licence fee, is being cut in most countries and the many new channels reduce advertising revenues. This has given advertisers and sponsors an important influence on programming, because they can pick and choose among several competing public and private channels.

The telecoms industry has also experienced a change in its relations with its customers. Gone are the days of cosy relationships with the single national PTT and the single national PSB. The ongoing integration of the European market has removed the protected national markets, and has forced most companies in the smaller European countries to close altogether or to allow themselves to be bought up by bigger companies. Moreover, massive investments in new technological development have led to a concentration of industries on a world-wide scale. The consumer electronics industry has already passed through several stages of the process of concentration in an attempt to stem the flood of goods from Japan and the USA. Few European companies maintain a lucrative global presence.

The actors meet in a number of fora, where a critical level of consensus has to be reached in order to create the new systems and open the new markets. The most important technical and standardization fora are the ITU, the CEPT, Eutelsat, ESA, the EBU, the EC and the Council of Europe.

The International Telecommunication Union (ITU) is the United Nations organization for the global regulation of telecommunications. The work is handled in the CCITT, which regulates wire-carried telecom services such as the ordinary telephone, and in the CCIR, which handles signal standards for over-the-air transmission such as broadcast television. Members of the ITU meet every four years in the World Administrative Radio Conference, WARC, to allocate the global use of the radio frequency spectrum. The International Frequency Registration Board (IFRB) has been set up to administer the global and regional use of all radio frequencies according to the guidelines laid down at the WARC meetings.

The European PTTs meet in the CEPT, the Conference of European Post and Telecommunications Administrations, in order to work out tariff agreements and other intra-PTT affairs. Previously this was the forum in which European telecommunications policy was made, but nowadays it is only one of several interest groups in the telecoms infrastructure sector fighting for the interests of its members.

Eutelsat is the European satellite organization owned jointly by 26 European PTTs. Officially it is a regional organization affiliated to Intelsat, the global communications satellite organization with headquarters in Washington, USA. Eutelsat was created to give Europe its own commercial satellite communications system independent of US controls. The European Communication Satellite system (ECS) provides European coverage, but the ECS satellites generate relatively weak signals, as they were originally designed for point-to-point telecommunications services between sites with 14–18-metre dishes. This makes home reception of ECS television programmes impossible. Television transmission, originally an incidental Eutelsat sideline, now accounts for some 70 percent of Eutelsat's revenue.

European governments, as a result of a French initiative in 1974, also set up ESA, the European Space Administration, to build and manage a European space programme parallel to that of NASA in the USA. European Ariane rockets, carrying the Eutelsat satellites into orbit, are launched from Kourou in French Guyana in South America.

The European Broadcasting Union (EBU) is the European association of public broadcasters. The organization has its own network for television programme distribution between European PSBs (using ECS satellites and terrestrial microwave links) and has a strong voice in the technological development of the media. For many years it has advocated the introduction of a new television signal standard designed to replace the existing PAL and SECAM formats. This position is based on purely technical considerations.

The EC acts mainly as an economic forum with a strong involvement in opening up the national telecom markets within the EC and strengthening European telecoms vis-à-vis the USA and Japan. The production of television sets is one of the few areas of consumer electronics in which Europe is still a major league player. The EC will do all it can to maintain this position. The EC also supports deregulation in the telecoms field and therefore treads a careful path between opening up to commercial television broadcasting while simultaneously strengthening European research and development of new transmission standards and broadcasting systems.

Table 5.1   *Actor participation in different fora*

Actors	EC	ITU WARC CCIR/CCITT IFRB	CEPT/ Eutelsat	EBU	CoE
Governments	M	M	I		M
Political parties	I				I
Public administrations	M	M	I		M
Consumer organizations	I			I	I
PTT		I	M		
PSB	I			M	
Media companies	I			M	I
Consumer electronics	I			I	
Telecoms industry	I		I		
Film industry	I			I	I
Advertisers	I			I	

M = member; I = exerts influence

The Council of Europe (CoE) is a forum of 26 European countries and addresses such issues as human rights and cultural policy. The CoE has been used by its member nations to hammer out an international agreement on television, regulating such issues as international broadcasting, advertising content, etc. Naturally membership of each of these fora is different, and non-members may be able to exert influence as well. Table 5.1 shows where each of the various actors can voice its concerns.

The decision-making

The approach towards European cooperation in the fields of industry and satellite operations varies radically from that in the fields of programming and broadcasting. Some explanation of successes and failures may be found in an analysis of the ways in which decisions are made.

Some actors involved in the policy-making process, also in radio and television, are new and come from sectors not traditionally associated with broadcasting, for example computer and telecom equipment manufacturers. This has created turbulence in the decision-making process, and has resulted in important issues moving from one forum to another. We can therefore expect actors to invest resources in defining the issues that are at stake, in an effort to move decision-making into fora in which the respective actors are in a particular position of strength.

An example of this is the EC, which has pushed hard to remove the development of the European telecommunications infrastructure away from the CEPT, and which has also tried to remove international broadcasting policy-making away from the EBU. This illustrates the telecommunications field's move from the area of public transport into the furnace of industrial policy. The common industry–government interest thus indicates an international forum where both sides are strong. The EC is a good example.

In general questions of media policy there is a preference among European governments for recommendations of the CoE variety rather than binding solutions such as those suggested in the EC Commission's Green Papers. On the hardware side, however, the opposite seems to be the case, with involved actors (governments, PTTs and media industry) preferring binding agreements on development and production costs, like those made by ESA and Eutelsat.

Private industry has traditionally combined staking (launching a product on the market in an attempt to set the *de facto* standard in the field) with its role in standardization organizations.

Decision-making by majority vote played no significant role in European relations prior to 1988. However, with the implementation of the Single European Act within the EC this has changed. One possible consequence is that decisions on specific issues, based on a more general consensus, are made by simple voting in competent EC bodies.

In standardizing bodies such as the CCIR a dual set of standards may be adopted because of unresolved differences. Majority decisions in the EC concern only the generic standards; the actual choice is left to national governments, national industry and the PTTs. Decisions made in the international fora seldom solve the predicament facing individual producers of consumer electronics, but remain on a more general level.

Next-generation television

Today's television standards date back to the early 1960s. The oldest television standard is the American NTSC (National Television Systems Committee). This standard has a 525-line picture and uses a 60Hz frequency. NTSC is used in Japan but was not accepted by the Europeans, who, during the late 1950s and early 1960s, developed two standards – the English/German Phase Alternation by Line (PAL) and the French Séquentielle Couleur à Mémoire (SECAM). Both standards have a 625-line picture and a frequency of 50Hz. They are still with us today. The PAL/SECAM signal has a bandwidth of 7 MHz. Nowadays there are over 100 million NTSC television sets in use and an equal number of PAL/SECAM sets. Therefore the standards are well established in a functioning organizational structure. However, the picture and sound quality of these standards is far from that of 35mm film and present-day stereo sound, not to mention the possibility of simultaneous sound tracks in different languages which are needed as a way of attracting a truly pan-European audience.

In 1990 European companies produced 85 per cent of the colour television sets bought within the EC. The production of TV sets amounted to 60 per cent of total EC consumer electronics exports. In this field Europe is running neck and neck with Japan, whereas the USA has only one producer – Zenith.

The European position of strength rests on the basic PAL and SECAM patents taken out some twenty years ago. These have been licensed very sparingly to companies outside Europe. However, the patent protection period is only twenty years. The SECAM patents have already run out, and the PAL equivalents will soon follow. This creates an industrial need for new patents in order to ensure a future role for European producers on the world market. Over the last ten years, European companies have developed a set of patents for a Multiple Analogue Components (MAC) technology based on a 1,250-line picture. The next step was to ensure acceptance of this technology in the various technical and standardization fora, in order to renew the European position of strength and to avoid the video standards fiasco in which European discord led to total Japanese market dominance.

The MAC standard and its Japanese competitor, MUSE, provide television viewers with cinema-quality pictures and sound in the same large-screen format. The estimated market for new high definition television sets is enormous. The American market, with only one national producer, is estimated by the US Commerce Department to be in the region of some 50 billion ECU.

The European companies which hold important MAC patents are organized in the Groupement d'Intérêt Economique, which is trying to repeat the PAL/SECAM performance by limiting the access of Japanese and Far Eastern companies to MAC patents. However, the group includes one non-European company, Intermetall, which, although based in Germany, is owned by ITT. Seemingly this company is not toeing the line in its dealings with other non-European producers of consumer equipment.

Recognizing the importance of the patents behind the next generation of television sets, Philips, Bosch and Thompson have been pressing the EC and the European governments to make the MAC standard compulsory for DBS satellites. The EC complied in 1987 and published a Directive making the MAC standards obligatory on all DBS satellites. Different MAC standards (D2-MAC and C-MAC) have since been implemented on all European DBS satellites.

However, MAC transmission signals of DBS satellite channels have to be converted back to PAL/SECAM as no commercial MAC television equipment is available and no commercial broadcaster is willing to risk his viewership figures. The digital-to-analogue conversion is expensive, and any compression encoding techniques used must preserve the possibility of reception on individual TVRO equipment. All this means is that the viewer does not benefit from quality enhancements, but has to pay for substantial extra equipment in order to receive the MAC signal at all.

The Japanese presented an analogue HDTV standard to the CCIR as far back as 1986. This standard, called Multiple Sub-Nyqvist Sample Encoding (MUSE), uses 1,125 lines and a 60Hz frequency. The MUSE standard is based on 10 years of research costing some 2 billion ECU. At the time it was supported by the USA and Canada, but opposed by European delegates. In 1987 the USA dropped its support for MUSE in the light of an internal US debate on whether or not the government should support the development of a US standard. Regular experimental broadcasting started in Japan in June 1989 via the Japanese DBS BS-2b satellite. Japanese companies have bought US film production companies in order to avail themselves of programme material in the MUSE format. Furthermore, in January 1991 Toshiba also began mass production of MUSE HDTV television sets.

The American Electronics Association (AEA) published an HDTV impact statement in 1988 in order to support its lobbying efforts in the US Congress. This paper contends that unless the USA develops its own HDTV industry, the US share of the world-wide PC market by the year 2010 will be only half of what it could be if the USA had a strong HDTV industry. In money terms this translates into a market of $110 billion, compared to a possible market of $220 billion. The AEA estimates that sales of HDTV sets and VCRs will reach $40 billion per annum before the year 2000.

MAC and MUSE HDTV standards are based on analogue signal transmission, but the Americans are concentrating on a fully digitalized transmission model in which picture and sound information are transmitted in binary code. This solution ensures that there is no loss in quality during transmission and requires significantly less frequency space. In April 1991, the American Federal Communications Commission (FCC) began testing six systems (four developed by US companies, one by the Japanese PSB, NHK, and one by NBD, Philips and Thompson). The FCC expects to adopt an all-digital standard in June 1993. The US government and US industry are clearly using the technology factor in order to create a new level of competition. The European answer may well be to stick to 'its' standard and to build up regional markets.

Electronic highway to the viewers

As communication technologies have developed over the last century, the 'wired society' has been gradually supplemented by a 'wireless society'. The development of the telecommunications infrastructure has never relied entirely on a single technology, instead preferring to maintain several overlapping networks. In television and radio transmission, three systems are used nowadays – cable, terrestrial broadcasting and satellite broadcasting.

Satellites are a risky business, but they have the potential to become an extremely successful means of distributing television and radio signals. The reasons are (Collins 1990: 6ff.):

- They provide programmes that are otherwise unavailable (particularly via terrestrial transmission).
- They provide a large bandwidth for higher quality picture and sound.
- They fulfil especially the requirements of smaller countries that seek access to the variety of programmes available in larger countries.
- Their growth is supported by the increasing demand for advertising and commercial broadcasting in Europe.

Shortage of terrestrial frequencies is a problem nearly everywhere in Europe; sometimes only two or three terrestrial television frequencies are available. Additional programmes have to be distributed either via cable or direct to the home via satellite. Clearly this creates a large potential market for satellites that are able to carry significant numbers of channels. The first satellites used for television broadcasting were the telecom satellites which transmitted a weak signal and required large dish antennae, and which are only economically viable when used in conjunction with a cable distribution system.

The next step was broadcasting to individual homes using Direct Broadcasting Satellites (DBS) with a very powerful signal. These are based on the World Administrative Radio Conference (WARC) concept of 1977 that allocated national 'footprints' to the respective states. The most typical DBS specification is the high-powered French–German TDF/TV-Sat that transmits to dish aerials of 30cm and upwards. More DBS satellites of this type have been launched, such as the British Marco Polo and the Swedish Tele-X.

Medium-powered satellites were introduced in Europe by the Astra consortium. This hybrid satellite combines a large number of transponders with a relatively strong signal. Technological development of the receiver equipment makes reception possible using cheap dish aerials of 60cm in diameter. The Astra broadcasts can be picked up all over Europe.

Currently the upper limit is about sixteen transponders per satellite (Astra), but several satellites parked at the same orbital position may be used to increase this figure. Moreover, special compression technologies are being developed to enable the transmission of an even greater number of programmes per satellite. The Sky Cable consortium in the United States, led by Murdoch, is planning to provide 108 channels by 1993, all of which may be received by means of just one dish antenna (*Newsweek*, 21 May 1990).

Different transmission technologies (terrestrial broadcasting, cable and satellite broadcasting) may be combined in order to enable a broadcaster to use some or all three systems simultaneously. For example, the German commercial broadcasters Sat-1 and RTL Plus use terrestrial transmission, telecom satellites with cable distribution, Astra and DBS.

Actors determining satellite television policy
During the 1980s European satellite policy was effectively privatized and commercialized in the sense that private companies (such as SES, Murdoch, etc.) took over much of the initiative and the decision-making from the public bodies (the PTTs, governments and the EC) that started the development in the late 1970s. The DBS projects of European governments have not achieved economic viability. The German government at present is not willing to finance the building of the third, reserve satellite which is necessary to guarantee a reliable DBS service to commercial customers.

The channels that French and German DBS carry are also broadcast via other satellites. This indicates that commercial operators have insufficient faith in DBS. The industrial lobbying which resulted in the EC directive on MAC standards, mentioned above, decreased broadcaster and consumer interest considerably, due to the unavailability on the market of cheap, mass-produced receiver equipment for D2-MAC and due to the lack of studio equipment designed to produce the new high-quality programmes. To date, MAC transmissions have been used by BSB (now dropped after its merger with Sky), by Sports 2-3 on the French TDF1, by the Swedish TV-3/TV-1000 on an Intelsat telecom satellite, and by SF Succe, a Swedish pay TV programme on the Swedish Tele-X DBS satellite.

As Collins puts it: 'The European satellite programme is much more strongly "pushed" by the lobbying power of the electronics and aerospace industry than it is "pulled" by demand from television or telecommunication users' (1990: 35).

The latest development in Britain demonstrates just how risky the satellite business has become: Murdoch's Sky Television and British Satellite Broadcasting (BSB) merged after having lost some £1.25 billion by 1990. Murdoch alone reported losses of £100 million over twelve months in 1989/90 and his News Corporation seemed to be in some financial difficulties. Prior to the merger, the programmes of these two operators reached 1.6 million (Sky) and 750,000 (BSB) households in Britain. Only the two (pay TV) channels Sky Movies and The Movie Channel will in future be kept separate. BSB was using the DBS satellite Marco Polo and transmitted in D-MAC (with conversion to PAL in the receiving cable systems); the new consortium will now use Astra and PAL (as Sky did previously) and so the new company is deserting the concept of DBS as well as moving away from the MAC specification.

Currently, the MAC and DBS concepts are in trouble. This might possibly change if and when HDTV takes off, as it requires a much greater bandwidth than is presently available. No other mode of distribution is currently able to carry the signal via satellite to cable systems or direct to the home. It is for this reason that the Astra consortium is considering HDTV capacity on its third satellite, due to be launched in 1992. But other actors are jockeying on the sidelines. American Zenith is developing its digital HDTV system, which may not require so much bandwidth. CCIR is currently not ready to accept any HDTV standard – and consumers may opt for enhanced PAL systems such as PAL-Plus. Technology is on the move and all investors have become very nervous. The Astra consortium decision may be an important indicator, as it has the biggest media investors as its clients – RTL Veronique (Netherlands), the Sky/BSB channels (owned by Murdoch), Premiere (Bertelsmann, Leo Kirch and Canal Plus).

Pay TV in Europe
New transmission technology is also paving the way for new television services. Thus pay TV services (around fifteen such services in 1990) have been set up in a number of European countries. Pay TV signals are scrambled and transported via cable systems (over-the-air transmission is the exception). Most scrambling technologies were developed outside Europe (for instance, FilmNet's SatPac technology by Matsushita or Tele-club's Payview in Hongkong) and are widely in use elsewhere. Because of this they have been heavily pirated (Hartshorn 1990). On the other hand, the MAC standard cannot be easily 'pirated', which makes MAC transmission interesting for pay TV operators.

Satellite radio in Europe
One satellite television channel can be converted into sixteen top-quality stereo channels with digital sound. The first European radio broadcasters that actually used satellites were 'propaganda' stations, traditionally transmitting on the overcrowded shortwave band that enables only very low-quality sound: Voice of America (VoA, Munich) and the BBC's World Service (London). The first

pure satellite radio channel, which started in 1987, was Cable One (Amsterdam/London), but it ceased operations after it was barred from Dutch cable systems.

At the end of 1989 about forty radio stations were transmitted via satellite and their number is still on the increase (Currie 1990). Satellite transmissions are also used to distribute programmes to commercial radio stations. This sort of network service includes the provision of continuous music and news programmes to local stations, a service that may be complemented by local contributions in the form of news and commercials.

Clearly there is a future for radio on satellites. The importance of this link will increase if digital radio becomes more widespread. Although some broadcasters transmit programmes in digital form to the respective satellite, they have to be converted back into analogue form prior to being fed into cable systems, as very few digital receivers are on the market as yet.

Choice of technology and economic interests

In the complex interplay between governments' and monopolies' attempts to control and defend vested interests, commercial staking by strong private media companies and attempts to develop pan-European approaches to broadcasting in several fora, two development paths can be discerned. These tie together programme production and broadcasting interests.

The first is an incremental, evolutionary development of the existing PAL/SECAM formats, adding stereo sound and enhanced picture quality in a new PAL-Plus format. This development will not make existing television equipment obsolete, but will, much like the move from black and white to colour television sets, provide consumers with new sets with a height–width ratio of 16:9 (like 35mm film), stereo sound and twice the picture scanning speed of today's sets. This does not bring out new details in a picture or allow for large flat panel displays, but makes the normal television picture more stable with less flickering.

The second approach is revolutionary and involves the move to a new level of picture and sound quality by introducing a new standard to replace NTSC, PAL and SECAM. Adherents of the revolutionary approach argue that a new standard should be implemented in order to exploit the new technological level of video and to overcome the technical shortcomings of existing standards. Changing the whole transmission and picture–sound system and getting programme producers, PSBs and viewers to invest in new equipment on a massive scale is beyond the means of any single

European nation. It is also beyond the narrow interests of the PTTs. The EC has become an important forum uniting government and industrial interests across Europe. Substantially greater investments than just the telecom network are involved and, correspondingly, international bodies with a wider scope of activities and more funds, such as the EC, are becoming interested. In some respects the revolutionary strategy can be seen as an extension of the evolutionary strategy – but a very costly extension.

The revolutionary strategy obviously involves a great deal of research and development and the production of new equipment, and therefore appeals strongly to industrial interests. The evolutionary strategy, on the other hand, has strong support among commercial television operators, who make money from advertising or subscriber payments. Using an American phrase, if it ain't broke, don't fix it, these interest groups point to the very low interest among viewers for better technical picture/sound quality.

Two competing programme distribution cartels emerge: the 'private cartel', which ties together advertisers, commercial operators and European medium-power satellite distribution; and the 'public cartel', which ties together PSB programming, PTTs' national DBS distribution and Eutelsat's European low- and medium-powered distribution.

Technologically the private cartel is geared to the PAL/SECAM picture format, whereas the public cartel is concerned with the development of MAC transmission standards and HDTV. The hardware industry involved in programme production and the manufacture of transmission equipment very much sees new transmission standards as giving it an important competitive edge. Therefore European consumer electronics and satellite industries have strong common interests with the public cartel.

What goes against this trend, however, is the reduced public funding of public broadcasters, which makes them reluctant to invest in the leading edge technology, which is very costly and whose potential take-up rate among viewers is unclear. Forced into a much more competitive stance, British Telecom (BT) has already invested in the private Astra satellite consortium, a strong proponent of PAL-Plus, in order to enter the market for transponder leasing and to become the major supplier in Europe. This move and others like it break the Eutelsat unity on the issue among PTTs. The British and Swedish DBS satellites (Marco Polo and Tele-X) carry both PAL and MAC signals in order to attract as wide a customer base as possible.

Heading the opposite way are the private pay TV operators, who prefer to use a new standard in order to attain a better encryption of their programmes – something PAL–SECAM and PAL-plus are not well suited for.

Conclusions

The technological factor has contributed little to the democratic and participatory visions discussed in Europe in the 1970s. Cable systems create new local structures and provide a potential strengthening of local communications. Linked to satellites though, cable systems turn into local distribution networks for centrally fed programmes. Satellites themselves are global and as such are centralistic technologies.

The European PTTs and the EC, together with the electronics industry, attempted to introduce satellite television in a regulated and controlled fashion. They tried to do so by (a) controlling the introduction of new satellites through their national PTTs and their European umbrella organization (Eutelsat); and (b) controlling the development of technical standards and norms of transmission (such as MAC).

The realization of both objectives met strong resistance from new actors, in other words commercial media and telecom companies:

- Astra, based on a US design and European financing, provides satellite services in what is basically an unregulated environment;
- commercial satellite broadcasters stick to the old PAL norm (except for pay TV) and thus make the introduction of the MAC family of norms very difficult;
- Eutelsat, as representative of the European PTTs, has taken up the challenge and provides its own new line of medium-powered satellites, but is deserting the MAC coalition;
- the DBS satellite specification seems to be without a clear future (a situation that may change if analogue HDTV picks up and requires this type of distribution network).

The situation has led to a basic shift of power among the actors and fora of decision-making. The traditional actors in media technology are the national PTTs in collaboration with the national public broadcasters and the national electronics industry. This structure developed technologies such as colour television, stereo radio, stereo television and the teletext systems. This 'cartel' also guaranteed that the norms remained 'European', though they were not always standardized because of ongoing national rivalries (such as PAL versus SECAM). This cartel's attempt to introduce a new MAC norm, one that would eventually lead to HDTV, is not succeeding due to the competing interests of the private cartel, which has opted for an evolutionary development in technology.

The European actors have not yet learned the Japanese trick of total packaging, whereby all parties involved – industry, government, PTTs, financiers and programme producers – reach a high level of agreement before launching into the necessary substantial research and development.

When an actor uses the technology factor as a strategic device to strengthen a market position, the end result may be that no new market is opened up at all.

The large multinational multimedia companies have successfully challenged the public broadcasters, but their success is mainly due to the trend toward liberalization of markets in Europe. Commercial broadcasters may also enjoy indirect help from national governments which seek political support in exchange. (The controversial incorporation of BSB into Murdoch's Sky operation was at some level approved by the Thatcher government, even though this broke several conditions of the licence given to BSB. Murdoch's chain of newspapers were always staunch supporters of the Thatcher government.) It is also evident that the EC favours their case through a policy of 'Television without Frontiers' and the EC TV Directive's policy of preferring economics over culture.

The more specialized fora such as CEPT are losing their influence on media policy and its broader implications. The specialized fora have a narrow focus and involve few actors. Conversely, the EC is increasing its media policy influence because of its close ties with the commercial interests involved and its influence on the media policies of its member governments. The involvement of many actors in the activities of a specific forum makes the forum important, especially if the decision-making process results in action and not just statements of intent.

The increased number of actors and the parallel weakening of public broadcasters have destroyed traditional coalitions and led to a diffusion and pluralization of technology policies. The result is not a clear framework for the media future of Europe, but rather a relatively high degree of uncertainty with increasing commercial influence, less planning security and mixed impacts on the process of European unification.

References

Baker, Simon (1990) 'SES Goes for a Hat Trick', *Cable & Satellite*, 9: 73–6.
Bell, Daniel (1973) *The Coming of Post-Industrial Society: A Venture in Social Forecasting*. New York: Basic Books.

Collins, Richard (1990) *Satellite Television in Western Europe*. London: J. Libby.

Currie, Tony (1990) 'Wired for Sound', *Cable & Satellite*, 1: 32–40.

Hartshorn, David (1990) 'The Year of the Decoder', *Cable & Satellite*, 3: 20–33.

Negrine, Ralph (1988) *Satellite Broadcasting. The Politics and Implications of the New Media*. London: Routledge.

Quester, George H. (1990) *The International Politics of Television*. Lexington, Mass.: Lexington Books.

Taishoff, Marika Natasha (1987) *State Responsibility and the Direct Broadcast Satellite*. London: Pinter.

6

Television Content: Dallasification of Culture?

Els De Bens, Mary Kelly and Marit Bakke

It is relatively simple to identify two main tendencies operating within the present European media arena. Firstly, technological developments continue to make it easier to transmit television programmes across national borders; and secondly, economic and commercial interests motivate media hardware and software operators to expand their markets. Programming issues, however, include a concern with not only technological and commercial logics but also cultural issues. Central here are concerns regarding television's contribution to the preservation and strengthening of regional and national cultures, and a concern to strengthen the role played by European actors in the software competition with American producers. Certain countries, such as France, and organizations such as the European Community and the Council of Europe represent these cultural needs more strongly than others.

In 1986 the Euromedia Research Group stated (McQuail and Siune 1986: Chapters 10, 11 and 12) that the fate of both national and European television programmes was caught between the industrial imperative and commercial forces. What does the picture look like five years later? And what are the prospects for the 1990s?

The preservation of cultural identity is still a relevant issue in the political media debate within different European countries. How to achieve it is quite another matter and one which is subject to much uncertainty. This situation is due to certain factors and forces which confront national broadcasting companies in their efforts to use television content as a tool for preserving national cultural identity.

Chapter 10 in *New Media Politics* (McQuail and Siune 1986) presented a model for analysing cultural aspects of media development in Europe. The key concept was control: control of content and control of communication networks. One way of attempting to ensure that a country's basic values are presented in TV programmes is to have national control over programme production. Given the possibility of controlling the content of programmes, there is still the question of the amount of home production. This is an economic as well as a cultural issue, and closely interrelated with the dynamics of international programme production. It is this economic context for television programme production in Europe which will be described in the first part of this chapter.

The next question concerns the kind of programming strategies that individual broadcasters have developed in this new competitive environment. In the second part of the chapter this is examined by looking at the different programming policies of commercial and public service channels, especially in terms of entertainment versus serious programming and of choices between domestic, European and American programmes. The third section presents the findings of an empirical study of the programmes transmitted by fifty-three European television stations during a two-week period in January 1991. It examines the types of programme offered and their country of origin. The results highlight the increased dependence of European broadcasters on both entertainment-type programming and on US fictional programmes. The fourth and final section examines some of the policy implications of both the economic context within which European broadcasters operate and their programming strategies for the future development of the European programming market.

The economic context of European programme production

As widely expected, the demand for television programmes has risen rapidly in Europe in the 1980s and this is likely to continue into the 1990s. As new delivery systems and commercial stations develop (whether terrestrial, cable or DBS) and the broadcasting hours of existing public service stations expand, each station seeks an increasing volume of programmes to fill its schedule. However, the finance available to many individual stations – both the newer commercial stations and older public broadcasters – has not increased sufficiently to enable a commensurate increase in original programme production. Hence, as will be illustrated below, increased competition has led, not to rapid expansion in European television production, but to increased imports, especially from the USA, and a decline in the European production of TV fiction (Lange and Renaud 1989).

This situation, it may be argued, is due to a number of inter-related economic factors including:

1   The high cost of programme production and the much lower costs of imports. One hour of US television drama tends to cost

5–10 times less than one hour of home production (Lange and Renaud 1989: 220).

2 Insufficient advertising expenditure to fund expensive programme production on the large number of new commercial stations (although expenditure on television advertising in Europe has increased). Because the new commercial stations may draw advertising money away from existing channels, there may be *less* money available *per channel* for programme production.

3 The non-increase or slow growth of alternative sources of funding such as the licence fee and cable or subscription fees (see Chapter 8).

4 The high launch and start-up costs of new commercial stations and their initial unprofitability, which leaves little for domestic production.

5 The highly diversified and fragmented nature of the European programme market as a whole, which has militated against the rapid development of a large pan-European programming market that might have allowed European production companies to introduce economies of scale and scope, enabling them to compete on more equal terms with the US audiovisual production industry.

Each of these factors will be discussed in greater detail below.

Market competition is usually expected to reduce the cost of the product. It is expected to provide the motivation to be technologically innovative, which in turn will bring productivity gains and consequent cost reductions. However, the cultural and entertainment industries, as Baumol and Baumol (1976), Locksley (1988) and Collins et al. (1988) have noted, are highly susceptible to 'the cost disease', where productivity gains are few. In these industries there have been few technological breakthroughs, while the largest cost – for the labour-intensive work of scriptwriters, producers, actors, journalists, etc. – has continued to increase as wages rise in line with those of the general population. Hence, relative to many other products, cultural products have increased rather than decreased in cost. They remain highly expensive to produce.

Television advertising grew in Europe in the 1980s, and is expected to continue to grow (Lange and Renaud 1989: 149). Yet the money available to European broadcasters is still only roughly half that available to US broadcasters (*Cable and Satellite Europe*, April 1989). Thus, the expansion in European advertising revenue has not been sufficient – to date – to fund expensive drama productions by new commercial channels on a large scale. Furthermore, the new commercial channels have taken a slice of the limited, if growing, advertising budget from existing public channels. The latter have been further squeezed by the fact that the licence fee has not generally increased across Europe, nor is it automatically index-linked in most European countries (Lange and Renaud 1989: 150). Thus, the capacity of public channels to expand their production has also been curtailed.

Further possible sources of revenue are cable and subscription fees. Cable, whilst increasing rapidly in smaller countries (see Chapter 5 above) has shown a particularly slow growth in larger countries, although Germany with 27 per cent of cabled households is now growing fast. However, little money is paid by the cable companies to broadcasters at present. Nor has subscription television provided a bountiful source of income, except in the case of Canal Plus.

The start-up costs of new television stations are extremely high, whether they involve buying up existing stations (TF1) or establishing new ones (Sky). New stations require considerable investment in a very high-risk venture by, mainly, large profitable commercial enterprises, newspaper publishers, and other major groups (see Chapter 3) already involved in film distribution or commercial broadcasting. Few of these new commercial stations – apart from Berlusconi's three stations in Italy – are making a significant profit as yet.

A serious drain on the resources of new channels has been the tendency for new stations, in their rush to fill their schedules with, at least initially, imported programmes, to bid competitively for these programmes against both other commercial stations and public broadcasters within the same territory. The main groups to gain in this competition are US programme exporters and sporting organizations.

The diversified and fragmentary nature of the European TV market as a whole has added to the difficulty of producing European programmes which compete with US products in terms of returns to the producer. The large, integrated US market of 88 million TV homes allows economies of scale and scope. The three large networks, although at present experiencing competition from independents and cable channels and hence a fragmentation of their own audience, still attract two thirds of the US audience at prime time and somewhat less overall, and are the largest spenders on production – nearly $4 billion annually (*Variety* 19–25 April, 1989: 41). Furthermore, as ownership of cable stations becomes concentrated, multiple systems operators have also begun spending on programme production. These factors, along with a strong, mature film industry, allow economies of scale and scope, not least through the planned time sequencing of programme releases through a series of 'windows' or 'exposures', each of which provides a return to the producer. Thus a film may be sequenced through theatrical release, video rental, pay-per-view, pay-cable, network television, independent television followed by basic cable. Large returns on film production are now made on the video market, and for television series on the syndication market. Given this integrated market, US producers can recoup costs at home and thus afford to sell cheaply abroad.

The European television market, although larger in total size than that of the US, with 112 million TV homes, is fragmented into five larger markets (Germany, France, Britain, Italy and Spain) and those of a further twelve smaller states (see Chapter 9), each with its own cultural differences, national broadcasting structures and legislation, legal differences regarding, for example, copyright and advertising, different policies regarding time sequencing of film release as well as differences in technical infrastructure – in extent of cabling, for instance. These differences have militated strongly against the development of general interest pan-European channels, as was the initial intention of Sky, which has now withdrawn from this project to concentrate on the British market.

Language difference is a further important factor dividing the programming markets of Europe. The largest language and programme markets are Germany, France and Britain, which include as markets not only these nation-states themselves, but also some peripheral European states or groups which share their language or culture, or which have traditionally imported media products from one of these larger states. These three countries are followed, in terms of market size, by Italy and Spain. There remain some twelve smaller Western European states, each with its own broadcasting system. Some also share linguistic and cultural similarities with adjacent larger states and form part of the larger programming region of these states (German-speaking Switzerland and Austria with Germany; French-speaking Belgium and Switzerland with France; Ireland with the UK); some share linguistic and cultural similarities among themselves, which may contribute to their forming a programming region (the four Scandinavian countries; the Netherlands and Flemish-speaking Belgium).

Response of broadcasters: programme strategies

Given the economic context of high production costs, low import costs and fragmented markets, what has been the response of

European broadcasting organizations – both existing public service broadcasters and the new commercial broadcasters?

Public service broadcasters have traditionally defined their programming responsibilities in terms of offering a wide and 'balanced' range of entertainment and informational programmes. The extent to which this is still the case will be examined in some detail in the next section. It is expected that intense competition for audiences within the national territory will have increased the tendency of public broadcasters to transmit entertainment rather than serious programmes – especially at peak viewing times, and to concentrate on low-risk, low-innovation programme policies.

Public broadcasters have also traditionally produced most of their own programmes. Again this will be empirically tested below to see whether increased competition has changed this pattern. The most frequently imported programmes are films and TV serials, which, of course, are high-cost productions. A pattern which has been noted before (Kelly 1988), namely that public broadcasters from the larger broadcasting markets of France, Britain, Germany, Italy and Spain import TV fiction from the US more frequently rather than from other European countries, will be further explored.

In smaller European countries the position of domestic production may be considerably weaker than in larger states. Due to the small size of their audience base, the amount that can be raised through either licence fees or advertising revenue is, of course, much more limited than is the case for larger countries. They are thus at a serious economic disadvantage relative to both larger European states and the USA. Furthermore, they may share language and cultural links with larger European states which make the latter's TV programmes particularly attractive (see also Chapter 9). Programmes may be directly imported by the domestic channel of the smaller country, or may be received through overspill or through the more extensive cabling of smaller states.

Many of the new terrestrial commercial stations are general interest channels, competing head on with public service broadcasters. Their policy is to attract and hold audiences as rapidly and cheaply as possible, even at the expense of national culture and domestic production. Hence, at least initially, popular US programmes are centre stage. The programming strategies of Berlusconi's three Italian channels provides the earliest prototype of this approach.

These strategies include: initial attempts to consolidate the home audience rapidly by a high level of imports and strip scheduling. Over time, however, the audience may tend to become bored with this kind of programming. Thus, after an initial period of intensive buying of US programmes, once such a generalist station is established within its home market the broadcasters may begin to move towards domestic production. On a wider front, programming strategies include attempts to achieve economies of scale and scope by expanding into other related media, especially film and cinema, and by expanding internationally through programme sales, co-production and co-financing agreements with other European broadcasters and those in the USA, and through the acquisition of television stations in adjacent states.

Programming policies in European markets are shaped by three divergent influences. Firstly, there is a strong pull, often expressed through high audience demand, towards domestic production and the domestic market. Secondly, there is a pull to the European market, especially for those smaller countries which share language and cultural affinities with larger countries. Thirdly, there is a pull to US programming, which is very cheap, but, over time, may not always be as popular as domestic programmes of the same type and quality – if one can afford to make them.

These three influences can again be seen in operation when the development of specialist satellite channels – including pay film, news, children's, sports, youth and arts channels – is examined. In recent years, programming strategies on these channels have changed and adapted to the exigencies of the European TV market. One such change is a recognition of the demand for programmes in one's own language. Thus the satellite channel Screensport, for example, is now available in three languages: English, French and German.

A second and related tendency is that, given the general recognition of the failure of early pan-European efforts, satellite stations are concentrating on building audiences in particular territories. Thus, Canal Plus's plan for expansion into Germany and Belgium is not to develop German and Belgian clones, but to develop in cooperation with indigenous media interests (Bertelsmann in Germany, RTBF and other Walloon companies in Belgium), and to develop an identity of their own relative to the country to which they are broadcasting. RTL is also moving in a similar regional direction: RTL Plus in Germany, RTL TVi in Belgium, RTL Veronique in the Netherlands.

A third tendency in specialist satellite channels is that US satellite-to-cable channels are continuing their move into European markets. Because of their existing US operations, experience and programme catalogues, they may expect to be able to survive in the niche markets of specialist channels (for example CNN, MTV and the Disney Channel).

General interest channels, however, are still the most prevalent and popular of all channels. As noted above, these stations, whether public or private, have to make two central programming decisions: firstly what entertainment/informational mix to offer, and secondly what mix of domestic, European and US productions. We investigated these decisions further by undertaking an empirical study of the programming schedules of European general interest channels. The results are presented in the next section.

The face of 53 European TV channels[1]

In order to investigate further the claims made above, an empirical analysis was undertaken of the programmes offered by 53 European TV stations.

The following working hypotheses were investigated by means of empirical data:

- Has the proportion of popular programmes, mainly entertainment and fiction, increased since the launch of various new commercial stations?
- Has the proportion of 'serious' programmes, especially in prime time, been reduced and is this trend present among the public broadcasting channels as well?
- Is the position of the American programming industry still dominant on the European TV market?
- Are there noticeable differences between the programming and purchasing strategies of the public and commercial channels?

The period sampled comprises the last two weeks of January 1991 (14/1/1991 – 27/1/1991). The public and commercial channels (53 in all) of the following countries were analysed: Austria, Belgium, Denmark, Finland, France, Germany (West), Ireland, Italy, the Netherlands, Norway, Spain, Sweden, Switzerland and the UK.

Stations such as MTV, Eurosport and the pay channels were not taken into consideration because of their thematic approach. Super Channel was not included either because of its dominant supply of music programmes (approximately 61 per cent).

Due to the Gulf War some TV stations changed their programme schedule (mostly to supply extended news bulletins). We did not take into account these accidental programme changes and analysed the regular, scheduled programme supply.

Trailers, announcements and advertising spots were not counted. A period of two successive weeks of programming might be considered unrepresentative since it takes almost no account of seasonal influences on programming. The analysis of the total programme supply of 53 TV stations is a gigantic task, however. Other authors such as Nordenstreng and Varis (1974 and 1986), Sepstrup (1989) and Young & Rubicam's research unit, Horizons Media International, who made somewhat similar studies, also limited their samples to one or two weeks.

The drawing up of a list of programme categories that can be used to classify the programmes is not an easy task. We have broadly followed the examples of the studies mentioned above. Since our study attaches much importance to fiction, we have subdivided this category into films and series/serials. All in all, ten programme categories were retained: *popular*: movies, series/serials, entertainment, music and sports; *serious*: information, culture, education, children, others.

The definition of prime time used was 7 p.m. to 11 p.m.

Comparative analysis of the programme structure of public and commercial channels

Several authors have pointed out that the ratio of 'serious' to 'popular' programmes on public service stations is on average 55 to 45 per cent, whereas commercial broadcasters programme popular programmes at a rate of about 60 to 70 per cent. In prime time, both public and commercial stations tend to increase the amount of popular programming.

Table 6.1 does not entirely confirm this trend. None of the PSB channels scores 55 per cent for serious programmes. Only the German and Norwegian public service stations reach a figure of 50 per cent. The Belgian, British, Swedish and Swiss public stations have a rate of ± 49 per cent serious programmes. In prime time, however, most of the public stations slide back to a lower percentage (with the exception of Norway's public station). Obviously, there are often differences between the public stations in each country: FR3 (France), WDR (Germany), NOS3 (the Netherlands) are examples of public service stations that have a higher proportion than the national average. The findings of this study thus indicate that the proportion of serious programmes on European public stations is decreasing. A similar study, also carried out by our research team, comparing the programming of 20 channels in 1988, 18 to 31 January, showed that the majority of the public stations broadcast at least 55 per cent serious programmes.

The reason for this change is the increasing competition of mainly new commercial stations, national and foreign. In several countries

Table 6.1   *Total and prime time programming (percentage of programmes; January 1991)*

	Popular		Serious	
	Total	*Prime time*	*Total*	*Prime time*
Austria				
Public	66	63	34	37
Commercial	–	–	–	–
Belgium				
Public	51	58	49	42
Commercial	78	82	22	18
Denmark				
Public	60	57	40	43
Commercial	–	–	–	–
Finland				
Public	64	76	36	24
Commercial	–	–	–	–
France				
Public	60	58	40	42
Commercial	62	82	38	18
Germany (West)				
Public	50	50	50	50
Commercial	78	93	22	7
Ireland				
Public	61	71	39	29
Commercial	–	–	–	–
Italy				
Public	63	72	37	28
Commercial	86	93	14	7
Netherlands				
Public	58	64	42	36
Commercial	76	89	24	11
Norway				
Public	50	47	50	53
Commercial	67	93	33	7
Spain				
Public	62	74	38	26
Commercial	74	83	26	17
Sweden				
Public	52	61	48	39
Commercial	73	82	27	18
Switzerland				
Public	51	50	49	50
Commercial	–	–	–	–
United Kingdom				
Public	51	63	49	37
Commercial	68	78	32	22

the percentage of popular programmes in public stations is 60 per cent or more (Austria, Denmark, Finland, France, Ireland, Italy, Spain). In all commercial stations the proportion of popular programming is situated between 62 and 86 per cent. In prime time this figure often increases to over 90 per cent (West Germany, Italy, Norway). Table 6.1 shows very clearly that in prime time the number of serious programmes on commercial stations is very low.[2]

The most important programme category in all stations (both public and commercial) is fiction. Table 6.2 shows clearly that the commercial stations fill their programming rosters with even more fiction. As far as entertainment is concerned, the public stations compete on an equal footing. Talkshows, quizzes, game shows, and so on are cheap programmes that attract viewers. They also offer the TV stations an opportunity to offer so-called 'home-made' productions. Such local programmes are very popular with the viewers. It might be noted however that they are often no more than exact copies of American game shows.

The percentage of fiction increases rapidly in prime time, especially among the commercial channels, while the public stations usually offer more entertainment programmes than fiction in prime time.

The third most important programme category is undoubtedly information (mainly news and current affairs). Here, the public stations score higher, with the exception of the commercial station Channel 4, which offers a large amount of information. In prime time the higher percentages of information among the public stations (on average around 25 per cent) is striking.

Domestic and imported fiction on European public and commercial TV stations

Tracing the origin of all TV programmes is rather problematic. Many programmes are labelled as 'domestic' but on watching them it often transpires that a large number of foreign inserts are used. It is, of course, impossible actually to view the complete programme supply of 53 channels over a period of two weeks. In similar studies (such as for example Nordenstreng and Varis, 1974, 1986; Morgan and Shanahan, 1991; Horizons Media International, 1987) foreign inserts are not taken into account either.

In order to assess the importance of foreign inserts, Varis and Nordenstreng made a thorough analysis of the programmes on Finnish TV during a two-week period (February 1973). They found that the overall share of foreign inserts in home productions stood at a mere 5 per cent, and on the assumption that the situation in other

Table 6.2   *Main programme categories of the 53 channels (percentage of total programming; January 1991)*

	Fiction	Entertainment	Information
Austria			
PSB FS1	43	9	11
FS2	17	12	15
Belgium			
PSB BRT1	29	15	18
BRT2	38	8	12
RTBF	32	15	17
Tele21	18	1	11
Com. VTM	47	22	15
RTL	61	9	13
Denmark			
PSB DR	27	10	12
TV2	25	16	18
Finland			
PSB TV1	30	5	16
TV2	33	7	14
TV3	31	28	3
France			
PSB A2	36	31	10
FR3	13	24	15
Com. TF1	35	20	13
La5	59	6	13
M6	31	5	5
Germany (West)			
PSB ARD	39	12	18
ZDF	40	13	21
WDR	13	6	24
Com. RTL Plus	43	23	5
SAT1	56	23	6
Telefunf	27	18	3
Ireland			
PSB RTE1	42	17	19
RTE2	32	10	9
Italy			
PSB RAI 1	21	23	20
RAI 2	29	20	11
RAI 3	16	18	14
Com. RETE 4	80	13	1
Canale 5	33	51	0
Italia 1	62	12	0
Netherlands			
PSB NOS1	25	33	16
NOS2	26	34	14
NOS3	13	5	24
Com. RTL			
Veronique (now RTLA)	35	31	6

Table 6.2 (*continued*)

	Fiction	*Entertainment*	*Information*
Norway			
PSB NRK	17	26	23
Com. TVN	46	14	11
Spain			
PSB TVE1	29	26	16
TVE2	36	10	5
Com. Ant	40	16	9
Tele5	49	22	3
Sweden			
PSB SVT1	26	5	3
SVT2	15	25	12
Com. TV3	36	16	10
TV4	11	13	4
Switzerland			
PSB DRS	21	12	19
TSR	42	8	16
RTSI	26	8	18
United Kingdom			
PSB BBC1	27	21	21
BBC2	24	9	8
Com. ITV	32	36	12
Ch4	28	18	25

countries was not very different they inferred that the share of foreign inserts in overall programming amounted to a maximum of 3 per cent.

The lion's share of foreign inserts is to be found in information programmes. Nevertheless, the present study classifies information programmes as fully home-made productions. After all, the concept and the final format of news programmes are the sole responsibility of the station's own newsroom; and the other studies referred to also treat information programmes as home productions.

The other programme categories such as 'music', 'entertainment', 'culture', 'education', 'children' and 'other' often use foreign inserts as well. For some TV programmes, especially music (particularly in the case of music videos), it was hard to trace the country of origin at all. In case of doubt, the programmes were counted as 'home' productions. Therefore the reader should be aware that the real share of home production is no doubt considerably lower than is claimed in the statistics.

It is often said that commercial channels rely more heavily than public channels on foreign imports. Our data (Table 6.3) confirm these findings. The share of foreign imports, however, never exceeds 60 per cent (Norwegian commercial station) and remains around 50 per cent. Exceptions are the commercial TV channels of

Table 6.3   *Origin of programmes on European TV channels (percentage; January 1991)*

Country	Home	Foreign
Austria		
Public	68	32
Commercial	–	–
Belgium		
Public	70	30
Commercial	43	57
Denmark		
Public	82	18
Commercial	–	–
Finland		
Public	64	36
Commercial	–	–
France		
Public	87	13
Commercial	70	30
Germany (West)		
Public	85	15
Commercial	49	51
Ireland		
Public	50	50
Commercial	–	–
Italy		
Public	74	26
Commercial	50	50
Netherlands		
Public	79	21
Commercial	46	54
Norway		
Public	76	24
Commercial	39	61
Spain		
Public	78	22
Commercial	81	19
Sweden		
Public	77	23
Commercial	44	56
Switzerland		
Public	73	27
Commercial	–	–
United Kingdom		
Public	85	15
Commercial	82	18

France, the UK and Spain, which programme a majority of home-made productions.

The general belief that public service stations of smaller states have to resort to foreign imports more often than their counterparts of larger countries is refuted: in the total programme supply of all public stations, the majority of the programmes is domestic.

As explained above, the ratio between home and foreign productions in the overall programming is not a very relevant parameter. Only a refined system for the viewing and analysis of all programmes could be expected to yield completely reliable results. This is why the present study emphasizes the ratio of home and foreign productions of fiction (films and series). The percentage of foreign imports is higher in fiction than in any other programme category. In general it is quite easy to trace the country of origin of fiction. Moreover, fiction constitutes the dominant programme category for most TV stations (see above).

The origin of movies Except for the French public stations, all stations buy most of their feature films abroad: 80 per cent for the 53 stations (see Table 6.4). There is no particular difference between the public and the commercial stations: both have to purchase their feature films on the foreign market. Smaller countries have to import almost all of their feature films because of their limited domestic film industry. The Swedish PSB stations are the exception to the rule and have a high domestic film percentage (41 per cent). However, only two successive weeks were analysed and we should beware of accidental coincidences.

By far the most important supplier is the USA: it accounts for 53 per cent of imported movies. Other imported movies mainly come from European countries (23 per cent); the three major suppliers are the UK 9 per cent, France 5 per cent and Germany 4 per cent.

Countries with linguistic and cultural affinities with one of these three countries prefer to import their films from those markets. There are no linguistic or cultural barriers for the purchase of American movies: the USA is the largest supplier for most European TV stations!

Table 6.4 reveals that commercial stations programme a greater number of American movies than the public channels; the French commercial stations M6 broadcast 78 per cent and La Cinq 73 per cent American movies; Italia 1 75 per cent, the Swedish TV3 81 per cent, and the Norwegian commercial station TV Norge 100 per cent.

The high percentage of US film imports by the French commercial stations La Cinq and M6 is astonishing because France has the

Table 6.4   *Origin of movies on European TV channels*
(percentage; January 1991)

	Home	Total foreign	From Europe	From USA	Other
Austria					
Public	9	91	53	35	3
Commercial	–	–	–	–	–
Belgium					
Public	5	95	57	36	2
Commercial	0	100	27	68	5
Denmark					
Public	10	90	33	44	13
Commercial	–	–	–	–	–
Finland					
Public	21	79	15	55	9
Commercial	–	–	–	–	–
France					
Public	62	38	1	36	1
Commercial	20	80	9	67	4
Germany (West)					
Public	41	59	29	28	2
Commercial	13	87	39	47	1
Ireland					
Public	5	95	14	81	0
Commercial	–	–	–	–	–
Italy					
Public	36	64	16	48	0
Commercial	34	66	7	56	3
Netherlands					
Public	25	75	21	41	13
Commercial	0	100	18	78	4
Norway					
Public	15	85	33	52	0
Commercial	0	100	0	100	0
Spain					
Public	19	81	32	43	6
Commercial	17	83	32	43	8
Sweden					
Public	41	59	31	28	0
Commercial	10	90	13	72	5
Switzerland					
Public	4	96	42	53	1
Commercial	–	–	–	–	–
United Kingdom					
Public	38	62	6	48	8
Commercial	30	70	5	63	2
TOTAL	20	80	23	53	4

strongest film industry in Europe and exports to other European TV stations; its own imports, however, are almost exclusively from the USA.

A comparison with the 1988 study on the origin of movies reveals some striking differences, shown in Table 6.5.

Table 6.5   *Origin of movies on European TV in 1988 and 1991 (percentage)*

	1988	1991
Home	29	20
USA	46	53
Europe	19	23
of which:		
France	6	5
UK	4	9
W. Germany	3	4
Other	6	5
Other	6	4

To date American movie imports in 1991 have increased and this is undoubtedly because of the many new commercial stations, which favour American movies.

Another striking difference is that the programming of domestic films has decreased by almost 10 per cent! The boom in new commercial stations has obviously not stimulated the European film industry; on the contrary it seems to have stimulated American film imports.

In the 1991 study the UK exported more films to European TV stations; the British stations however imported hardly any films from other European countries, and their foreign movies came almost exclusively from America. A strange coincidence: the two European countries, France and the UK, that can sell their feature films to other European TV stations very rarely programme a European movie (Table 6.4)!

The 4 per cent 'other' category refers to all the other countries of the world; almost half are imported from Australia. The share of Australian imports is more important for series.

The origin of series   Here again the share of foreign productions is significant: 83 per cent of the series are imported (see Table 6.6). Only the UK (PSB as well as commercial stations) programmes a majority of domestic series. France, with its high share of domestic movies, broadcasts 45 per cent domestic series on its public channels, 39 per cent on its commercial ones. In Germany almost

Table 6.6   *Origin of series on European TV channels*
(percentage; January 1991)

	Home	Total foreign	From Europe	From USA	Other
Austria					
Public	18	82	8	74	0
Commercial	–	–	–	–	–
Belgium					
Public	9	91	17	61	13
Commercial	1	99	11	74	14
Denmark					
Public	15	85	36	36	13
Commercial	–	–	–	–	–
Finland					
Public	12	88	30	49	9
Commercial	–	–	–	–	–
France					
Public	45	55	9	44	2
Commercial	39	61	9	52	0
Germany (West)					
Public	45	55	16	34	5
Commercial	1	99	4	79	16
Ireland					
Public	7	93	22	53	18
Commercial	–	–	–	–	–
Italy					
Public	5	95	5	90	0
Commercial	12	88	0	67	21
Netherlands					
Public	17	83	30	39	14
Commercial	11	89	9	74	6
Norway					
Public	0	100	50	43	7
Commercial	0	100	12	78	11
Spain					
Public	11	89	17	49	23
Commercial	8	92	6	59	27
Sweden					
Public	33	67	18	46	3
Commercial	5	95	19	64	12
Switzerland					
Public	0	100	14	66	20
Commercial	–	–	–	–	–
United Kingdom					
Public	52	48	0	32	16
Commercial	55	45	0	32	13
TOTAL	17	83	16	56	11

half of the series on the PSB channels are domestic; the commercial stations, however, broadcast 1 per cent domestic series!

The French and British stations mainly import from the USA and the Australian market and hardly at all from other European countries. France and the UK produce a number of TV series which they can export abroad, yet themselves buy very few series on the European market (a similar scenario was noted with regard to movies).

In the UK there is no striking difference between the purchasing policy of public and commercial channels (Sky One was not taken into account); in France the commercial channels programme more American software. In Germany, the American series are mainly programmed by the commercial channels (RTL Plus 97 per cent; SAT 1 84 per cent). The PSB stations also buy series on the US market but they also import more than France and Great Britain from other European countries.

All small countries have to rely on foreign imports. Austria, Belgium (French-speaking), Ireland, Switzerland, Norway (commercial station) and Sweden (commercial station) import their series mainly from the USA. The PSB stations of smaller countries (such as Denmark, Finland, Norway, the Netherlands) buy more of their series on the European market.

On the Italian channels, both public and commercial, the American domination is very strong. The Italian PSB channels programme more than 90 per cent of American series; the Berlusconi channels less: 67 per cent! Again the linguistic and cultural arguments do not work here: Europe is becoming more Americanized.

On the Spanish channels half of the series are American: 49 per cent for PSB; 59 per cent for the commercial stations.

Australia and Brazil are also important suppliers of series for the European market. In fact more series were imported from Australia (5 per cent) than from France (1 per cent), Germany (3 per cent), and the rest of Europe (2 per cent); only the UK beats Australia (10 per cent). Thus, when compared with individual European countries, Australia scores highly.

The share of the Brazilian imports is half that of the Australian: 3 per cent. The Brazilian telenovelas seem less successful with European audiences, and their share, in comparison with the 1988 study, is not growing.

A comparison with the 1988 study reveals some interesting trends, as shown in Table 6.7. Here we find that the amount of domestic series has decreased in favour of American series. Most of the TV stations (public as well as commercial) give peak placing to

Table 6.7 *Origin of series on European TV in 1988 and 1991 (percentage)*

	1988	1991
Home	37	17
USA	36	56
Europe	14	16
of which:		
France	2	1
UK	7	10
W. Germany	3	3
Other	3	2
Other	13	11

American movies and series, so that during prime time the share of American fiction is even higher.

This drastic fall of domestic series and increase of American imports cannot be imputed only to the policy of the new commercial stations. Many public stations also programme American series. Is this programme policy the result of the competition between public and commercial stations? Are public service broadcasters trying to raise their audience ratings by scheduling more popular American series? Or is the European TV programme industry not capable of meeting the increasing demand for TV series? Europe seems to find it difficult to win a share of the international TV market. Australia and Brazil have succeeded better. The question is whether the European programme industry has to follow the Australian recipe: imitation of American TV formulas, thus stimulating the globalization and homogenization of the international TV market.

European broadcasters, however, know that their viewers prefer domestic fiction even if it is not of top quality. But home-made fiction is often much more expensive than imported drama, especially low-priced American drama. Audience research has revealed that in all European countries American series and films as a general rule guarantee higher positions in the ratings than imported European drama. This encourages broadcasters, especially those of the commercial stations, to include more American drama in their programming schedules. Over a long period of time this 'overdose' of American fiction could cause a 'Dallasification' of the European TV culture.

Research findings on Flemish viewers reveal that American fiction is often preferred to fiction imported from other European countries. Because of the dense cable network (91 per cent of

Flemish TV households are connected to cable), Flemish viewers have a rich choice of about 25 TV stations. They are exposed daily to an overdose of television fiction. Home productions by Flemish stations, especially news, fiction and entertainment, receive high ratings on the whole. Of the imported fiction broadcast by the Flemish stations, American series (more than films) attract on the whole bigger audiences than fiction from other European countries! But there is more: when Flemish viewers switch over to a foreign station for fiction, their preference is mostly for American fiction. The large number of foreign stations and recently the many new commercial channels available on the Flemish cable network have had a cumulative effect on the viewers' preference for American fiction. Will the new transmission channels in Europe, notably planned for cable networks and/or DBS reception, grow into the highways along which American TV fare will definitively conquer Europe?

Policy implications for the development of the European programme market

The broadcasting systems of Europe produce a total volume of films and TV programmes far larger than that of the USA, and broadcast an estimated total number of at least 260,000 hours per year, an increase of 125 per cent since 1980 (Lange and Renaud 1989: 108). Indeed the EC countries alone produce a larger volume of films and TV programmes than the USA (de Vries 1989: 13). Yet imports from the USA have rapidly increased, while the majority of programmes and films made in each European country never leave the country in which they are produced; the European Commission has calculated that this is the case with 80 per cent of the films made in the European Community (de Vries 1989: 13).

The empirical study revealed two major trends: the new commercial channels have stimulated popular entertainment programming and imports of American TV fiction. The new commercial TV stations programme mainly entertainment and fiction; the PSB channels, especially during prime time, also schedule a large number of popular programmes. The process of commercialization has had a downmarket effect on the overall TV programme supply. Commercial channels as well as PSB stations are in search of high audience ratings. Television in Europe thus becomes increasingly an entertainment medium. If PSB stations give in to this levelling down strategy, if they increasingly imitate the high entertainment profile of the commercial stations, they run the risk of abandoning their *raison d'être*.

Our empirical study shows that the European broadcasting industry is highly dependent on the USA for its film and series imports. While the production of film and series is growing in the USA, the production of feature films and TV drama has declined in Europe. While over 800 feature films were produced in Europe in 1970, this number declined to just under 700 in 1980, and even more rapidly in 1987 to under 500. The production of TV drama has also declined. The outflow of revenue from Western Europe to the USA for programmes is estimated to be in the region of at least $800 million annually, while this can be trebled to include film and video rights. This amount is increasing annually. Nor is this compensated for by US purchase of European programmes: only 2 per cent of programmes on US screens come from Europe, and these are mainly British programmes on minority channels, such as public service TV or specialist cable channels. European countries earn about 900,000 ECUs from programme exports – three quarters of this accruing to the UK (de Vries 1989).

Contributing to the decline of Europe's film industry is the continuing fall in cinema attendances and hence the need to find new sources of finance for film production. However, cinema exposure is only one source of revenue and films may be marketed through a planned sequence of 'window' releases. In the US film industry, home video release now contributes more to total return (43 per cent) than do cinema release (35 per cent), television (11 per cent), or pay TV (9 per cent).

Likewise with US TV fiction. Increasingly such fiction does not recoup its production costs with a sale to the major networks. Typically the deficit after sale to the networks is between a fifth and a third of the cost (*Television Business International*, February 1989). Indeed full costs may not be covered and profitability reached (if at all) until the show is released into domestic syndication, perhaps up to five years after its first US run. Prior to this it may be, as with film, marketed through a series of 'windows'.

The lesson of the US market for European companies would appear to be the need not only to generate more finance through co-production and co-financing, but to consider the whole audiovisual industry as an integrated sector, and to be particularly aware of the need to coordinate the marketing of audiovisual products if their full revenue potential is to be realized. As the television industry, both public and commercial, is already an important financier of film production in Europe, further developments in this direction should be encouraged.

A further pointer from the US audiovisual industry is its ability to capitalize on popular hits and to exploit film and TV drama

successes through the production of long series, spin-off programmes, books, toys, etc. It is thus involved in a scale of
production which capitalizes on economies of scale and scope which
will help to offset losses on those films and programmes which are
not hits.

Large rather than small firms are at a distinct advantage in such a
market. They must be capable of long-term deficit financing as well
as capable of moving into or negotiating satisfactorily with adjacent
markets to capitalize on spin-off effects and sequenced exposures.
Concentration in ownership of private broadcasting stations is thus
occurring not only in Europe, but also in the USA. Also, there is
increasing involvement of US companies in European productions,
cable and satellite companies, and by European companies in the
USA.

One of the central policy questions which arises, given the
emerging patterns of multinational and multimedia ownership in the
audiovisual industries in Europe is the interrelationship between
concentration in ownership and competitiveness in the international
market place on the one hand (see Chapter 3) and, on the other, the
consequences of these for programme diversity, a diversity which
should adequately reflect the wealth of European national cultures
and subcultures.

A number of economic, political and cultural factors will contribute to the evolving relationship between national, European and
US programme markets. At the national level, two factors contribute to the vitality of home-produced programming. The first is
audience demand. Here the evidence to date appears to indicate
that audiences may prefer TV fictional programmes from their own
country to US programmes (Silj 1988), but not always to other
European programmes. The second is the commitment of public
service broadcasting to home production. However, as noted
above, competition from commercial stations has frequently eaten
into the finances of public service stations and thus the amount
available for high-cost fictional programmes has been reduced.
There is a need for greater political will to support public service
broadcasting – if high-cost home-produced programmes are to
continue to be made. This is especially the case for smaller
countries.

At the European level audience demand is not so clear. It is
possible that, in their choice of foreign fiction, audiences may
choose to view US products rather than fiction from other European
countries. The European programming market may thus be weakened not only by the attractions of US products, but also by the fact
that it is itself fragmented not only in terms of nation-states, but also

in terms of regions which share language and cultural similarities. These linguistic and cultural regions may also be characterized by traditions of cultural and media dominance between a larger and richer core state and smaller adjacent states. There thus exist strong tendencies towards regional European audiovisual markets, rather than a generalized and unified market. Another, related area that needs further research is the role that subtitling may play in the creation of a more unified European market.

Some economic and political factors may in the future reinforce a Europeanizing trend. Concentration in media ownership across Europe is one such trend, as well as the economics of the audiovisual industry which would appear to favour larger companies which can gain from economies of scale and scope. Counterbalancing this growth in concentration is increasing concern that the dominance of a few multinational and multimedia conglomerates in Europe (see Chapter 3 above) may lead to less rather than more diversity.

Political factors which may contribute to a Europeanizing tendency are the quota regulations of the Council of Europe and the EC (see Chapter 4 above). Some would argue, however, that neither the EC's nor the Council of Europe's media policy offers efficient strategies and support. The EC's media policy is mainly economically inspired and market-driven. The EC Directive of October 1989 imposes soft quotas for European productions. For smaller states this Directive offers little protection for domestic productions.

It is undoubtedly in the cultural interest of European nations, as well as of Europe as a whole, to recognize that the dominant economic and industrial logics that motivated commercialization of television and the rapid development of new communication technologies in the 1980s have had the cultural consequence of supporting neither nationally based production nor European production, but rather, of massively supporting Hollywood. Because of American dominance, Europeans should be alarmed at the growing uniformity of TV fare which is frequently at the cost of their own cultural identity. It is a major challenge to European TV stations, commercial as well as public service, to fight this continuing American 'cultural' invasion. Facing the homogeneous, uniform American software industry, Europe can muster a unique weapon, her cultural diversity. National governments face an important task: TV media policy needs a more cultural approach.

Notes

1 The data for this empirical research were collected by the Department of Communication, University of Ghent, Belgium. Detailed TV programme guides were the main source. The assistance of several members of the Euromedia Research Group as well as of several broadcast corporations was indispensable.

2 If Sky One had been taken into account as well, the percentage of popular programming of the British commercial channels would probably be higher. The three Finnish stations were counted as public stations though they provide broadcasting time to commercial broadcasting organizations. This explains the high percentage of popular programmes on Finnish television. In fact the third Finnish station has become a commercial station in the meantime.

References

Baumol, H. and Baumol, W.J. (1976) 'The Mass Media and the Cost Disease', in W.S. Hendon, H. Horowitz and C.R. Waits (eds), *Economics of Cultural Industries*. Ohio: Association for Cultural Economics.

Collins, R., Garnham, N. and Locksley, G. (1988) *The Economics of Television: The UK Case*. London: Sage.

De Bens, E. (1985) 'L'influence de la câblodiffusion sur le comportement télévisuel des Belges et sur les stratégies de programmation des services publiques belges', *Bulletin de l'Idate*. Montpellier, 21 November: 310–30.

De Bens, E. (1986) 'Cable penetration and competition among foreign stations', *European Journal of Communication*, 1(4): 477–92.

De Bens, E. (1988) 'Der Einfluss eines grossen ausländischen Programmangebotes auf die Sehgewohnheiten', *Publizistik*, Sonderheft, Heft 2–3: 352–65.

De Bens, E. (1989) *Dallasification as a result of increasing TV channel competition*, ICA Congress, San Francisco, 6.

Geerts, C. and Thoveron, J.V. (1980) 'Télévision offerte au public. Télévision regardée par le public', *Etudes de radio et télévision*, RTBF: 85–102.

Horizons Media International (1987) 'Television Programming in Europe 2, 1986/87 Summary Report'. London: Horizons Media International (now known as 'Young and Rubicam Media in Europe Ltd').

Hoskins, C., Minus, R. and Rozeboom, W. (1989) 'Programs in the international market: unfair pricing', *Journal of Communication*, 39 (2): 55–75.

Kelly, M. (1988) 'National European or American Programmes: trends in European television', *Administration*, Dublin, 36 (1): 13.

Lange, A. and Renaud, J.L. (1989) *The future of the European Audiovisual Industry*. Manchester: European Institute for the Media.

Locksley, G. (1988) *Broadcasting in Europe and the New Technologies*. Luxembourg: EC.

McQuail, D. and Siune, K. (eds) (1986) *New Media Politics: Comparative Perspectives in Western Europe*. London: Sage Publications.

Manschot, B. (1988) 'De internationale verspreiding van televisiefictie' (The international distribution of TV fiction), *Massacommunicatie*, 2: 145.

Morgan, M. and Shanahan, J. (1991) 'Television and the cultivation of political attitude in Argentina', *Journal of Communication*, 41.

Nordenstreng, K. and Varis, T. (1974) 'Television traffic, a one way street? A survey and analysis of the international flow of television programmes material', *Unesco Reports and Papers on Mass Communication*, 70.

Nordenstreng, K. and Varis, T. (1986) 'La circulation internationale des émissions de télévision', *Unesco Etudes et Documents d'Information*, Paris, 100.

Pragnell, A. (1985) *Television in Europe*. Manchester: European Institute for the Media.

Sepstrup, P. (1989) 'Implication of current developments in West European broadcasting', *Media, Culture and Society*, II: 29–54.

Silj, A. (1988) *East of Dallas*. London: British Film Institute.

de Vries, Gijs M. (1989) *The European Film and Television Industry*, Report drawn up on behalf of the Committee on Economic and Monetary Affairs and Industrial Policy of the European Parliament.

Wober, J.M. (1989) *Screening America for Britain*, Research Paper, London: IBA, May.

PART III

PRESSURES ON NATIONAL SYSTEMS

7

Public Broadcasting in a State of Flux

Kees Brants and Karen Siune

A system of public service has to a greater or lesser extent been the central feature of broadcasting in Europe. In the 1980s this feature came under pressure from the commercializing tendencies of new electronic media, the appearance of media tycoons in an expanding market, political ambiguity and, more generally, an ideological move from a cultural to more of an industrial policy orientation. Most countries, one way or another, both welcomed the new media and, at the same time, seemed to treasure the 'old order' of public broadcasting.

The nature of public service broadcasting

Public broadcasting in Europe is relatively lacking in norms; in fact, there is no uniformity even in the terminology used. Quality, accountability, non-commerciality, access, all seem to be elements of the treasured public broadcasting system. Different actors, however, emphasize different elements. Governments, from their regulatory and political point of view, will stress the public and financial aspects of the organization and impartiality in news coverage. Here the emphasis is on accountability (other than through market reactions), on government-regulated licence fees and on balance, both in programme genres and in political content. The media industry will object that regulation is interference in a natural, commercial market system and that a true public service is, of course, one that the *public* wants: entertainment programming, not regulated and cheap.

Public broadcasters, on the other hand, will view their role from a different angle. According to the European Broadcasting Union its members serve or aim to serve the entire population of their respective countries; ensure diversified and balanced programming aimed at all strata of the population; effectively produce and/or

arrange to have produced under their control a substantial proportion of the programmes (Lange and Renaud 1989: 69–70). Some
public broadcasters emphasize alongside this their more missionary
and educational role, as, for example the director-general of the
Belgian (Walloon) RTBF, who added that they have a mission to
fulfil towards cultural and other minorities; that they make a
valuable and important contribution to improving general culture
and education; that they make possible free expression and that
they provide a state-independent news and information service
(Burgelman 1986). Even media researchers are not in agreement,
and emphasize different elements of the definition of public service
broadcasting (see Kuhn 1985; Blumler et al. 1986).

In spite of these differences, the 'old order' of public broadcasting
in Europe seemed to agree on at least a few elements:

- some form of accountability to (political representatives of) the
  public, other than through market forces, and realized through
  some form of administrative organization;
- some element of public finance – where advertising is another:
  any profit made is used for programming, programmes are not
  made for profit for its own sake, as in the private commercial
  system;
- (close) regulation of content, ranging from the more general
  rules of balance, impartiality and serving minority interests to
  banning certain kinds of advertising, violence and pornography;
- universal (geographical) service whereby the audience is
  addressed more as citizen (for whom programmes should have
  an added value) than the consumer; and
- protection from competition – if not a public monopoly, then
  some form of competition-decreasing measures.

The question is whether all European countries still have (elements of) such a public system. In other words, what does the West
European broadcasting scene look like at the beginning of the
1990s?

A look at Europe

In taking a closer look at the old European broadcasting order
which existed until the beginning of the 1980s, one has to distinguish
several types, as the picture in Europe has always been as diverse as
the map of the continent itself: a non-commercial, purely public
monopoly, such as could be found in most Nordic countries; a

public monopoly with mixed revenue sources from licence fees and advertising, as was the case in Austria, Finland, France, Greece (with payment of a levy on the electricity bill), Ireland, the Netherlands and Portugal; and a dual model in which a public system co-existed with a commercial one, as in the United Kingdom (although commercial broadcasting was heavily regulated) and Italy, where at the end of the 1970s private stations had effectively broken the public monopoly.

Spain and Luxembourg are two exceptions. The former had a public monopoly with no licence fee and financed almost entirely by advertising (and until 1988 by a subsidy from general taxation). The latter has a purely commercial system – still the only one in Europe – although some might argue that it has no system at all. Looking at it from a different, less financial and more organizational and content angle, there existed two further models: a federal type as in Germany and a linguistic one, as in Switzerland and Belgium (which excluded advertising as a revenue source). The first two countries fell within the mixed revenue type, while Belgium had a public monopoly, strongly politicized, heavily regulated and financed only through licence fees.

Table 7.1 *Number of TV channels in Europe 1980/1990*

	1980		1990		
	Public	*Commercial*	*Public*	*Commercial*	*Foreign cable*
Austria	2		2		12
Belgium	4		4	2	21
Denmark	1		2		25–30
Finland	2		2	1	
France	3		3	3	15–20
Germany	3		3/5	4	5–10
Greece	2		3	4	
Ireland	2		2	(1)	10–20
Italy	3		3	6	
Luxembourg		4		2(4)[a]	20–23
Netherlands	2		3	(1)	15–20
Norway	1		1	1	10–20
Portugal	2		2		
Spain	2		3[b]	3	
Sweden	2		2	3	15–20
Switzerland	3		3		12–20
UK	2	1	2	5+	

[a] Two are based in Luxembourg but beamed to other countries.

[b] One is regional.

In 1980 the seventeen countries of Western Europe had, taken together, 41 television (and 61 radio) channels, predominantly of a public nature. As Table 7.1 indicates, there have been widespread changes. In 1990 there are 36 commercial channels (with Ireland and the Netherlands having made the legal provisions for terrestrial commercial television), a majority of which are national satellite stations. The number of public channels (including new satellite channels) has risen too, although less dramatically: from 36 to just over 40. Together with special interest and other satellite channels owned by media moguls, there are more than a hundred television channels in Europe.

In all European countries, dual or mixed systems have replaced the public monopolies which existed ten years ago. Pure public monopolies without advertising no longer exist. Even the number of countries with public broadcasting that combines licence fees with advertising has decreased. The majority of countries now enjoy a dual system whereby public stations have to compete with private commercial ones. However, the changes have not been as dramatic everywhere as may have been expected in the mid-1980s. Luxembourg, with its population of less than half a million, is still the only country with a purely commercial system, although the RTL symphony orchestra suggests that even Luxembourg has a slight public service element.

Table 7.2   *Typology of national systems 1980/1990*

System	1980	1990
Pure public	Belgium, Denmark Norway, Sweden,	
Mixed revenue	Austria, Finland France, Germany, Greece, Ireland, Netherlands, Portugal, Spain, Switzerland	Austria, Denmark, Netherlands, Portugal, Switzerland
Dual system	Italy, UK	Belgium, Finland, France, Germany, Greece, Italy, Ireland, Norway, Spain, Sweden, UK
Pure commercial	Luxembourg	Luxembourg

In the following a closer look is taken at how countries have moved along the line from public monopoly via mixed revenue (licence fees and advertising – and dual system – to pure commercial system (see Table 7.2). Countries have been grouped into three levels of change: minimal, medium and strong.

Countries with minimal change

The first category comprises Austria, Italy, Luxembourg, Portugal and Switzerland. A plebiscite in 1989 favoured the abolition of the public monopoly in Austria, which still exists on terrestrial channels, but to date only the legalization of private radio is proposed. The Swiss, too, are expected to open up their legal system for private initiatives, including those concerning television. At the beginning of the 1990s the Swiss had a commercial pay TV channel.

Italy is perhaps a special case, as chaotic changes had already taken place between 1976 and 1981. The RAI monopoly was successfully challenged in 1976, resulting in a 'Wild West' period with several, at the time unregulated, private stations, most of which were soon incorporated into Berlusconi's Fininvest. RAI responded with a third public channel and has since held its ground (40 per cent of the audience share and a steady income flow from advertising) against the six current main commercial networks.

Luxembourg, commercial to begin with, is certainly unique and would find itself uncomfortable in a minimal position in view of the fact that it has been instrumental in many changes in the European television scene. The national system of the Grand Duchy has changed very little, but is turning out to be a haven and literally a satellite for others to broadcast from. It has provided refuge for media industries restricted in their commercial ambitions in their respective countries, making available satellite facilities for, or helping to set up, RTL TVi (French-speaking Belgium), RTL Plus (Germany), M6 (France) and RTL Veronique (the Netherlands).

Countries with medium change

In this category – where we find all the Scandinavian countries, Greece and the Netherlands – moderate changes have taken place and policy initiatives are expected to trigger more. In both Denmark and Sweden advertising has been introduced: in the former the monopoly of the public broadcaster was abolished in 1988 by the introduction of a second channel, which is expected eventually to be totally financed by advertising. In Sweden the success of Scansat TV3 and the popularity of other satellite stations prompted the government in 1989 to open up the Tele-X satellite for national commercial TV distribution. Norway, which has had a UK-based but Norwegian-owned commercial satellite station (TVN), has also changed the law recently to allow for the introduction of a private commercial channel, TV2, a channel with a monopoly on domestic terrestrial advertising and one which will be strongly regulated.

In Finland, the commercial Oy MTV, which was incorporated in the public system, will be given a new television channel that will be the only one allowed to carry advertising. In Greece, a radio and television law has legalized private local radio and television, the latter on a temporary (experimental) basis. The Netherlands is one of the few countries (with Germany and Italy) that started a new (third) public channel in reaction to commercial satellite initiatives. RTL4 (formerly RTL Veronique), a CLT subsidiary partly owned by Dutch publishers, has commenced commercial (Dutch-language) programming from Luxembourg and now has more than a quarter of the viewing audience. The government has proposed the introduction of national commercial television, and there are several candidates interested in running it. Publishers, however, are hesitant about its economic viability in view of the success of RTL4. With this Luxembourg station beamed at the Netherlands, the country already has a dual system in practice and is likely to have one officially in the future. For now it still falls officially into the category of mixed revenue.

Countries with strong change
In this category we find a strong contingent of six countries. A short overview shows diversity – both in strength and in scope – in the kind of change. Big countries, big changes, one might say, but it is one of the smallest that has made the biggest step, from a pure public to a dual system, with the public broadcasting stations struggling to keep a fair share of the audience.

In Belgium public broadcasting used to have a monopoly, with no advertising, but in 1987 in French-speaking Belgium (RTL-TVi) and in 1989 in Flanders (VTM) commercial broadcasting started. Spain has never had a licence fee and the national public television service is now financed entirely by advertising revenues. In 1983 a third television channel was introduced, in addition to the two RTVE channels, for public broadcasting in the regions. A law allowing the setting up of private television was passed in 1988, resulting in three new channels: Antena 3 (La Vanguardia/ABC), Tele 5 (ONCE/Berlusconi) and Canal Plus (El País).

France, Germany, Ireland and the United Kingdom highlight the movement towards a more privately organized broadcasting system in Europe. Probably the most dramatic changes have taken place in France, where change of government from left to right (and in a way back again) has changed neither the pace nor the direction of an outspoken government policy which aims both at promoting French culture and at stimulating the French communications industry.

In 1980, broadcasting in France was a strict public monopoly with three stations, TF1, Antenne 2 and the regional FR3; in 1990 the country is heading towards a predominantly commercial system. Those ten years have put France on the map of media change. After President Mitterrand had supported decentralization of the public function the year before, a new law broke the state monopoly in broadcasting in 1982. It was the government itself that initiated new commercial stations such as Canal Plus (pay TV; now public–private), La Cinq and M6, which were then auctioned off to the private sector. The French publisher Hersant and the Italian Berlusconi now have a majority share in a not very successful La Cinq, while Luxembourg's CLT has a majority interest in M6.

In 1987, the then liberal–conservative government took a step which was unique for Europe and put the public TF1 up for sale. To support its cultural aim it initiated a new public satellite station, La Sept. There are now three public and three private stations, with the main competition between TF1 (with some 40 per cent of the audience) and Antenne 2 (with 25 per cent). The position of the public stations (two thirds of A2's income comes from advertising too) is delicate.

Germany has established itself firmly as a dual system. The (re)union with the GDR will not change very much in this respect, but as yet it is unclear how the unification will affect the decentralized public system. There is no national broadcasting system nor a national policy for the media in Germany, since legislation is handled by the eleven (and since 1990 sixteen) Länder all of which have their own media laws. Until the arrival of private television – made possible in 1984 – television was provided by ARD (produced in the Länder but distributed nationally, ZDF (produced and distributed nationally) and a third, regionally organized programme.

Since different Länder have different laws and varying attitudes towards private initiatives, some Länder have provided favourable regulatory environments for terrestrial commercial transmissions, and for the current four main commercial satellite-to-cable services: SAT 1, RTL Plus, Tele 5, Pro 7. With 27 per cent of the country cabled they have a varying reach, but on the whole RTL Plus and SAT 1 now have more than 50 per cent of the audience share. In response, the public system has started two new satellite channels: Eins Plus and 3 Sat.

In Ireland, after the successful operation of pirate radio for more than a decade, a new Radio and Television Act has legalized private commercial radio stations. Furthermore, the introduction of (terrestrial) commercial television is proposed and expected towards the end of 1991, although there are doubts about its economic viability. Thus, Ireland has moved to a dual system in radio; television will follow in 1991/92.

The United Kingdom has known a dual system since 1954, when, alongside the public BBC, a network of private, regionally based ITV companies was introduced. These companies derive their income solely from advertising, but are regulated by the Independent Television Commission (ITC), formerly the Independent Broadcasting Authority (IBA). Both BBC and ITV, however, have a public function and are accountable to parliament. The Conservative government, with its strong adherence to deregulation and privatization, has, in a way, proposed to re-privatize the IBA. In the 1990 Broadcasting Act it introduced a new, commercial Channel 5 and an auctioning of the regional 10-year franchises of the ITV channel 3. For the BBC nothing has changed, but – depending on the government at that time – changes are expected when the BBC charter has to be renewed in 1996.

Two direct-to-home satellite organizations started operating at the end of the 1980s: Murdoch's Sky Channel, which after an unsuccessful European adventure has retracted to the British Isles, and British Satellite Broadcasting (BSB). Towards the end of 1990 they joined forces to form British Sky Broadcasting with three to five channels on the Astra satellite, a combination which triggered a fierce discussion on cross-ownership. Since Britain is only slightly cabled (approximately 2 per cent) and government support is only verbal (subsidies clash with the monetarist policy), the success of this venture is largely based on the sale of relatively expensive dishes.

On the whole one can see a considerable movement between 1980 and 1990. At the beginning of that decade public broadcasting was in a strong, often still monopolistic situation. Ten years later it had to compete with a growing number of private commercial channels.

Actors on the move

Different actors are active with regard to developments in national broadcasting; some are in favour of and stimulate new technological and commercial initiatives, while others oppose them or try to make them conform with the traditional values of the public system. Governments, still the most dominant actors in regard to decision-making, are torn between old loyalties, political and cultural obligations, economic considerations and commercial pressures.

represented.

Regulatory bodies as such are of less interest than is their com-position, because it reflects the variety of actors and their relative positions of strength. It is expected that the law reflects actual positions and not just wishful thinking (unlike the laws concerning local media mentioned in Chapters 11 and 12).

At the European level (see Chapter 4), the Green Paper of 1984 formed the incentive for the European Commission's Directive, and in spite of the original opposition by the Council of Europe, the latter's final Convention eventually converged with the EC's Directive in a pro-market stance. The fight for the 'nomination' of a regional capital for the financial sector after 1992, with London, Frankfurt and Milan all claiming top status, has, in a way, its counterpart in the field of communications. London and Luxembourg are increasingly becoming the headquarters of media tycoons and the decision-making centres for satellite developments in smaller countries, whilst Paris and possibly Berlin are making headway as well.

At the national level, monetarist and neo-Keynesian governments alike favour the socio-economic prospects of a commercial European media industry, but, with the exception of France, their attitude so far has been reactive rather than proactive: firstly, to tolerate or welcome private commercial initiatives, as in the cases of Belgium, Finland, Germany, the UK and others which will follow shortly; secondly, to allow advertising on those public channels that had licence fees as their only source of finance; thirdly, to start up more terrestrial or satellite public channels, as in the case of Denmark, Italy and the Netherlands.

At the same time, most countries (with the exception of Sweden, Finland, Austria and Switzerland), have tried to regulate these new developments by law. Support and regulations seem to have several motives: cultural (protecting national identities – e.g. France); industrial (both economic – supporting national industries, as in the case of France – and ideological ones – the ideal market place for ideas is the economic market, as in the case of the UK); and financial (shortage of resources – e.g. Ireland). One way or another, these motives are intertwined with the crisis in which public broadcasting institutions and their supporters have found themselves, namely in legitimating the privileged access to limited resources typical of a public service function (Syvertsen 1991).

There has been a change in political ideologies as well. Historically, as Syvertsen points out, in most European countries there has been an alliance between intellectuals, cultural elites and the labour movement in supporting public broadcasting throughout its first fifty years. After half a century, however, this alliance is now fragmented and the institutions can no longer look to one defined coalition of interests for support and legitimacy.

Originally, social democrats and parties of the left defended the public broadcasting system, with conservatives and others opting for a more commercial, preferably self-supporting system. On the other hand, some christian democratic parties have always opposed the 'dark side of capitalism': commercialization also meant glorifying profit-making and personal greed. Social democrats, christian democrats and conservatives all over Europe now seem to have joined forces. The staunchest defenders are to be found among the public broadcasters themselves and those critics who, at one point, considered public broadcasting institutions another 'ideological state apparatus', the mouthpiece of typical class interests.

The question is whether a myth is being created around public broadcasting, conveniently forgetting that a fair amount of pro- gramming is entertainment-focused and hardly different from private stations (see Chapter 6). For some, public broadcasting has become a fetish, the last bastion of a truly democratic, participa- tory, cultural stronghold against mediocre, mass cultural Dallas- type programming. On the other hand, the question is whether we can simply apply such notions as 'economic' versus 'cultural' primacies in the light of media tycoons and others who have entered the scene, or is the situation more complex?

In analysing the actors in the media field there seem to be four different logics at work (see Burgelman 1989) which at times interact and strengthen each other. Firstly, there is a cultural– educational or cultural–pedagogical logic which was, and in general still is, the driving force behind the concept of public broadcasting. In this logic, broadcasting and more generally the new communica- tion technologies have a culturally dynamic role to play in informing and educating an audience to become, or function as, full members of an optimal democracy. Until the beginning of the 1980s this was the dominant logic in Western Europe.

Secondly, there is a state logic which drives the need for regulation. This state logic seems to be wavering: the breakdown of the public monopoly is a result of and has an effect on this logic, as it is linked with a more general change from neo-Keynesian (regula- tion) to more neo-liberal (deregulation) politics. On the one hand we see a deregulatory tendency in most countries of Europe, as far as the organization and privatization of broadcasting is concerned, on the other there is a re-regulatory tendency of a more ideological nature which can take several, sometimes conflicting, forms: protec- tion of the national culture/identity; regulation of programme content (notably advertising, violence and pornography); guaranteeing balanced programming as in the British proposal to introduce a Broadcasting Standards Council and some sort of Fairness Doctrine; rules against cross-ownership as a protection of diversity.

Thirdly, there is an economic logic where profit maximization is the driving force, the market the natural battlefield and the public both sovereign consumer and arbitrator of success or failure. With profit and commercialization having lost their negative connotation, even in the discourse of public broadcasting, interference in that market – as in the case of anti-monopoly rules or quota claims – goes 'against nature'. Especially where the state and the economic logic coincide, as is the case in France and (at least in the political discourse) in the United Kingdom, the economic logic dominates the cultural one.

Finally, there is an administrative logic, a policy of 'muddling through' with its often unplanned effects. We perceived this logic as a counter-pole to an innovative logic guided by the new visions or new goals which can be attained by means of the new media. Non-decision-making from political actors often results in regulations created according to an administrative extension of existing rules for established media. Lack of a coherent media policy can lead to passivity among decision-makers in public bodies and such passivity can create great changes for policy-makers outside the traditional political system (McQuail and Siune 1986: 1–7).

With most countries showing a lack of any systematic or comprehensive policy for the media, it is precisely in this political vacuum that actors with an economic logic operate. Nevertheless, the issue of control is still around.

New media, old issues

Governments have a long tradition of regulating broadcast mass media. To an increasing extent modern governments have, generally speaking, become regulative governments, whether they be called (neo-)corporatist, (neo-)Keynesian, welfare or interventionist states. In most of the traditional areas of governmental regulation, political and administrative authorities interfere with greater intensity than just a few decades ago. This general conclusion could be the explanation for an ongoing regulation of the broadcast media as well; media policy is following the main trend.

An alternative theory could be that since modern governments have taken on the task of regulating private activities which, until recently, were totally unregulated, they have given up the regulation of other areas either because of lack of energy or lack of relative concern. But the answer to this alternative hypothesis is that, although 'energy shortages' may occur within governments, the concern for the broadcast mass media is still there and many actors put pressure on governments to show their interest in the development of national broadcast media. So regulation will continue.

Although, with the possible exception of terrestrial broadcasting in Austria, all public monopolies have been abolished in Europe over the past ten years, public service broadcasting is still there. Albeit in a precarious financial situation, the number of stations has not decreased, and their existence is generally guaranteed by law.

The question has to be posed as to whether the technological, commercial threats to that system and the more favourable political climate all over Europe towards private commercial ventures will reveal a different picture for the 1990s. Generally speaking, we treat media regulation as the dependent variable, as a response to the situation or as a result of the traditions within a national system. The elements emphasized in national laws are particularly related to matters of organization, finance and content, and to a lesser degree to (the assurance of some form of) access. Is the regulatory system of public broadcasting in a state of turmoil? With the service provided by broadcasting in Europe showing more and more private commercial rather than public features, there is also a movement away from government to market-induced regulation if we take Europe as one entity. With that in mind, let us take a closer look at the different fields of control that are in question.

Control of organization

All over Europe we see signs of change, of a loosening grip. With the success of neo-liberalism we see a gradual retreat of the ruling state and more emphasis on the *laissez-faire* principle of the market. In some countries – notably the UK, the Netherlands, Italy and France – there are rules to limit cross-ownership, but in most countries such rules have not been very successful. The European Parliament has shown its concern, but has to date not proposed any concrete measures. Most countries, notwithstanding their political 'colour', have some form of controlling body more or less directly linked to government. On the whole, regulation of public broadcasting still exists – while for private stations regulation is either limited, not forcefully adhered to or not successful.

Control of finance

Whereas in the 1980s the main source of income for public broadcasting was the licence fee, for the 1990s income in most countries is increasingly dependent on advertising, which is less controlled than the licence fee set by national governments. In general it can be said that a multiplication of channels means a diversification of income sources and a slackening of control. Rules on sponsorship, product placement and 'natural breaks' do not change this trend.

On the other hand, with the apparent success of government spending cuts there is growing pressure on the labour-intensive public broadcasting institutions to save money through rationalization and, in general, to cut costs. Competition from the less labour-intensive commercial stations, of which government control is minimal, has formed an extra impetus for this trend.

Control of programming

There are four levels at which some form of control over programming is involved. In the first place there are regulations for the protection of national culture or identity. The quota regulation of the EC Directive (see Chapter 4), which has to be implemented in national laws, however much it has been toned down and only refers to programmes of a European origin, is one example. Secondly, all European public broadcasting institutions have to maintain some kind of balance in their programming, be it political or in diversity of genres (information, culture, entertainment, etc.). The new private channels are more loosely controlled content-wise, notably with regard to that element of balanced programming.

Thirdly, some countries try to ban programmes of a particular nature, notably sex and violence. Finally, as with the previous regulation intended to protect the young, countries try to limit or ban the advertising of certain kinds of products. The EC Directive and the CoE Convention have special regulations on the advertising of cigarettes, medicine and alcohol. Some countries, such as France, have tougher regulations for public than for commercial broadcasters.

Control of access

This is a tricky regulatory issue, as countries seem to have different definitions of access, and some give it no weight at all. Access can firstly be defined as a concession to broadcast to the nation as a whole (universal availability). With the advent of cable and satellite the scarcity argument for regulating access has lost most of its power, but 'must carry' rules (some cable stations must carry terrestrial channels) and the support of regional and local stations is still an area of control.

Secondly, access can be defined as the relative openness of a system. With the new audiovisual media and their apparent abundance of channels, the problem of access has, however paradoxically, become more problematic. On the one hand, abundance is choice, but on the other, the choice is generally limited to the commercially strong. But access can, thirdly, also be defined as regulating air time for specific groups in a society, such as minorities, political parties, etc.

There is a trend away from what could be called an 'old model of regulation' (guaranteeing quality, access, etc.) to a new model, inspired by the economic logic, whereby regulation only guarantees an optimal and fair market, a market which facilitates the media performance regulated in the old model.

Conclusion

A great deal of change took place in the European media structure during the late 1980s, and in the early 1990s the question can be raised again as to whether deregulation has become the proper label for the situation. The answer, subsequent to the experience gained during the work on *New Media Politics*, is that it is still not a sufficient term for Europe. The hypotheses are: (1) that regulation continues in Europe with respect to national media, and (2) new means of regulation are used side by side with the old ones when we look at national reactions to the challenges to the national media structure, challenges arising from local and transnational media.

The developments are a combination (see Murdock 1990) of liberalization (introducing competition where previously a public monopoly reigned), commercialization of the public sector (through spot advertising, sponsorship, merchandising, co-productions combined with aiming at an international market) and deregulation which can take the form of re-regulation (a loosening of restrictions for private operations, combined with a tightening of normative and balancing rules). Where deregulation takes the form of decreasing public expenditure and reducing the bureaucracy in a public system, liberalization and commercialization may well become a financial necessity when the squeeze is put on the public broadcasters' budget. Liberalization, commercialization and deregulation are then all part of a rather closed universe of discourse, where definitions become self-fulfilling prophecies.

To what future, finally, will these developments lead for public broadcasting in Europe? This will depend on a few factors, one of which is the level of financial support. On the whole, countries in Europe are hesitant to raise licence fees in view of commercial competition and declining economies, and some countries (France) have indeed lowered them. In general, the situation in the richer countries will be less gloomy. But that will, secondly, depend on political support. Thirdly, the future of public broadcasting will depend on the combination of audience support and the willingness of advertisers still to 'go public'.

The final factor that will influence the future of public broadcasting is the reaction of the public broadcasters themselves: will they adapt, adopt, or perish? That is the topic of the next chapter.

References

Blumler, J.G., Brynin, M. and Nossiter, T.J. (1986) 'Broadcasting Finance and Programme Quality: An international review', *European Journal of Communication*, 1 (4): 343–64.

Burgelman, J.C. (1986) 'The Future of Public Service Broadcasting: A Case Study for a "new" Communications Policy', *European Journal of Communication*, 1 (2): 173–201.

Burgelman, J.C. (1989) 'De ontwikkeling van de audiovisuele media in de jaren 90', *Communicatie*, 19: 21–31.

Kuhn, R. (1985) *The Politics of Broadcasting*. London: Croom Helm.

Lange, A. and Renaud, J.L. (1989) *The Future of the European Audiovisual Industry*. Manchester: European Institute for the Media.

McQuail, D. and Siune, K. (eds) (1986) *New Media Politics: Comparative Perspectives in Western Europe*. London: Sage.

Murdock, G. (1990) 'Redrawing the map of the communications industries: concentration and ownership in the era of privatization', in M. Ferguson (ed.), *Public Communication: the New Imperatives*. London: Sage. pp. 1–16.

Syvertsen, T. (1991) 'Public Television in Crisis: Critiques Compared in Norway and Britain', *European Journal of Communication* 6 (1): 95–115.

8

Public Service Broadcasting: Reactions to Competition

Olof Hultén and Kees Brants

Public service broadcasting in a changing world

This chapter will deal with the effects of increased competition and commercialization on the traditional public service organizations in Western Europe, and the ways in which they react to this. Political influence and regulation include many 'thou shalts' and 'thou shalt nots'. On the one hand, such guidelines do not define public service efficiency or success very well; on the other hand they can be very inhibiting in a competitive situation. Commercialization of broadcasting is a process on multiple fronts. Here we shall consider public service organizations' reactions to increased competition from commercial broadcasters for audiences, programmes, talents, broadcasting rights and financial resources, as well as for political support.

The factors of competition are, as in other consumer industries, price and quality of products, production resources, market strategies, packaging and product branding. Other important factors of competition are innovations, the control of supply and distribution, and efforts to influence the rules of the game by lobbying regulators and legislators.

How public service broadcasters define their business and how they formulate their strategies is crucially significant in determining their choice of responses to changes in their environment. The commitment of the political establishment to preserve a strong public service system is the second decisive factor, and more important than the manner in which the public system is financed.

The pressures for change
The previous chapter describes the changes in the European regulation of public service broadcasting. These changes form a very complicated and mixed pattern. The national regulatory

environment is weakening. External pressures on national public broadcasting today as a rule include international competition and legislation.

In his analysis of national debates on the regulation of television, Vincent Porter (1989: 5–27) points to three issues which are at stake. First, the relative importance of the market versus regulatory bodies in shaping the new television order. Secondly, the appropriate balance between public and private sector television, and thirdly, what conditions can be imposed on the private sector by regulators.

An asymmetrical regulatory system has emerged in Europe – the roles assigned to the public and to the private sector are different and, consequently, the regulations for each sector differ as well. All predictions about future developments in European television will have to take this lack of symmetry into consideration (see Chapter 2). It does constitute a destabilizing force in the broadcasting system as a whole and it certainly creates frustration among European public broadcasting organizations.

The strengths and weaknesses of traditional public service organizations

No doubt every public broadcasting system in Europe has taken stock of its strong and its weak sides. A number of decisive factors, political, structural and economic can be judged to be either an advantage or a disadvantage.

Advantages of public service broadcasting given appropriate political support, are:

- predictable revenues;
- no financial risks;
- universal availability;
- high audience reach and profile; and
- diversified programming and production capabilities.

Disadvantages of public service broadcasting are:

- limited freedom to operate;
- multitude of programming obligations;
- inflexible cost structure; and
- politically determined organization.

Given these strong and weak sides, there are three possible strategies open to public service organizations faced with increased competition from private broadcasters: adaptation, purification and compensation.

Adaptation means competing with more or less the same logic as commercial stations, running the risk of diluting or abandoning the traditional spirit of public service.

Purification – or restriction to public service only – at the other extreme in effect means withdrawing from competition, concentrating on the kind of programmes that private stations do not bother to offer. The goal here is to focus on what only public service can do, or is expected to do. As far as can be judged, no public broadcasting organization has chosen this strategy for itself. Nor have any been forced to do so by regulators, yet.

Opponents to public service broadcasting favour a strategy of purification, obliging the state to preserve the existence of a traditional cultural and minority service alongside a dominant commercial system. This strategy, which in practice means marginalization of public broadcasting, is most often proposed by supporters of commercial television, but also by cultural commentators critical of public broadcasting imitating the tricks of commercial television. Only occasionally is purification suggested by public broadcasters themselves.

Compensation indicates a middle way of avoiding both the logic of commercial television and the role of a marginalized cultural enclave. Such a strategy tries to build on the strengths of established public broadcasting, such as news and current affairs, in-house productions and regional presence. A new sort of balance has to be found between traditional public service values and the necessity to act successfully in a market dominated by commercial forces.

Those defending a strategy of compensation, including most public broadcasting organizations, want to please and serve television viewers without falling into the trap of commercialism.

Commercialization and competition

In essence, commercialism in broadcasting is the production and supply of information and culture within a market structure, for profit (McQuail and Siune 1986: Chapter 11), but in practice definitions of commercialism are vague and diverse. They refer to several things: the structure of the broadcasting media, modes of financing, and the processes and effects of broadcasting itself.

Central to commercialization is the concept of competition, the struggle for limited resources. Commercial competition requires commercial responses, whatever current public service ideals have to say. A broadcasting regulation which tries to reconcile unregulated competition and commercial expansion with the traditional ethic of quality and comprehensiveness, without expecting significant contradiction or tension, is unrealistic and overoptimistic (Blumler 1989).

The two sets of actors, private and public broadcasters, are interdependent on each other in three areas: input resources (events, programmes, talents), consumer demand (viewing time) and, increasingly frequently, financial resources. A recipe for asymmetric regulation has to face this interdependency.

The main reasons for the apparent failure of the market to deliver the ideal public service result, according to Blumler, from the special conditions of television markets: (1) increased competition tends to drive costs up rather than down, while (2) demand (viewing time) is more or less inelastic, creating (3) uncertainty in the market place.

In his model of competitive strategies, Michael Porter introduces two perspectives of competition, direct competition and extended competition (Porter 1980). Direct competition is the narrower relationship between already established companies involved in a particular market. Nowadays this situation is the rule in Western Europe, where few countries maintain the traditional monopoly system (see Table 7.1, p. 103). An analysis of extended competition widens the perspective by adding new entrants, substitute products, suppliers and customers, to the direct relationships between established competitors.

Porter's concept of extended competition is helpful in describing the changes in the environment of all public broadcasting organizations in Western Europe, albeit each country represents a unique case in the evolution from traditional monopoly towards transnational competition.

New entrants

It has been, and for terrestrial broadcasting still is, the privilege of regulators to control entry to the market. New technologies have, however, changed the conditions for entry. With the rapid diffusion of cable systems, and the access to direct reception from satellites in individual homes, entry is today more or less open. Governmental control is in practice very difficult, if not impossible. The cases of Germany, the Netherlands, Sweden and the UK illustrate this.

To bring some common order to the international level, the Council of Europe and the European Community have established a set of minimum rules for transnational satellite distribution (see Chapter 4). Thus an analysis of competition in television must be extended beyond the national context.

Substitutes
Fifteen years ago, it was expected (or feared) that video would become a serious challenge to conventional television. Today, video is more a substitute for another substitute for broadcast television, namely pay television. New direct substitutes for broadcast television are satellite and cable television channels. Direct broadcast satellites still do not amount to much of a threat in Western Europe, although several such services are being developed in Europe, notably by BSkyB in the UK. Technological forecasts predict a continuing dominance of cable reception.

Customers
Public broadcasting, totally financed by licence fees, ideally serves only one customer, the viewing and listening audience. One classic criticism of public service broadcasting, however, has been that the audience has never really entered into the thinking of traditional public service broadcasting. Viewers could simply be ignored because they had no financial influence on the broadcaster. The fee was determined by public authorities and collected by some public body, usually the PTT. Small wonder that the public broadcasters had their eyes fixed primarily on the politicians.

The introduction of advertising in public broadcasting opened up a market on a new front. Much energy has been invested in the protection of public broadcasting from undue influence by advertisers. It is a matter both of definition and honesty to establish the extent of real influence advertising has on public broadcasting. Often a comparison is made with the press, where the dependence is supposedly no problem.

Suppliers
The most important suppliers are film distributors, rights holders, promotion agents and production companies as well as specialists and professional talents. All television stations need such crucial key resources. Joint venture partners, investors and financiers are other suppliers of increasing significance to public broadcasters as well.

Different phases of competition

We can distinguish the following five phases of competition, few of which, however, are found in pure form anywhere. The traditional *monopoly* phase is today a thing of the past. During the *entry* phase, there is no real threat to the established order. This comes only as competition gains a certain momentum, in terms of household coverage and advertising volume. Competitors will then, in the *battle* phase, be able to acquire strategic programmes and events and to outbid public broadcasters for stars and personalities. Public broadcasters during the battle phase encounter problems selling advertising time at the prices and under the conditions to which they are bound. The costs for acquired as well as in-house productions increase.

During the *consolidation* phase, uncertainty can be reduced by agreement between competing broadcasters on price levels for certain programmes and resources. A division of labour can prove mutually acceptable. Strategic alliances or mergers are other approaches to limiting uncontrolled competition.

Perhaps the UK is the only example of a country where competition has reached maturity. The BBC and ITV, after thirty-five years of competition, have actually developed such a degree of consensus on their mutual interests that the duopoly is now being opened again to new entrants. A new process is about to start.

Italy could become the second country to reach a stage of maturity, as parliament, after fourteen years of more or less uncontrolled battle between public and private television, in November 1990 legitimized the present status quo in a new Broadcasting Law.

A few countries, such as Greece, Ireland, Norway and Sweden, are in the entry or early battle phases. As mentioned above, the UK also fits in here in terms of the 1993 implementation of the new Broadcasting Act concerning independent commercial television.

Belgium, Germany and France have been in the battle phase for some years now, the Netherlands and Spain only since 1990. In these countries, public and private broadcasters are engaged in strong, direct confrontation. Denmark, perhaps, also belongs in this group, although competition here is fought between two publicly regulated television organizations, one exclusively financed by licence fees, the other primarily by advertising.

The competitive tactics of public service broadcasters

As Blumler notes with regard to television in the USA, the conditions for competition in the market and the processes that guide organizational strategies leave no broadcaster unaffected. It is often, wrongly, assumed that non-commercial licence fee funds somehow shield public broadcasting from competition, and thus act as a guarantee for a traditional public broadcasting service. Public broadcasters in Western Europe are obliged to act in certain prescribed non-commercial ways, but they are also under pressure to perform well and to be cost-effective. They are compared to their competitors, to which they are linked through the same audiences and various interrelated resources.

Schedules
Composition of programme schedules, especially during peak time, is of central importance to every broadcaster in competition. As advertising revenues became increasingly vital to many public systems as early as the 1970s, some such adjustments were already introduced prior to the changes caused by market liberalization and the advent of new technologies. The need to deliver audiences to advertisers requires close attention to programme schedules and to audience research.

Public broadcasters with no advertising to sell quite naturally tend to take a closer look at their programme schedules, too.

The extent of 'dilution' of content or reduction of 'standards' of cultural quality as a result of more competitive scheduling is not easy to measure, partly because category systems are very generous. The general picture which emerges is that changes have been made by every public broadcasting system, in order to keep what are defined as satisfactory audience shares during peak viewing times. Even so, there is obviously quite a long way to go before public broadcasting in Western Europe approaches its most commercial rivals. We can, however, expect further concessions to market forces in many countries in the coming years.

Another way of reacting to increased competition, which is easier to detect than shifts among content categories, is quantity of broadcast hours. Extended broadcast time is clearly the most common reaction to growing competition. We have found an increase in average broadcast time on public channels of about 30 per cent during the latter part of the 1980s. This must be considered to be a significant change, especially since most public television budgets have levelled out in real terms (see Chapter 6).

A third kind of change in public broadcast schedules would be to alter the overall composition of output. This, it seems, is not a viable strategy for Western European public broadcasters. A traditional mixture and balance of entertainment, information, news, children's programmes, education, etc. is the essence of public service and the *raison d'être* of the licence fee system much preferred by public broadcasting organizations. The BBC expression: 'a full range of programmes and the best of its kind', encapsulates the ideal of public broadcasters.

Programme acquisition

One area where competition is felt early on is in the acquisition of programmes, especially those that head the list of viewers' preferences, such as sports, movies and television series. Sourcing strategies, that is, the supply of programme material and broadcast rights, are of crucial importance to every broadcasting organization, in order to control spiralling costs and to guarantee a steady input of attractive programmes.

Public broadcasters restricted to their national markets have to organize their own way of sharing acquisition costs. Besides pooling resources with public broadcasters in neighbouring countries, it is increasingly common to include other rights besides those of broadcasting. Spreading the costs of acquisitions against revenues from other sources, such as video, cable, pay TV and pay-per-view TV, is an approach taken by a number of public broadcasters. Again, it is easier for a commercial broadcaster to pursue this strategy, a broadcaster who is free to operate on the national and international market at his own discretion. Public broadcasters, in most cases, have to rely on contractual agreements and sub-licensing deals.

In sports and news, the European Broadcasting Union (EBU), to which all public broadcasting organizations belong, has for many years played an important role in acquiring broadcasting rights and programme material. The importance of the union is growing, especially among its smaller members, as commercial competition grows stronger. The rapid evolution of EBU news exchanges and the intensified cooperation in the field of sports are good illustrations of this point.

The price for the broadcasting rights of attractive sporting events has increased dramatically in recent years, due not only to added demand from new entrants but also as a consequence of the exploitation of related commercial activities and ancillary rights, such as merchandising, sponsoring, video rights, etc. Between Moscow 1980 and Barcelona 1992, for instance, the price the EBU had to pay to secure the Olympic Summer Games for its members increased more than twelve-fold.

In order to guarantee maximum exposure for sponsors of sports, some members of the EBU created Eurosport in 1989. It is a satellite-delivered, advertising-supported specialist cable channel in which to date seventeen members of the EBU participate in cooperation with News Corporation International.

The EBU and Eurosport have been accused of being illegal cartels, breaking §85(1) of the Treaty of Rome. The case was brought to the EC Commission in 1988 by a competitor, the private satellite channel Screensport. The EC Commission determined that EBU practices have to become more open to non-members. The EBU has proposed a model for sublicensing. In May 1991 the Commission ordered the channel closed, awaiting further restructuring.

Control of supply lines and of programme costs is increasingly necessary in a competitive situation. Paying more in cash for broadcasting rights is one way, however costly. Offering ancillary revenues to sellers is another approach. Sharing the costs of package deals with other television organizations is yet another. Co-financing and co-production of programmes, finally, are methods increasingly often used by broadcasters to secure exclusive broadcasting rights. Independent producers as well as major film companies cover their growing production costs by inviting capital and offering distribution rights in return.

In this context, another aspect of programme supply is worth mentioning. The burden of huge facilities and large staff numbers has been considered one of the chief disadvantages of public broadcasting organizations. On the other hand, access to and control of in-house production resources can also be seen as a competitive advantage. The depth and competence of RAI's own staff and facilities has proved a decisive factor in the organization's successful competition with Berlusconi's channels. A broadcasting organization totally dependent on external supplies of programmes can in the long run become the victim of prices beyond its own control.

Financial strategies

One of the competitive disadvantages of public television is its dependence on politically regulated resources. Most organizations are involved every year in budget discussions with governments or special parliamentary committees. In a few countries, the licence fee is tied to an index of some kind (as in Sweden and the UK), the value of which is supposed to reflect the broad effects of inflation on broadcasting budgets. In most countries (such as Finland, Germany and Switzerland), licence fee increases have to last several years at a time.

Most public broadcasting organizations have been pressed by governments to cut their costs. A regular procedure is to allocate budgets not fully compensated for inflation. Many organizations also work hard on their own to rationalize and save expenses in order to free resources to meet the competition. Although public broadcasters cannot influence the revenues by increasing the licence fee, some of them have introduced ancillary services, some of which are described below. Other, and more common, strategies aim at cutting the cost of present operations, or at increasing output at no added costs.

It is no easier, it seems, for a public service organization supplemented by advertising revenues to achieve budget increases, than it is for those totally dependent on licence fees. With increasing competition for advertising, public broadcasters feel the burden of asymmetric regulation. ARD, for instance, has been forced to reduce its advertising tariffs by an average of 20 per cent for 1991, as a result of audience losses. Ireland's RTE saw its advertising revenue cut by 10 per cent in 1990 as a result of governmental protection of the interests of private broadcasters.

Public broadcasters argue for more liberal advertising conditions in order to make it easier for them to attract necessary commercial revenues. Faced with a choice, advertisers will invest in channels where they reach their target audiences at the lowest cost per thousand viewers. In order to do so, they quite naturally want to have an influence over the time during which their advertisements are broadcast.

Some public broadcasting organizations have met with sympathy from governments on this point. More hours of advertising are sold on public channels in Western Europe today than a few years ago. New and more flexible time slots and tariff structures are allowed. Advertisers are given more influence.

Another source of revenue for public television in Europe is sponsorship. Traditionally, such revenues were clearly defined as off limits for public broadcasters in Europe, with a few exceptions (Austria, Italy and from 1986 onwards France). But attitudes have changed. In the Council of Europe Convention and the EC Directive, sponsorship is defined and recognized as a legitimate source of income under certain conditions.

In European commercial broadcasting, sponsorship is an important adjunct to selling advertising spots. Most public broadcasters today accept and actively seek sponsorship, because it is increasingly often a condition for access to attractive big international live events. Sponsorship, however, is still regarded as something requiring careful attention by management, in order to refute suspicions of undue influence on programme content. On the whole, its economic significance to the budgets of most public broadcasting organizations is expected to remain small.

Other kinds of contemporary commercial practices in television, such as product placement and bartering, are not practised by public broadcasting, but will no doubt also come to exert an influence on public channels. Merchandising, however, is used by public broadcasters to capitalize on the market value of their programmes by the sale of books, records, games, puppets, etc.

The establishment of new channels financed by subscriptions has been discussed by some public broadcasters. The BBC has introduced subscription services for national distribution, as well as TV Europe, a satellite channel for European cable subscribers. A2 and SRG are part-owners of cable channels.

A widely used method to supplement licence fee revenue is to sell in-house facilities, such as archive productions as well as production facilities and special services. Only a few big public broadcasting organizations have been successful in selling programmes on the international market. Re-selling programmes on the domestic video markets has proved easier and is practised by all public broadcasters.

Improved marketing and corporate image

In competition with commercial broadcasters, public service organizations have had to develop a better understanding of audience behaviour, preferences, needs and attitudes. Marketing and audience research thus have become strategic tools for public broadcasters as well. New audience ratings services have been introduced, a direct consequence of competition.

Audience research departments have been a part of public broadcasting for many decades, although in most cases they have fulfilled a rather low-key, cultural function. In countries where spillover from neighbouring countries early on gave rise to competition for viewers' time, ratings were usually meant to compare performances. Hence, broadcasters did not have to legitimize their existence by means of them; such foreign competition did not threaten their revenues nor influence their costs. Ratings and other forms of audience information were intended as a general measure of satisfaction among the audience as a whole and with specific content areas. Research served the function of providing simple feedback on how well public service broadcasters were fulfilling their obligations.

With growing competition for audiences, for funds, for programmes and for political support and legitimization, the function of audience research has entered a new phase.

Many public broadcasting organizations fear that they will lose their political legitimacy if viewers desert public channels beyond a certain limit. Much energy is now being devoted to defining the parameters of success for public broadcasting, in terms of quantity as well as quality of service. The uncertainty created by competition and uncertainty about what political establishments actually expect of public broadcasting are significant stress factors.

The methods of researching the audiences show this transformation: from occasional studies by diary or interviews to daily surveys by telephone interviews or people meters, from a few reports per year on the viewing and listening preferences to daily computerized reporting on various substrata of the population.

Cooperation and alliances

Growing competition also forces public broadcasting organizations to look for strategic alliances and joint ventures with other partners. German-language public broadcasters, ARD, ZDF, ORF and SRG, for instance, cooperate extensively in acquisitions and production as well as in satellite channels (3SAT and EinsPlus). The Nordic public broadcasters have for twenty years co-produced and exchanged programmes, especially children's programmes. In recent years they have also arranged for joint sales and screening efforts, as well as joint programme acquisitions. The BBC has created joint commercial distribution ventures of its own productions in the USA.

The range of commercial joint activities open to public broadcasting is narrower than alternatives open to commercial broadcasters. A public broadcasting organization must not, for example, expose licence fee revenues to entrepreneurial risks. Another limiting factor is the ideological resistance to the 'old monopolies' or 'traditional public service' expanding on the market, thus making it difficult for commercial actors to enter and succeed.

Conclusions

As this chapter has made clear, public broadcasting organizations in Western Europe have reacted to increased competition in many different ways. Competition, direct or extended, by commercial broadcasters, whose programmes are distributed by terrestrial networks, cable networks or by satellite for direct reception is nowadays the rule for all public broadcasters.

Although public broadcasters are criticized by many for being or becoming commercial, no public service organization is in fact commercial in the true sense of being totally dependent on commercial revenues and of operating for profit. In fact, all public broadcasters are still dependent on governments for their budgets.

With a few, rather insignificant, exceptions, all public broadcasters in Western Europe have decided to fight back in one way or another in order to remain strong and to provide attractive services in their countries. No one has chosen what we call the purification strategy, in other words, to reduce a traditional full range of programmes to a narrower range of information and culture output, basically offering only programmes which are of no interest to commercial networks. The dominant strategy is, however, not to adopt the same strategies as commercial competitors, but rather to try to do what public broadcasters define as the essence of their task: to offer a full range of programmes and the best of their kind. This is a very high ambition indeed, the success of which requires cost-efficient in-house production skills, managerial competence, marketing and strategic excellence, self-confidence, as well as a solid financial base, which entails political support.

Increased competition has pushed cost increases in television to a much higher level than the general level of inflation. To cope with this situation public broadcasters have tried combinations of strategies, all of which aim at making these organizations more market-oriented. The actual speed and determination of this market adaptation depends on a range of factors, amongst which, in the long run, the level of asymmetry in broadcasting regulation will be of crucial importance.

References

Specific details of the reactions by PSB organizations can be found in the accompanying volume *The Media in Western Europe*.

Blumler, J.G. (1989) 'Multi-channel television in the United States: Policy Lessons for Britain'. New York: Report for the Markle Foundation.

McQuail, Denis and Siune, K. (eds) (1986) *New Media Politics: Comparative Perspectives in Western Europe*. London: Sage.

Porter, Michael E. (1980) *Competitive Strategy: Techniques for Analyzing Industries and Competitors*. New York: The Free Press.

Porter, Vincent (1989) 'The re-regulation of television: pluralism, constitutionalism and the free market in the USA, West Germany, France and the UK', *Media, Culture and Society*, 11 (1): 5–27.

9

Small States in the Shadow of Giants

Werner A. Meier and Josef Trappel

This chapter deals with specific problems of small Western European states as far as the process of change in the audiovisual media is concerned. Smallness as a characteristic feature determines freedom of manoeuvre for the large majority of European states. This chapter starts by defining the subject, then analyses the structure, describes basic features and arranges them into a framework in order to explain some of the media policy reactions in small states.

With reference to a previous analysis by Denis McQuail and the Euromedia Research Group (McQuail et al. 1990), an attempt is made to apply the policy model to the context of small states. The 'two-step-model' presented in that article provides the overall framework for analysing the peculiarities of small states. At least five terms are of vital importance, namely:

- dependence;
- shortage of resources;
- market size;
- vulnerability; and
- corporatism.

It is quite obvious that small states follow the process of internationalization in the fields of technological development and of policy-making. Four different models of policy-making in relation to the different types of electronic media are identified below. These features characterize the present position of small states on their way to deregulation and privatization.

Sometimes, of course, developments in small states are not at all different from the processes found in larger European states, but most aspects of the process of change affect small states to a much larger extent than big states. In any case, small states have to act and react under different conditions from those in bigger states such as Germany, the United Kingdom, France, Italy and Spain. Therefore the general focus of this chapter is on small states, although some of the findings presented here may hold for big states as well.[1]

The 'small state' as a pragmatic concept

It is not easy to define what exactly is a small state: 'Despite the long and intensive tradition of research into the problems of small states, a continual, constructive research process is not evident. . . . A definition that is, at least partially, unanimous and satisfactory overall has not been achieved' (Höll, 1978: 260). According to the respective demographic, political, economic, sovereignty and neutrality perspectives, differing elements of the definition come to the fore. In any case, it also seems relevant to consider dynamic elements (see Mouritzen 1983: 240)[2], such as flexibility, adaptability or readiness for innovations, as well as the rather more static criteria of size (geographic area, population, GNP, etc.). In the following, empirical evidence will be given in order to identify the structural features and media political strategies of small states in the electronic and broadcast media in Western Europe.

In a global perspective, even the five big European countries seem rather small. The (inter)dependence between the USA and its external markets seems quite similar to the relationship between big and small European states.

To enable comparisons to be made, the following will consider small countries with a broadcasting system which is nationally institutionalized. For the purposes of inclusion in this chapter a country must have a public service broadcasting organization which provides at least one fully fledged television channel. Because of the important factor of the home market, the discussion below is limited to those countries which have more than one million inhabitants.[3] Basically, the idea is to find out to what extent media structures and national media policies are determined by small state characteristics.

Characteristic features of small-state media systems

Dependence
Dependence is expressed initially by the fact that, as a general rule, small states in their strategies have to pay more attention to the decisions of sizeable countries than is the case the other way round. Dependence is shown in great efforts to be flexible towards the dominant powers of the relevant political–economic environment. Even the suprastate institutions call for greater efforts to adjust to them, as a general rule, since such organizations are set up and run in accordance with the needs and interests of the dominant members. This can be shown, for example, with the help of the EC Directive and the Council of Europe Convention on Transfrontier Television.

These two documents on the one hand ensure a much greater choice for television viewers by offering free access to foreign programme providers. On the other hand small states are in danger of losing some of their cultural sovereignty. Article 3(4) of the EC Directive gives member-states the right to issue stricter or more concise regulations for their own national programme providers, in order to make allowance for certain specific circumstances. In the same instance, however, this national 'negative protectionism' hinders domestic companies on the market, because according to Article 2 of the EC Directive even small member-states are obliged to allow the reception and re-transmission of broadcasts from those member-states which have not issued comprehensive or strict regulations for their respective national programme providers. As a result, programmes from larger states dominate the European satellites and small states do not have a fair chance to compete.

A similar regulation can also be found in Article 28 of the European Convention on Transfrontier Television of 5 May 1989. The disadvantages affect primarily public broadcasting institutions – be it in the field of programme obligations or advertising, which are ascribed a particularly important role in small states, and whose role extends well beyond that of simply offering a service. The dominance of supranational markets is especially threatening to the essential public service functions of small states. At the same time the conditions for large, multimedia corporations from large European states are improving, whilst small-state media enterprises with a limited home market can, at best, satisfy themselves with filling market niches. In general, small states have to make adjustments which tend to go against their own broadcasting rules and regulations, because the newly promoted idea of broadcasting as predominantly an economic service in no way corresponds with those broadcasting obligations set in accordance with most of the national constitutions of small states. To meet the new market standards, small states have to adapt their whole broadcasting system to a much larger extent than big states with their already re-regulated systems.

Even those small states not in the European Community attempt to comply with the EC Directive. Large parts of the content of the EC Directive and the Convention of the Council of Europe are identical, so parts of the EC regulations will also be implemented by non-member-states. For example, Switzerland and Sweden chose the EC Directive, as well as the Convention, as guidelines for new media laws.[4] Not only was this a requirement for the EES (European Economic Space) negotiations between the EC and EFTA, but small non-member-states simply have no other option in terms of meeting at least three policy goals: firstly, to confirm their willingness to adopt a common European legal framework; secondly, to demonstrate their readiness for the ongoing process of European integration; thirdly, to be in a position to compete with foreign companies relying on large home markets.

In television programming, especially in those small countries which are integrated within larger language markets (see Chapter 6), there is a tendency to imitate the entrepreneurial strategies of large channels and corporations in order to keep up with innovations. For example, the introduction of midday news programmes or breakfast television does not necessarily correspond with public demand, but with foreign programming patterns.

In contrast to other economic sectors such as banking, insurance and the manufacturing industry, the conquest of the international media market by small-state enterprises can only be realized by means of a sufficiently large home market. None of the dominant European media corporations dealing with audiovisual software originates from a small state. The media environment largely determined by these corporations is also for this reason detrimental to small states, or at least it does not take into consideration their specific needs and obligations.

Shortage of resources
Shortage of resources refers to the availability of capital, know-how, creativity, talent, competence and a professionally trained workforce in the media. In terms of culture, politics and economics, the following structural characteristics can be discerned.

The successful establishment of an audiovisual cultural industry in small states tends to be the exception rather than the rule – an industry that is in a position to provide national channels with regular home productions, which act as an arena for independent and diverse small-state self-awareness, and that in this way effectively convey opinions, values, ideas and artistic creativity. Within the fields of entertainment, as well as films and series, institutions in small states see themselves as being less able to provide their own attractive, creative programmes, the harder they try. As a general rule, small states lack either the educational and training opportunities or the financial resources necessary for programme production – or both, which only makes it even more difficult to strengthen the national audiovisual culture industry. This is why young national artists seek success in larger states and markets, which offer more attractive opportunities in all respects. This can be observed more frequently in those small states which share their language with a larger country.

Even in the field of news and current affairs, it is more difficult for small-state media to create their own, relevant view of the world (see Meier 1983). Commentary on and evaluation of international events by foreign correspondents does not always contain national components specifically designed to suit the respective small state, as is expected of professional journalism, especially in television.

Shortage of resources is not only visible in the production of cultural artifacts by small-state media, but also in the conceptualization, establishment and implementation of media policy strategies and measures. In the internal as well as external representation of media policy matters and their implementation, small states have to cope with a lack of admininistrative competence and authority, due to a lack of staff resources or of an extensive administrative bureaucracy, which is unaffordable for small states.

Market size

A basic element of small states is their limited market for production as well as for consumption. Small states consist solely of 'minority audiences'.

In the permanent contradiction between market and cultural values, the size of the audience is of importance for two reasons. Firstly, an economic media unit (newspaper, publishing house, film studio, radio station, television channel, etc.) can only achieve a profitability which ensures its existence if there is sufficient demand for the products by consumers and advertisers. The potential market size also increases the use of 'economies of scale'. Secondly, such synergy effects can still, however, be successfully utilized in larger markets, even where the potential audience is limited to a specific sector of society.

The establishment of specialist channels, common in large countries, is difficult in small states, as the size of the home market and resources are insufficient to provide a commercially successful service, since the production costs of television programming are roughly the same for small and large states in Europe. It is more than a symptom that all attempts by small-state media enterprises to gain a foothold in larger markets to date have failed for various reasons. The European Business Channel (EBC), despite its bilingual, professionally made programmes, was unable to build up a European audience outside Switzerland that was attractive to advertisers. In summer 1990 EBC went bankrupt subsequent to the withdrawal of money by its banks and business partners. The Swiss pay TV channel Teleclub has almost reached saturation point with 80,000 subscribers in German-speaking Switzerland. With an increasing number of clients in Germany, it will now attempt to satisfy German demands in programming and, in doing so, will have to neglect Swiss legislation.[5] Moreover, the recently established pay TV channel Premiere will sooner or later become the market leader in a unified Germany and will thereby marginalize the Swiss programme provider, unless these competitors merge or collaborate.

Vulnerability

Usually small-state markets do not represent a worthwhile target for multinational corporations, unless the small market is chosen as a test market. Only an enterprise with a certain size of operation and attractive market and competitive advantages (regional/national monopolies) excites international interest. Again, small states sharing a language with large states are more likely to fit into the business strategies of multinational corporations. In the case of the Nordic countries, the Anglo-Swedish satellite channel TV3 did not target one country alone but extended its service to at least three countries in order to gain a sufficiently large audience.

It is primarily national sovereignty in the field of broadcasting which proves to be vulnerable. Thus pirate activities – not necessarily originated by foreign enterprises – plunge small-state media regulations into deeper economic and legislative crises than is the case in big states. Belgium, for example, carried out fundamental changes in the system, as national frontiers for broadcasting shifted with the introduction of new transmission technologies. Not technology itself, but the vulnerability of broadcasting sovereignty and political weakness in implementation, were responsible for the transformation of the media regulations.

Small states come under economic pressure as a result of 'modern piracy'. In some cases a portion of the advertising volume is transferred abroad. Increasing transnational television transmissions enable centrally guided advertising campaigns which are not broadcast on small-state channels, but on long-range, language-regional, big-state channels. Both these tendencies affect not only national and regional television in small states, but often to an even greater extent the respective country's print media, especially magazines.

Corporatism

In his political analysis Katzenstein allocates to Sweden, Norway, Denmark, the Netherlands, Belgium, Austria and Switzerland structures of democratic corporatism (Katzenstein 1985: 21). He distinguishes three components: the economic and political social partnership, the importance of interest groups, and the inclusion of all social powers in negotiations (Katzenstein 1985: 32). Small-state media policy can be understood in terms of the acceptance of neo-corporatism as: 'the cooperation of the state and large interest organizations in realizing goals described as overlapping' (Lehmbruch 1983: 408).

In Sweden, for example, a country with very elaborate media laws, employers and employees were involved in all decision-making considered to be of any importance. Representatives of relevant professional and trade associations in Belgium, Finland and Greece determined the way in which private television was to be introduced in these countries. The shape and implementation of broadcasting policy, particularly in Austria and Belgium, with their massive political influence in personnel decisions, can be described as neo-corporatism.

This model has proved efficient in small states since the war. With growing internationalization and the legislative engagement of supranational organizations, the traditional roles of media policy actors are changing. In place of the search for broadly supported compromise solutions in the corporate tradition, individual decisions by actors appear to be pushed through, because the available scope has been exhausted. It was, for example, pressure from regional newspaper companies which finally led to the introduction of private radio and the admissibility of newspapers as owners in Finland. Quite similarly the press in Greece exerted political pressure in order to gain control of the newly introduced private commercial television channel. After the basic political decision was taken to introduce national competition in television, Belgian newspapers successfully demanded control of this new sector. On the other hand, the issue of a statutory instrument on experimental local broadcasting in Switzerland in 1982 is typical of the best of corporate traditions in that the departments responsible for broadcasting followed the recommendations of a broadly constituted commission of experts.

Until recently, and in their own separate ways, small states have by and large clearly followed corporatism as a model for media policy. But since the mid-1980s working partnerships in the most deregulated countries have become increasingly difficult.

Characteristic small-state media policy since the early 1980s

In the early 1980s the media regulations of small states intended electronic and print media to be functionally equal. The press could claim freedom of opinion in accordance with Article 10 of the European Convention on Human Rights. Interference in media matters was seen as an offence against a basic human right.[6] On the other hand broadcasting was supervised by the state, and was obliged to provide a public service. This emphasized cultural, political and educational duties more than economic ones. Diversity in programmes, basic objectivity, balance and political impartiality were the requirements entrusted to broadcasters.

This duality between a private press and public broadcasting, a 'journalistic division of power', met with broad political agreement. Of course, the model was safeguarded somewhat differently in the different small states. For example, Switzerland relied on a generally formulated constitutional article (Article 36 of the Swiss Constitution) and a law dating back to 1922 ('Federal Law of 14 October 1922 concerning the use of telegraphs and telephones'). In Austria a new broadcasting law was passed in 1974, which confirmed the competitive equality of the press and broadcasting. It was not intended to open the broadcasting system to private, commercial bidders.

Arising from the structural description above, there follows an attempt to describe some of the basic political processes in media policy. The description takes into consideration the five characteristic features outlined above, and views the national government as the dominant actor.

Firstly, small states pursue a relatively conservative regulatory policy. Proof of the efficiency of the existing enterprises compared with internal and external challengers is central. On the whole the media policy can be classified as lacking innovation, due to the non-existence of an institutionalized media policy, as is evident in lack of conceptional coherence and poor execution.

In the second process, small states, in contrast to larger European states, appear to be more committed to traditional broadcasting regulations and duties towards culture and society. For this reason governments enable their respective public service broadcasters to enlarge their services in order to ensure survival in a market environment.

Thirdly, because of the ongoing trend towards concentration of political powers, manifested in the dominance of associations and interest groups, small states show a tendency to take single measures at short notice, making *ad hoc* decisions instead of developing integrated concepts and strategies. Relatively few major actors determine the media policy discourse.

Fourthly, in addition to the internal pressure brought by the smaller number of interest groups, governments are subject to the growing influence of supranational institutions, even on national matters.

In the fifth process, small states renounce the media policy instrument of media-specific anti-trust laws in an attempt to strengthen the domestic media enterprises, which are already limited in number.

Dynamism of the 1980s
It seems that media policies of small states follow the path of the bigger countries quite closely, but with a considerable time lag. To a certain extent the opening up of the market in large European countries can be regarded as the initial signal for change in small-state politics. Italy's basic ruling, for example, on the licensing of private radio in the 1970s and of private television in the early 1980s, led to a rocking of the political consensus in Switzerland and Austria. Pirate stations were set up on the northern borders of Italy, and German-language radio programmes were transmitted. Developments in media policy in Germany, the UK, France and Italy in many ways acted as a guideline for small states. Even though the influence on the Nordic countries is less obvious than it is in those countries that share their language with big states, and taking into consideration the time schedule of the transformation to privatization, small states have generally followed the guidelines given by large states.

Since the WARC conferences of 1977 and 1979, and with the technical possibility of receiving foreign television programmes via satellite since 1982, national legislators have been called upon to make decisions concerning the newly allocated frequencies and their uses (VHF and satellite). Along with the new frequencies commercial interests suddenly made themselves heard. Commercial competitors from small states, however, were backed by noticeably fewer political and economic resources than commercial enterprises from large European countries.

The two pan-European organizations, the European Community and the Council of Europe both had something to say about this internationalization of programme and transmission markets. Whilst the Council of Europe continually made allowances for the cultural concerns of the media in its reasoning, the publication of the so-called Green Paper[7] was for the EC a step in the direction of entering a previously unspecifically regulated area. The aim consisted of establishing step by step a joint market for audiovisual programme producers and broadcasters. The free flow of broadcast programmes should not only help to improve the economic position of Europe, but simultaneously help to forge a European identity. As a result of the overall conception of the Green Paper, tailored to the broadcasting structures of big states, the interests of small states found little consideration.[8]

To facilitate a dynamic re-orientation of national media policies, the following actors appointed themselves to prominent positions: political parties, associations and existing media enterprises. In Belgium, Greece and Austria political parties almost entirely control decisions; power and lobby interests are articulated via the parties and their representatives.

In contrast, Finland's interest groups put their claims direct to the public. The stubbornness of newspaper entrepreneurs and their local radio association (Paikkalisradioliitto), founded specifically for the purpose, has been instrumental in the licensing of independent, commercial radio broadcasters. Under the banner of 'hand over the media to the media', the print media enterprises in Austria, Belgium, Greece and Switzerland all hold similarly strong positions. Political parties, which are in favour of the introduction of private commercial broadcasting, usually run into difficulties with their policies because of their divided stance. Whilst on the the one hand they are interested in retaining control over public broadcasting, they are on the other hand trying to capture markets through new and independent competitors. This threatens the strong position of public radio and television institutions. Compromise solutions in the form of short-term trial regulations or non-commercial private broadcasters are often the result of this dilemma.

Models of small-state media policy

The concept of deregulation as a form of withdrawing state control and implementing market mechanisms has also won political ground in all small states. Despite structural and media policy similarities, a certain variance in coping with the change of paradigms can be noted throughout Europe. The four differing and 'ideal' models outlined below are an attempt to identify these variations.

1 *'Protectionism'*: In the field of electronic media the state exercises its responsibility and authority by means of strict and comprehensive regulations. Market mechanisms play only a secondary role. The means used are limitations on access and regulations concerning cultural and social obligations. Appointments to high-ranking positions within public broadcasting organizations are determined by the relative power of the political parties.

2 *'Wait and see'*: Although the public audiovisual media still enjoy protection to a large extent, new concepts are discussed and models are drawn up. The first cautious steps towards a certain type

of deregulation have already been taken, without threatening the interests of the dominant actors in order to stabilize the media system as a whole.

3 *'Experimental position model'*: Competition is slowly introduced in formerly protected sectors by means of short-term licensing of vendors and services. The measures taken are designed primarily as a way of gaining time and experience, in order to give all affected participants the opportunity of adjusting to a new situation.

4 *Regulated market:* The licensing of private competitors is absolute and takes place within the limits of certain legal constraints. State control is limited to the minimum. Market mechanisms define this sector, state intervention is regarded as an inopportune interference. Cultural obligations are defined and probably fulfilled only if they do not clash with economic requirements. This model represents a provisional end to developments.

An analysis of the media policies of small states in Europe in terms of the four models is contained in Table 9.1.

Table 9.1 *Broadcasting policy in small states in 1991*

Medium and type	Model 1	2	3	4
Television				
Public service	A, G, CH, F, N	H, S, D, B		I
Pay TV				CH, B, H, S
Private commercial national		D		B, G, F
Private commercial regional		D	B	F
Radio				
Public service	A, N, G, H, CH, D, F	B, S		I
Private commercial national/regional			CH	F, B, D, G, I
Non-commercial		G	CH	S, N, D

A=Austria, B=Belgium, D=Denmark, H=Netherlands, CH=Switzerland, S=Sweden, N=Norway, I=Ireland, G=Greece, F=Finland

It indicates that:

- In general the classification of new services is shifting towards a regulated market model.
- Pay TV has been institutionalized to date exclusively as a private service.
- As a general rule public broadcasting services (radio and television) in small states are still strongly regulated.
- Not more than half of the small states analysed have introduced private commercial television channels at the national level. The most careful policy design can be found in Denmark's new TV2, which has to fulfil public service obligations and is established on a non-profit basis, although basically financed by advertising.
- Private non-commercial radio services are characteristic features of Scandinavian countries.
- The introduction of additional media and services in small states has been achieved basically in the form of 'experiments' and 'regulated markets'.

The decision of the Belgian and Greek governments to introduce private commercial national television currently places these two countries at the far end of the spectrum. Entry is still limited by legal requirements, but the circle of competitors has been extended from the existing monopolists to include leading press companies. Finland's model, of the peaceful and controlled co-existence of public and private competitors, can be seen as a longstanding experiment, which will presumably end in 1993. Private and public broadcasters will then transmit programmes independently. Finland will implement the market model, which has governed radio policy since the admissibility of private enterprises.

In the field of radio, private stations have usually been introduced ostensibly as an 'experiment' or a 'trial' – insofar as pirates had not taken the lead already, but they have in fact been subject to market mechanisms. Sweden, with 'neighbourhood radio stations' which were the result of a compromise solution implemented by a coalition government, exemplified a model which was then copied by its Nordic neighbours (Denmark, Norway).

Summarizing the table, three different types of media policy can be identified: Ireland, Greece, Belgium and Finland strongly orient their media to market constraints. In contrast, Sweden, Norway, the Netherlands, Switzerland and Denmark follow this path, but more moderately. Austria appears to be the only country where this process has not yet started.

Current issues on the agenda

We have shown that, as a general rule, small states gain little or nothing from the changes of the 1980s where there is no intervention in the form of national policy and the establishment of international relations. Based on the elements of the small states' characteristics and models, we will highlight some relevant features that may contribute to the ongoing debate.

Firstly, broadcasting in small states faces increasing difficulties in fulfilling its cultural and social obligations. These can be defined as the maintenance and promotion of specific national or regional peculiarities. Maintaining and enlarging this function require a certain infrastructure for programme production. Strong political support and the allocation of public money are needed to ensure the financing of these productions beyond hardware costs.

Secondly, as a result of the politically motivated policy of privatization, broadcasting, in particular television, is becoming more expensive to the population of small states than to that of the big states. The enlargement of programme services brings with it an increase in costs (see Chapter 6). These are met increasingly through the advertising budgets of industry. The general public, or, more precisely, the consumers of the advertised products, indirectly bear the increasing cost of the new television services, regardless of whether or not they use them. Taking the size of the market into consideration, these additional costs are distributed amongst fewer consumers than in big states and are thus proportionally higher. Therefore it appears particularly appropriate for small states to increase the proportion of direct payments (licence fees) in the total budget.

Thirdly, apparent economic necessities and political calculations mean that the media policies of small states are reactive rather than active. Media, one of the crucial fields of cultural policy, deserve a higher priority in national policies.

Fourthly, in small states the contradiction between economic competition and cultural obligations is particularly obvious. Whilst larger states can fulfil both requirements to a certain extent, small states reach their limits considerably earlier for structural reasons.

Finally, media business is progressively networking and tends towards cross-ownership over all media, whilst policy is usually oriented towards measures which treat the different media separately. Finland, Denmark and Switzerland illustrate the importance of high-level policy groups (Media and Culture Commissions) which consider conceptualizations of media policy over a longer period of time.

Notes

1 The viewpoints in this chapter reflect our experience as citizens of the small states of Switzerland and Austria.
2 Mouritzen uses the term 'behaviour' as a criterion.
3 Austria, Belgium, Denmark, Finland, Greece, the Netherlands, Ireland, Norway, Portugal, Sweden, Switzerland.
4 In both chambers of the Swiss parliament, on the grounds of 'Europeanness', a formula for advertising regulation was chosen which broadly corresponds with the EC and Council of Europe approach.
5 In the Teleclub licence the promotion of European, particularly Swiss, filmmaking was set as a duty. Article 4 reads that the majority of feature films where practicable should be films of European origin. At least every two months a Swiss feature film should be shown. (Teleclub licence of 23 August 1989.)
6 For example, the freedom of the press enjoys almost universal protection in Swedish legislation. See The Swedish Institute, *Mass Media in Sweden*, Stockholm 1990.
7 Commission of the European Community, *Television without Frontiers*, Brussels 1984.
8 Whilst the European Convention on one occasion mentions the protection of small states in Article 10(3) in the context of European quotas, the EC Directive does not contain a similar paragraph.

References

Höll, Otmar (1978) 'Kritische Anmerkungen zur Kleinstaatentheorie' *Österreichische Zeitschrift für Politikwissenschaft*, 3: 259–74.
Katzenstein, Peter J. (1985) *Small States in World Markets: Industrial Policy in Europe*. Ithaca/London: Cornwell.
Lehmbruch, Gerhard (1983) 'Neokorporatismus im Westeuropa. Hauptprobleme im internationalen Vergleich', *Journal für Sozialforschung*, 4: 407–20.
McQuail, Denis and the Euromedia Research Group (1990) 'Caging the Beast: Constructing a Framework for the Analysis of Media Change in Western Europe', *European Journal of Communication*, 5: 313–31.
Meier, Werner A. (1983) *Ungleicher Nachrichtenaustausch und fragmentarische Weltbilder: Eine empirische Studie über Strukturmerkmale in der Auslandsberichterstattung*. Bern/Frankfurt/New York: Lang.
Mouritzen, Hans A. (1983) 'Defensive Acquiescence: Making the Best out of Dependence', in Otmar Höll (ed.) *Small States in Europe and Dependence*. Vienna: Braumüller: 239-61.

10

The Global Village Stays Local

Hans J. Kleinsteuber

In 1968 Marshall McLuhan, in his book *War and Peace in the Global Village*, forecast that emerging technologies would lead to new forms of global communication and conflict. As the village became global, local peculiarities would seem to disappear. Other authors have come to quite different conclusions, arguing that the introduction of local radio means that we are entering the 'third age of broadcasting' with a growing emphasis on local affairs (Crookes and Vittet-Philippe 1985: 1). During the 1980s local media were a topic of increasing importance and relevance in Europe. It seems that the local element has become stronger in many parts of Europe, mainly because of changes in the field of radio.

This chapter focuses on local media in Western Europe, but it should be kept in mind that wide-ranging changes are currently taking place in Eastern Europe. The 'real socialist' type of centralized supervision allowed only a few substantive local elements in the media. This system of control is widely disappearing, but the shape of things to come is not yet clear. Certainly the local element will be strengthened.

Concepts of 'local'

'Local' would appear to be a pan-European term derived from the Latin word 'locus', literally meaning 'the place'. It is found in many European languages and refers to a small place separated from large-scale entities, or the part and not the whole. As well as this international meaning, the term also carries some other connotations. Some of these are more of a European type, others are much more an expression of national characteristics. In English the term also includes elements of the neighbourhood, the village, the town, county, district or parish (*Concise Oxford Dictionary*).

The overall impression is that local means something nearby, something cosy – the connotations are positive and supportive.

In systematic terms 'local' refers to a relatively small entity or space. On a scale that extends from big to small, it may look as follows:

global   =   the whole world
continental =   one of the continents of the world (say, Europe)
national   =   containing one (nation) state
regional   =   containing parts of a (nation) state (federal state, province, county or geographical region)
local   =   containing a part of a region, sometimes with a central function (metropolitan area, city, town, village)
sublocal   =   containing parts of a locality (section of a city, neighbourhood)

In the field of media research and media policy, the following dimensions of local seem to be relevant:

● In terms of *technology*, local refers to technical distribution systems limited to one locality. This makes sense particularly for local radio and television stations with a transmission power that reaches only the locality. Furthermore, cable TV systems are usually limited to a local community or parts of it, as their technical structure does not make sense for larger entities.

● In *legal* terms, local defines a station that has acquired a licence to serve a local community. The same applies to cable TV systems.

● In terms of *economy*, it refers to local financing. This may include the capital invested in local media as well as local revenues, that may come from local advertising, donations or subsidies.

● In terms of *programming*, it defines programme material that has been produced locally. The most important aspect here, of course, is local news, but sports, music, discussions, etc. could also be included.

● In terms of *access*, it describes a situation where the opportunity is given to communicate personally on a local level with local people, either professionally or as amateurs.

Technology

As Harold Innis pointed out in 1951, media technologies are not just a neutral instrument in the hands of those who use them, but carry a kind of 'bias' that favours a certain kind of use and makes it quite difficult to employ the technology contrary to its built-in bias. In his theory, radio and television have an especially strong bias towards space, as their signals travel long distances without delay but are difficult to store. Print media have more of a time bias as they take longer to transport, but may store information long into the future.

In the field of electronic broadcast media, there is a clearcut relationship between certain technologies and their primary use as media, as outlined below:

global	=	satellites, esp. telecom satellites
continental	=	satellites, esp. hybrid satellites (of the Astra specification); direct broadcasting satellites (DBS)
national	=	DBS; large networks connected by microwave links and transponders
regional	=	small networks, (high-power) transmitters
local	=	(medium-power) transmitters, cable systems
sublocal	=	(low-power) transmitters, cable systems

Licensing

The establishment of local print media does not require a permit, at least not in the Western liberal model. In the field of broadcasting, however, in all countries – even in Italy since 1990 – a licence to broadcast is required. The licence usually includes a limit on the time during which a certain frequency may be used with a fixed transmission power. Often the type of organization of the broadcasting institution, the financing, and the programme content are regulated as well. Usually regulations on the local level (see Chapter 12) are less strict as control is more difficult to impose. One important result of this was the setting up of local pirate stations that, at times, played a prominent role in introducing local radio in Europe and are still important in some countries, such as the Netherlands.

In Europe, with its extreme diversity of political cultures, there are quite a number of ways of licensing and supervising local media, for example:

- It goes without saying that pirate radio, such as in the Netherlands, does not have a permit. In Italy local stations were unlicensed, but legal, in the period 1978–1990. In 1990 a new broadcasting law changed this situation.

- In France and in many southern European countries local radio started out as illegal 'radio libre' without regulations, but was later legalized by means of a licensing process administered by special bodies established for the purpose.
- In countries of northern and central Western Europe licensing is carried out by the national governments or some other national public body prior to the commencement of broadcasting. This is the case in Scandinavia, in the UK, the Netherlands and in Belgium.
- The local station is an outlet of a much larger organization, but it maintains its local character; this model applies to BBC local radio and to the local stations of commercial network TV in Italy or France.
- Licensing is administered by special bodies in the region, such as the federal states of a national state: this is the case in Germany's Länder.
- Licensing is conducted by regional bodies that reflect the interests of minority and/or ethnic regions in a country, such as the autonomous regions in Spain.
- Licensing may be carried out by local government (as is the case with cable systems in the USA and in some European countries): this principle may be found in Denmark, the Netherlands and partially in Belgium for local radio stations.

This pattern still leaves one question unanswered: how local are the licensees? Are the owners of the licence and/or the operators in fact part of the local community, or do they come from outside, interested only in the exploitation of a commercial market?

Financing

Financing of media is always based on a limited number of sources. Often there is a combination of several means of gathering revenue. In local media, the following sources seem to apply:

- for newspapers, sales over the counter or by subscription;
- the sale of advertising space in the print and advertising time in the broadcast media;
- for public broadcasters, licence fees paid to the respective national organization;
- financial contributions and subsidies from governments or governmental institutions on all levels (national, regional and local), perhaps for cultural or educational reasons.

In the real world of local media there are pure models with a single source of finance as well as mixtures of several sources.

A few examples follow:

- The traditional local newspaper is financed partly through sales and partly through advertising.
- Some local papers and all commercial radio stations are financed entirely by means of advertising revenue. Commercial local radio can be found in most of Europe apart from Sweden and Austria.
- Local public radio stations may be financed entirely (such as the BBC's local stations) or partly (local public radio stations in many European countries including the Netherlands, Italy, France, Germany) by licence fees.
- The audience may pay a radio membership fee or give donations, as they do for the community radio stations that can be found in most if not all Western countries today, such as associated radio in France, democratic radio in Italy, community radio in Britain, local radio in the Netherlands, Nærradio in Scandinavia. In the USA, public radio (NPR), public television (PBS) and community radio fall into this category.

An important aspect of local media always concerns the limited amount of financial resources available. Somehow the situation may be seen as a closed system or a zero sum game: local advertising as the prime source of income is clearly limited. Thus, a successful commercial radio station might divert so much revenue from competing local newspapers that their very existence is endangered. Using this argument, newspaper companies in local markets have demanded that they be given preference in the awarding of local radio licences. Such a 'dual monopoly' may contribute to the financial soundness of a local media company but creates problems of media power and its abuse. Such monopolies may dominate the locality, since it is such a small market for information. In some parts of Europe today local radio licences are held by local newspapers in cross-ownership (as is the case in Norway, Denmark and Germany).

Further funding may be based on donations by individuals and local organizations (such as political parties, trade unions, churches, sports clubs and many other organizations). In some parts of Europe (especially in northern Europe) games such as bingo provide broadcasters with significant amounts of revenue.

Financial resources may also be drawn from outside the local system (broadcasting fees, government subsidies), but again the extent of this is definitely limited. The result is that the revenue available to some existing media may decrease or that money is drawn away from some fields where it was spent before (such as when churches become active in broadcasting and cut their financing of other activities). Politically, the consequences of these developments will be mixed.

Advertising is always a primary financial source of income for local media, but it is not necessarily financed by local companies. All these considerations underline the fact that the local level may be seen as just one subsystem among others in a larger (national or even international) system with many relations between the local subsystem and its non-local environment.

Local content

Marshall McLuhan once argued that the 'content of any medium is always another medium' (McLuhan 1964: 23). This somewhat theoretical concept becomes very real in the analysis of local content in local media. The simple fact of placing the media 'hardware' in the locality – the newspaper being printed or the transmitter located on the spot – does not at all determine that the 'software' is local in any way. All programme content might actually come from outside sources and may just be distributed locally.

An American development which has been copied in Europe (France, for instance) is for local radio stations to be organized as 'robots', in other words they work automatically. Broadcast material is either pre-loaded or fed from outside, perhaps by satellites. But even if some content is local, as it is in nearly every local medium in Europe, it can be quite difficult to judge what share of all reporting or programming is substantially local and what is imported.

It is possible to discern a kind of hierarchy of increasing local content.

1   Only the transmitter is local (robotized programming).
2   Programme origination is local but programmes consist of material produced outside the community (such as canned music, syndicated news).
3   News programmes are produced locally but consist of imported material. For example, material from central news agencies is simply repeated, as in Italy, where small commercial stations simply re-read RAI news.

In view of these possibilities of using imported material, the typical local producer provides purely local content for only a fraction of transmission time. The 100 per cent local station would transmit only music from local bands in a local style and would present, in the local language or the local dialect, local news or

hand, commercial stations that are usually licensed
amming only avoid excessive local content because of
derations. By nature of the business logic, commer-
ters and publishers attempt to reach as large an
readership as possible, because this guarantees the
tion for advertisers with the least costs.

way, it has to be to realized that an anti-local bias is
ommercial programming; often consumers get a local
y, rather than the real thing. The result is the afore-
pseudo-local content of many of these media. In fact,
the hierarchy of concepts of local as described above,
the move away from technology (which is almost always
maller the actual local content.

gest quality of local, namely the ability to communicate
d exchange ideas on the local level, is restricted mainly to
ercial types of 'alternative' media that offer access to all
nbers of the community who show a special interest in it.
70s there was a great deal of experimenting in small local
rs of this type, but only a few have survived. The 1980s
mergence of the local radio station of the non-commercial
many parts of Europe. Individuals showed a greater interest
participation than in former decades, and many became
involved in radio initiatives. They wanted to arrange
nming themselves and not leave it to non-local, distant
rs. Only the amateurs that run these stations can guarantee
local content, as they founded the stations for exactly this
e, namely to become active locally . The question remains, of
, whether or not many people in the local comunity are
red to listen to these stations. But this is not the main concern
se who choose to become amateur broadcasters. In any case,
ms that these non-commercial local radio stations represent
of the original promise of local media than any other of the
sed variations that claim to work for the local community.

rences

zinger, J.P. (1900) *Lokalpresse und Macht in der Gemeinde*. Nuremberg:
ürnberger Forschungsvereinigung e.V.

wn, R. (1978) *Characteristics of Local Media Audiences*. Farnborough: Saxon
House.

okes, P. and Vittet-Philippe, P. (1985) *Local Radio and Regional Development in
Europe*. Manchester: European Institute for the Media.

chs, W.A. (1984) *Presse und Organisationen im lokalen Kommunikationsraum*.
Augsburg: Maro.

nis, H. (1951) *The Bias of Communication*. Toronto: Toronto University Press.

sports with only local themes. Obviously such a station would not
appeal to audiences of any significance.

Syndicated material – produced by somebody else outside the
community and only distributed locally – is much cheaper to buy on
the programme market than material that is locally produced with
local talents. As a consequence there is a bias towards non-local
material. In actual fact many of the European local stations
broadcast international pop music, presented by a local disc jockey
who has hardly any connections with the community. The most local
element of this programming might be the DJ's local dialect or
language and the commercials for local businesses. The result could
be called a station with pseudo-local content.

Looked at this way, local media may be no more than the local
outlet of a centralized distribution system or may come close to it.
On the other hand, even if only a small share of programming is
substantially local, this might be to the advantage of a locality where
there used to be no local content at all in the available media. As
mentioned, local content is relatively expensive and cheaper alternatives are available. But there is always the problem of pseudo-local
content, in which the positive connotations of being local are used in
practice to sell internationally standarized programme material.

Access

A central theme of local media is, of course, access. The media next
door mean a good opportunity to get into personal touch with the
interactive potential of media, either to communicate problems of
local concern to the local journalist or even to become active as an
amateur broadcaster. Local access means that the media producer is
only a local telephone call away, or that the medium is housed
around the corner and may be easily reached and entered. Local
media presents an opportunity for the individuals who are responsible for them to become widely known in the community – they may
be met in their office or even on the street. Journalists or amateurs
can easily establish contacts with community leaders, interview the
mayor on topics of local concern, or talk to the local sports hero, the
clergyman, the school dean or just to ordinary people.

Radio in particular provides an opportunity for narrowcasting in
the sense that a low-cost transmission is available, that even
sublocal stations are possible. Segments of larger cities could be
served by 'neighbourhood stations' (as evolved in Japan). Or special
groups in society can establish their own stations: ethnic or social
minorities, citizens' action groups, universities, can establish separate information systems. Examples of this are Arabic-language

stations in France, stations for immigrants in Britain or for labour migrants in many parts of Europe.

All this might happen, but it is just one possibility. Empirical research shows that the interest in local news is there, but that it is quite limited – usually not much happens in a typical locality anyway. And those who are part of the local power structure show a keen interest in controlling the local media: often close relationships arise between the political and economic leaders on the one hand and the local media representatives on the other, both united in common interests – and sometimes also in ownership. Can this really be changed with the introduction of new media technologies?

Much of the news in a locality is traditionally diffused via interpersonal communication, in the local bars and churches, in clubs, associations or at parties. Is it desirable to substitute these, often quite effective, means of distributing information among small audiences by impersonal, technical media systems? Why should somebody stay at home and listen to the radio when the same kind of news may be received easily in public places – only this time from real people? Or even worse: as was described above, commercial local radio may be particularly successful when it presents international music and light entertainment in pseudo-local surroundings. It should not be forgotten that commercial media prefer the consumer to be a passive recipient. The more and the longer a person listens to local commercial radio, the more revenue the station earns from advertisers. Local media, of course, have the potential to activate local citizens, inform them about local activities, send them to places – but this kind of mobilization may conflict with the commercial message, which encourages passivity on the part of the listener.

All media, even the local ones, are technical systems that basically present 'one-way' information, which makes them fundamentally different from any kind of person-to-person communication, which is always interactive. In technical systems the citizen can 'talk back', but only by using much smaller and less powerful channels, such as a telephone call or a letter to the editor. Some local actors might see this as an advantage in local politics. Assuming a conflict in local politics, the responsible politician may be interested in hiding behind the communication barriers of a technical media system and use it to prevent public confrontations. In this way it becomes difficult for citizens to express their concerns or their anger, even on a local level. In the USA most if not all political campaigning is conducted nowadays in the electronic media because they enable new kinds of political marketing, mostly derived from advertising campaigns, which shield the politicians

from unfriendly confr[...]
Europe.

Local media present – [...]
ways of local communicat[...]
they fulfil their promises.

Some conclusions

The first and most fundamen[...]
that most local media are n[...]
precisely, locality in most cases[...]
there is much less real localism [...]
of the content of a local new[...]
consists of centrally produced n[...]
canned music, etc. Much of the [...]
flage for a system of local dis[...]
material.

There are two reasons for this s[...]

1   Many stations are licensed fo[...]
    element of local service is writte[...]
    licence (see Chapter 12)
2   Local content suggests close pro[...]
    neighbourhood orientation, both o[...]

Pseudo-local media, it seems, is what[...]
up as. The central rationale behind the li[...]
is financing. Local news and other kind[...]
much more expensive to produce tha[...]
'imported' from far-away places. Once ag[...]
structure of centres and peripheries, me[...]
producers provide a large hinterland wit[...]
Costs are also a prime reason for the lack o[...]
in large cities in Europe (see Chapter 11). Fu[...]
broadcasters in certain places are forced t[...]
television because it may have been a prere[...]
licence. This makes sense for the national calc[...]
to do with earning any local money.

In the field of electronic media, public serv[...]
Europe engage in relatively little activity on the[...]
tions include the BBC radio stations in the UK). [...]
that public media are not well prepared for local [...]
much more the result of lack of financial resources [...]
by the local newspaper industry, which is keen to [...]
advertising market.

Jarren, O. and Widlock, P. (1986) *Lokalradios*. Berlin: Vistas.

King, D.S. and Pierre, J. (eds) (1990) *Challenges to Local Government*. London: Sage.

Kleinsteuber, H.J. (1991) *Radio – Das unterschätzte Medium: Erfahrungen mit nichtkommerziellen Lokalstationen in 15 Staaten*. Berlin: Vistas.

Kleinsteuber, H.J. and Sonnenberg, U. (1990) 'Beyond Public Service and Private Profit: International Experience with Non-commercial Local Radio' *European Journal of Communication*, 5(1): 87–106.

McLuhan, M. (1964) *Understanding Media*. New York: McGraw Hill.

McLuhan, M. (1968) *War and Peace in the Global Village*. New York: Simon & Schuster.

Webster, B.R. (1975) *Access: Technology and access to communications media*. Paris: UNESCO.

11

Models of Local Media Development

Els De Bens and Vibeke G. Petersen

Patterns of local radio

Local independent radio started in Western Europe in the mid to late 1970s in a spirit of protest. Local radio stations that form part of a national broadcasting organization, such as the BBC, are not included in this chapter. They are to a large extent centrally controlled and financed and generally share the public service obligations of their parent institutions. In most countries they existed prior to the emergence of the independent local radio stations and were thus part of the target of the protest. There was dissatisfaction with the existing broadcasters, mainly public service monopolies because of their political bias, limited public access, and little attention to life outside metropolitan areas. There was a growing demand for local self-determination and self-expression in cultural, social and political affairs. And there was increasing commercial pressure, not least from the press, for access to the electronic media on more liberal terms than those available.

These forces, operating in various combinations, contributed to the break-up of traditional broadcasting patterns. Ten to fifteen years later it seems clear that the commercial interests have proved the most tenacious. Looking ahead to the 1990s a consolidated pattern emerges of commercial networks criss-crossing the media landscape, with only an occasional dissenting station interrupting the flow of pop music. There are strong trends towards increased commercialization with the resulting fare of bland programming, networking and increased press ownership of radio stations, all of which makes it hard for the pioneering protest radio stations to survive.

Between the beginning and the projected consolidation, the development has gone through a wide range of different stages, some of which are common to many countries, while others are unique attempts to control the process. In the following we try to present a coherent framework for dealing with the diverse experiences.

Given the large number of different types of local radio across Western Europe, a rigid framework of clearly distinct models would not capture the essential feature of the phenomenon, namely its local roots. It is therefore inevitable that the proposed models will constitute a less than perfect picture. There are, however, some broad characteristics that seem to dominate development in groups of countries, such as the idealistic pioneers, rapidly overtaken by commercial interests in Italy, France, Belgium, Ireland, Luxembourg, Greece and Spain; the cautious 'top down' approach in Scandinavia and the Netherlands, where commercialization is still being held in check; and the seemingly undramatic incorporation of a third tier of radio broadcasting in Switzerland, Finland, West Germany and the UK.

'Free' radio marked the beginning of the end of the public service broadcasting monopoly in most of Western Europe. Legislators approached the phenomenon (in several cases after witnessing long periods of illegal activity) with the primary aim of keeping local radio local. It was supposed to be a complement, not a competitor, to established media. This involved imposing regulatory restrictions that were at odds with market forces. At the same time, financing of the new stations was by and large left to the inventiveness of the broadcasters. The result has been a continual – and often successful – pressure from local broadcasters for more liberal rules.

So far, local radio is still in transition from an idealistic past to a commercially viable future, and its impact on overall media development looks modest. To the extent that the commercial strategy succeeds, local radio will, however, become more of a threat to existing national (and regional) radio because of its ability to compete for listeners and advertising income.

The free market model

The beginnings: idealism, clandestineness and struggle   In countries like Italy, France, Belgium, Luxembourg and in some ways Ireland, Greece and Spain, private local radio stations have developed along similar lines. In all these countries the emergence of local private radio was triggered by two dominant factors: a strong resentment of the absolute monopoly of the public broadcasting system (in the case of Luxembourg, resentment of the monopolistic position of the commercial broadcasting corporation CLT-RTL) and the absence within these systems of genuine local radio.

Towards the mid-1970s the demand for more decentralization, for small-scale local broadcasting offering complementary and alternative programming, with more open access facilities, became urgent.

In Italy, France and Belgium, the private local radio stations which were launched all shared some common characteristics: they were engaged in a sort of struggle scenario, that is, they wanted to break the national broadcast monopoly; they were illegal and were persecuted; they broadcast at irregular periods; their transmission range and coverage was small; their revenues came from benefit activities and supporters. Most of these pioneers were ideologically committed. They belonged to grass-roots movements, student and minority groups.

Italy was the first country where the monopoly of the public service corporation was disrupted. The protagonists of liberalization found an ally in the Constitutional Court with its rulings on freedom of expression on the basis of art. 21 of the charter of the Republic. Liberalization was granted, however, only on the local level; the national level remained an RAI monopoly. Thousands of FM radio stations were launched in the mid-1970s. The struggle and illegal pioneer stage were fairly short: as early as the mid-1970s private local radio stations were allowed to broadcast. A legislative framework, however, was not created, so that the thousands of radio stations, operating in legislative chaos, ended up in a life and death struggle.

In France and Belgium the fight for liberalization was to take longer and to be more difficult. In these two countries the public broadcast monopolies had become real bastions, often highly politically biased. In France 'les radios militantes', 'les radios de combat' and 'les radios vertes', all small-scale non-profit radio stations, demanded liberalization; they were persecuted, and under President Giscard d'Estaing new laws (August 1974 and July 1978) were enacted which condemned all attempts to break the public service monopoly. In addition to these militant radio stations, some commercial stations were also active. However, the latter were persecuted less often than their idealistic colleagues! The pressure for liberalization was so strong and irreversible that, when the Mitterrand government came to power in 1981, it was evident that the 'radios libres' would be legalized (July 1982).

In Belgium we can see the same scenario: the majority of the first 'free' radio stations originated in grass-roots, student and minority movements. Again they were harassed by the detector service of the telecommunications authority and had to move around in order to continue their clandestine broadcasts. Towards the end of the 1970s dozens of free stations popped up, no longer confining themselves to militant and environmental topics, but giving attention to local information, socio-cultural actions and music. As time went by an increasing number of commercial radio stations were established, their programming mainly non-stop chart music. They all demanded legalization. Finally, they were 'tolerated' and legislation followed in the early 1980s (in the French-speaking part of Belgium in 1981, in Flanders in 1982).

In Luxembourg the first private station started its broadcasts in 1983. The 'battle scenario' began: equipment was confiscated and the station moved to Arlon in Belgium. By the end of 1987 no less than thirty-one illegal stations had emerged, the majority still adhering to the old pioneering idealism and only one third commercially inspired. They are now 'tolerated' and awaiting legislation fairly soon in 1991.

In Ireland the story has been similar, though with some differences. The current local private radio stations are a direct development of illegal stations dating back to 1975. The majority of these local private stations were commercially inspired from the start. The old pioneers' idealism is echoed in the so-called 'community radios', which are non-profit stations. These stations form a minority and are exceptional media phenomena for Ireland since there is widespread reliance on advertising throughout the media. During their pirate period all these private local stations were harassed and persecuted to a lesser extent than those in France and Belgium. The government postponed legislation until 1988.

During the early 1980s several local illegal radio stations were launched in Greece. Some were commercially inspired (pop music) but others were contesting the PSB monopoly, which was closely linked to the socialist government. In 1986 the conservative mayors of Athens, Piraeus and Salonica set up municipal radio stations. They were still illegal but soon they became very popular. In 1987 municipal and private local radio stations were legalized.

Subsequent to the legal establishment of private radio stations in 1987, local radio thrived in Greece. The private local stations became more popular than the three municipal ones. Advertising was allowed from the beginning so that commercialism took over. By 1989, 120 licences had been granted and hundreds of other stations had applied for licences. In Athens alone, scores of private local radio stations are actively competing with the municipal station, which is losing its audience. Some of these private stations are doing quite well and taking away advertising from the PSB stations. Networking is illegal but practised nevertheless. The old pioneers' model had little chance in Greece since from the very beginning advertising was the main source of income.

In Spain, local radio was not allowed to develop under the Franco regime. In 1968 a few local radio stations emerged, but they were, of course, persecuted. After the Franco era (1939–75), a new law created 'autonomous' regional PSB radio stations. In spite of this decentralization policy, private local radio initiatives were taken. The first illegal local radio station was Onda Libre (1977) in Barcelona, but it disappeared because of financial difficulties. In several regions the municipal authorities launched (illegal) radio stations. Legalization of these municipal stations started after 1979 (Transitional Plan for FM Radio Distribution). Meanwhile hundreds of smaller local private stations have emerged, but they are still operating illegally. As they try to break the monopoly of PSB and of the municipalities, their future is uncertain. Some of them stick to the old pioneers' model, while others have gone commercial and are establishing illegal networks.

In Greece and Spain municipal authorities have played an important role in the attempts to break the PSB monopoly. In Greece both municipal and local private radio stations have been legalized, whereas in Spain only the municipal radio stations have been legalized so far.

The post-monopoly period: commercialism Except for Italy, where until recently legislation was completely lacking, and Spain and Greece where legislation is partly lacking, the legal frameworks of the different countries show some similarities. Legislation was inspired by the ideas of the idealistic pioneers' model: limited range of transmission and of coverage, local programming quotas, demands for pluralism, guarantees of open access, a ban on networking and advertising. The private local radio stations, however, frequently flouted the regulations, especially the ban on networking and advertising. Financing was one of the major problems as public funding was almost entirely excluded, and benefit and volunteer actions did not last in the long run. Again the authorities gave in and the ban on advertising was lifted in France in 1984, in Belgium in 1985. In France a fund was created by means of which some of the profits of the rich stations would be transferred to the poor ones (compare the Robin Hood concept of the Scandinavian model). This fund was to keep alive the small non-commercial radio stations in France, but it never worked.

Once advertising was allowed, the road to commercialization lay open. Local commercial stations turned out to be attractive to advertisers and thus their advertising budgets showed a rapid growth. Via networking they enlarged their audience and made life difficult for the remaining non-commercial radio stations.

In Ireland and Greece advertising was from the beginning the legal source of financing; the same model applies in Luxembourg. In Ireland, the non-profit community stations also rely on advertising but their goal is not a commercial one. Four of the twenty-four local stations that have been licensed are community radio stations; one has already been trapped by commercialism (it is now fully commercial), and the fate of the other three is open to question. It should be noted that in France, Italy, Belgium, Luxembourg, Greece and Spain, small-scale, non-commercial local radio stations are still active. As they all have to rely on goodwill and on benefactors, their future looks rather gloomy. Especially in Italy, France, Greece and Belgium they are finding it difficult to survive: their number is constantly decreasing.

As a result of increasing commercialization, a process of concentration is taking place. Networking is inevitable in order to stay in the market, even if the law forbids it. In Italy, four large networks control 100 minor stations (in 1988); in France, eight networks control almost all local private radio stations (1989). In Belgium the situation is the same: five major networks have been established (1989). In Spain networks of local radio stations are growing. In Ireland and Luxembourg, where advertising is the main revenue, networking will be inevitable.

In Italy, France, Belgium and Greece newspapers participate in local private radio, especially in the networks. In Ireland and currently in Luxembourg newspapers are also involved. Ultimately, private local radio, intended by the pioneers to be a complementary, alternative medium, has stimulated the process of concentration – a rather disappointing turn of events!

As a result of commercialism the programming content of the local stations has drifted away from their original goals. The commercial stations have been reduced more and more to non-stop hit music channels, interrupted only by commercials and short information bulletins. Their audiences are growing and consist mainly of young people.

In the free market model, private local stations have forced their way onto the radio scene; legislators have followed step by step, always giving in to commercialism. In these countries the local radio phenomenon has never been part of a coherent media policy. The model has developed along *laissez-faire* lines. Recently (7 November 1990) a new law was passed in Flanders which attempts to restore the old pioneers' model: limited range of transmission and coverage, local programming (80 per cent), networking forbidden, etc. It is, however, doubtful whether this law will be applied . . .

Finally, it has to be stressed that the public service broadcasting institutions in these countries are fighting back. They are losing listeners and advertising revenue to the local private stations. These radio stations have revealed two needs: more local information and more popular music aimed at young audiences. This has resulted in further decentralization and popularization of the existing public service stations.

The Scandinavian model

Local radio came into existence in the Scandinavian countries in 1979–81 – at a time when the broadcasting systems of Sweden, Norway and Denmark were very similar. Each country had a national public service monopoly institution, financed through licence fees and broadcasting a limited amount of television (2 channels in Sweden, 1 each in Norway and Denmark) and a few radio programmes (1 channel in Norway, 3 each in Sweden and Denmark). Organized within these institutions and ruled by the same guidelines, a small number of local/regional radio stations provided the only electronic media service below the national level. This set-up had developed within a tradition dating back to the 1920s and enjoyed a high degree of political consensus.

It is therefore not surprising that the first departure from the monopoly in all three countries was very similar in structure as well as in goals. Although not stated in equally explicit terms, these goals can be summarized as follows: to create a third tier of broadcasting which would allow local communities to speak to and about themselves on their own terms; to put broadcasting at the disposal of 'ordinary' people in order to widen the scope of freedom of speech and information and to democratize access to the electronic media; and to increase the level of local information.

There were national variations: in Sweden the new medium was seen primarily as a means of strengthening the existing local civic, cultural and spiritual associations which are the traditional pillars of social life in the country; in Norway, emphasis was placed on the potential of local radio for creating a stronger social and cultural identity in small communities, an important concern in this large but sparsely populated country.

As opposed to the situation in, for example, Italy and France, there was virtually no pressure for access to broadcasting in Scandinavia from the bottom up. Grass roots movements, minority groups, special interest organizations and local activities of all sorts, which were later to crowd the airwaves, did not voice a strong interest, nor did they engage in pirate activity to any noticeable degree. It should perhaps be mentioned that the commercial lobby, which might have seen an opportunity for a new market, was concentrating its endeavours on getting advertising into the national radio and television services.

Idealistic beginnings   Thus, the regulators could quite freely design their local radio regimes and choose the instruments with which to further their goals. Legislation breaking the public service broadcasting monopolies was passed in Sweden in 1979 and in Denmark in 1981 (in Norway a clause in the existing law was used for the first time in 1981). In all three countries a number of licences were issued for an experimental period lasting a few years. In the spring of 1985, when these experiments were about to be replaced by permanent systems, Sweden had 1,013 licence holders, Norway 318 and Denmark 90, broadcasting in about 60, 90 and 40 local areas respectively.

The availability of frequencies in sufficient numbers to ensure that almost every local community had its own station – to be shared by an assortment of different interests – was in itself seen as a guarantee of plurality. The need for traditional public service obligations such as impartiality and diversity would be fulfilled by the sheer number of broadcasters. The most appropriate instrument for the regulators to use would therefore be rules on structure rather than on content. To keep local radio local, a maximum transmission power was set which allows for a coverage area of about 10 km (with some concessions to cater for special geographical and demographic problems), and local programming quotas were imposed, albeit in fairly vague terms.

To widen the freedom of speech and media access, the range of applicants eligible for licences was made very broad: religious and political groups, cultural and social associations of all kinds, educational institutions, city councils (except in Sweden), and individuals (only in Denmark).

In all three countries commercial enterprises were excluded, with the notable exception, however, in Norway and Denmark, of newspapers. The press had – successfully – claimed that it would suffer, if not immediately then in the long run, from being left out of the pervasive media development from print to electronic means of information exchange.

The particular Swedish concern, that local radio was to be a means of strengthening the organizational structure of religious, cultural, civic and political life, was expressed in the rule that only associations set up with a goal other than broadcasting and in existence for at least a year prior to application, could receive a licence.

The issue of financing, which was to play the main role in later regulatory changes, was settled by way of exclusion: there was to be no commercial income from advertising and sponsorship, no enforced licence fee, and no state support (in Denmark, about $1 million in seed money was given by the state to selected stations). Local public subsidies, listeners' contributions, support from the broadcasters' background organizations and various fund-raising activities (in Denmark radio bingo became an important bread-winner) constituted the somewhat precarious economic basis for the new broadcasters.

It is perhaps not surprising that the Scandinavian countries were unwilling to abandon their non-commercial broadcasting systems. It is also in keeping with the development of local radio elsewhere in Western Europe to view the new medium as an extension of the public service ideal rather than an addition to the commercial sector. But in effect the legislators placed it in between the two sectors – without the financial security of the public system or the advantages of free market forces of the commercial one. It can be argued that only the Swedes acted realistically by putting local radio in the hands of already existing organizations with available funds of their own. The Swedish system has, incidentally, gone through the 1980s virtually unchanged.

In Norway and Denmark the experimental period offered plenty of evidence to back up the design of the new broadcasting system. Applications for a licence came in by the hundred, and those who received one acted by and large according to the rules: they dealt with local affairs in most of the programmes, they stayed within their assigned area, and they managed to scrape together enough money to keep their stations on the air. It also became clear, however, that new sources of income were necessary if the under-taking was to have a future. This issue was complicated by several factors. The options were mainly to allow advertising or to institute public subsidy. Neither country had any (recent) experience of broadcast advertising – disregarding the relatively few instances of illicit advertising on the local stations – and there were considerably divergent opinions among the political parties as to the desirability of starting commercial broadcasting at the local level, when no decision had yet been taken about advertising on the national channels. Disagreement over public subsidy was no less pronounced.

Clash of ideologies   The political consensus which had surrounded the introduction of local radio was thus replaced by an ideological clash over the character and role of the new medium. The focal point of the conflict was the question of financing, but it involved other issues as well, such as the delimitation of the local area, networking, and the right of newspapers to own radio stations. According to one view the purpose of local radio was to give voice to those who are not normally heard – minorities, special interest groups, and grass-roots movements; to strengthen community life, and to offer information on local affairs. The message of local radio was essentially regarded as a cultural and social one and therefore to be kept out of the commercial market place. In Denmark particularly, this view was accompanied by support for a public subsidy scheme. The local coverage area was to remain within the rather narrow limitations of the experimental period (10-watt transmitters, or a range of about 10 km). The press was to be excluded from ownership of local stations in order to prevent the formation of local information monopolies, networking was to be banned, and a requirement for local content of programming was to be maintained. According to the other view, local radio was supposed to express community life in a broader sense. Local business life, majority interests and the press were to be as fully involved as minority and cultural interests. The role of the regulators was to clear the way so that competition in a free market place could provide the local community with the media of its choice. This entailed commercial financing, flexible arrangements with respect to coverage area, some allowance to be made for networking and the inclusion of the press as licence holders.

The first of these two views had its roots in the notion of local radio as an extension of the existing public service system and resembles the initial motivation for breaking the existing monopoly. The second reflects the experience of the first years of local broadcasting and – perhaps equally important – a marked change in the media environment during the same period. The advent of satellite television gave added impetus to the discussion of the introduction of broadcast advertising, and traditional resistance had begun to wither away in the face of the increasing commercialization of transfrontier television. Furthermore, the prospect of a multitude of new foreign channels made it important to create viable domestic alternatives.

As could be expected, the political divergences resulted in compromise solutions. In both countries advertising was allowed (Norway in 1987, Denmark a year later). There is a maximum limit of 10 per cent of broadcasting time for advertising. Apart from opening up this source of revenue the regulatory frameworks have kept an emphasis on localism, in Norway more explicitly than in Denmark. The Norwegian local radio stations still have to broadcast mostly local content programming, whereas this requirement has been dropped in Danish law and replaced by the much vaguer demand that programming must be connected to the local area. A local area is defined as a municipality, about the same as during the experimental period, and transmitter power is limited accordingly. Networking is forbidden. In Denmark, however, it is possible for a station to obtain a licence covering several municipalities (by using as many transmitters as it takes) if the local authorities agree to join together – an option that is becoming increasingly common as broadcasters press for wider coverage because of economic problems.

The question of press ownership of local radio stations has gone through a series of regulatory changes. In Norway it was first forbidden again, then allowed, which is where it stands today. A similar development occurred in Denmark. It is worth noting, however, that the Danish press has shown only little interest in acquiring licences – in spite of heavy lobbying to be given the right to do so.

Half-way to commercialism   In line with the attempts to safeguard the principal goals of local broadcasting, namely that it be local and accessible to 'ordinary' people, measures have been introduced to counter the predictable effects of commercialism. Through a central fund money is channelled from the rich to the poor stations. In Norway, local stations must pay a levy of about 20 per cent of their advertising income to a central administrative board which in turn gives grants to stations with 'a low advertising potential' – primarily those in sparsely populated areas. (This levy has been lowered to 5 per cent as of January 1991.) The Danish scheme differs by being based on objective criteria. Here, all local stations pay 10 per cent of their total income to a fund. Stations earning less than a fixed amount of money per broadcast hour are entitled to a subsidy from the fund for up to 28 hours of broadcasting per week, the actual sum being calculated on the basis of the money available in the fund. In practical terms, this means that when the overall income of all radios is low, the subsidies are small – which was the case during the first year of commercial financing – and many stations that do not consider themselves rich find that the system is spreading poverty instead of distributing wealth. The system is likely to be abolished in the course of 1991.

Looked at from the economic point of view, all three Scandinavian local radio systems are still very much anchored in their idealistic origin, living on a shoestring and largely operated by unpaid amateurs. In Sweden 2,300 licence holders spent only about

$5 million in 1988 on broadcasting 215,000 hours. In Norway 330 radios have an estimated annual output of more than 600,000 hours, and in 1988 they earned only about $3 million in advertising revenue. In Denmark 350 radio stations broadcast 750,000 hours per year on a total income of about $12 million.

In many respects the Scandinavian countries – particularly Sweden – have remained faithful to their original local radio intentions. The regulatory changes of the past few years in Norway and Denmark are attempts to fit a solution to the financial problems into the exisiting regimes. It is not entirely clear, however, that these attempts will be successful in providing adequate scope for a plentiful and varied offering of local radio. The present half-way position between idealism and commercialism is a political compromise, difficult to police because of its decentralized character, and imperilled by the logic of commercial competition.

The Dutch way

The Netherlands have always had a unique broadcasting system. The so-called 'pillar' structure of licensing interest groups and according them national broadcast time in proportion to their size has secured diversity of opinion and some measure of access for minorities. This has not, of course, satisfied all sectors of society. Commercial lobbies have found advertising regulations too restrictive, and local groups have, as in other countries, felt a need for their own channels. True to tradition, two parallel outlets have developed outside the 'pillar' structure in order to cater for these interests: a vast number of pirate radio stations, plugged into the cable networks, have earned advertising money, and a smaller number of (legal) community radios have been in operation since the mid-1970s, first on an experimental basis, and since 1984 as an integral part of the Dutch cable system.

Although the Dutch and the Scandinavian local radio regulations spring from different media structures, they share the most important goals and means of obtaining them. Networking is allowed only to a limited degree and only through the connection of adjoining cable networks. Programme content must be directed towards the local community – one way of ruling out networking on a large scale. The press may deliver news to a local radio, but the broadcast remains the responsibility of the radio station in order to preserve some competition in the provision of local information.

Licences are given exclusively to organizations representative of local cultural, social and religious life, thus leaving out commercial interests. Until early 1988, local radio could only be distributed through cable, and the coverage area of the individual station therefore needed no further definition. With the introduction of over-the-air broadcasting at the local level, transmission power has been limited to cover the same area, which generally has a radius of about 10 km.

On the issue of financing, the Dutch system suffers from the same lack of realism as did the early Scandinavian rules. When advertising becomes more widely available as a source of income, some of the regulations designed to hamper commercialization can be expected to crumple. The Dutch authorities, however, have already shown a willingness to persecute illegal broadcasters with some vigour – they have greatly diminished the number of pirate radio stations during the last few years – and they may still be unwilling to give up their carefully balanced broadcasting system.

A model of pragmatism

In some European countries, private local radio has been instituted as a simple, small-scale addition to the public service and commercial radio systems rather than as a radically new venture. To varying degrees this holds true for Germany, Finland, Switzerland and the UK, where the notion of a third tier of broadcasting as an alternative to the existing national and regional/local ones is influenced more by the general liberalization in the field of broadcast media than by a sustained pressure for a qualitative change.

Given the difficulties of generalizing about the development of local radio in any one country, it is clearly not possible to generalize for a number of countries without leaving out some national peculiarities which may in fact merit more attention. The existing media regimes in the four countries in question are quite different, but historically they share the feature of being less centralized and monopolistic than most of their European counterparts. The UK and Finland have had commercial alternatives to their public service television for the past 35 years, in the UK public service radio has had competition at the regional and local level from Independent Local Radio since 1973. In West Germany and Switzerland regional cultural and linguistic independence has traditionally been important in media politics. Consequently, the need for reform – as expressed by pirates in the politically tightly controlled systems of Italy and France and by large sections of the political parties in the monolithic systems of the Scandinavian countries – has been less acute.

Late beginnings   With the exception of Switzerland, which passed a decree on experiments in local broadcasting in 1982, these four countries introduced private local radio rather later than others – in West Germany in 1984, in Finland in 1985, and in the UK in 1989. The original Swiss local radio decree, which was the most similar to the idealistic model that was common in Europe at the time, was changed in 1984, 1985, 1987 and 1988. Each time restrictive measures were relaxed in order to adjust the experiment to the economic realities of the market place.

In Germany, where media legislation is the prerogative of the Länder or states, local radio is subject to different regimes. Some states have issued licences to state-wide networks, some to individual stations within confined local areas. In most states, no legal distinction is made between what could be termed a fully fledged commercial radio system and a community-type system, while North Rhine-Westphalia has developed a complicated two-pillar arrangement with the aim of letting commercial exploitation of part of a frequency support non-commercial broadcasting on another part.

The UK came very close to initiating an experiment with community radio in the mid-1980s. The Home Office had picked out locations for twenty-one stations and written guidelines, according to which preference would be given to applicants who offered 'services which would be additional to and different from our existing local radio services'. Most of the stations would be allocated a coverage area of 5 km.

The plan was dropped, however, with the official explanation that proper regulations for such stations were lacking, and that the whole area of radio broadcasting was to be looked into. The resulting Bill was published in December 1989, and in the accompanying press release the idea of community radio is revived in the following way: 'In the course of the 1990s, 200–300 new stations could come on air, including neighbourhood and community-of-interest stations. Local audience demands and the extent to which the service would broaden the range of local programmes would affect local licence allocation.' It appears from the Bill that there will be no difference in the licence conditions for community radio and other independent local radio services.

As a forerunner of the new regime, in 1989 the IBA added a new set of radio stations to the existing ILR stations by licensing 23 so-called incremental stations (local radio stations in existing ILR franchise areas). By and large they are governed by the same rules as the ILR system, with the notable exceptions that they do not have to provide a broad range of programming, and are not obliged to carry a news service.

When the Finnish government decided in 1985 to open up the airwaves for private local broadcasting, it did so with the goal of promoting local freedom of expression. Consequently, a minimum of 20 per cent in-house programme production was imposed on the licensees, who were also obliged to sell surplus air time to local non-commercial interests. Licences are issued to commercial as well as to non-commercial stations. The latter category has not, however, been much in demand: out of forty licences, four were for non-commercial radio, and they have all changed their licences into commercial ones. When twenty-six new licences were issued in May 1989, six were non-commercial. It would seem that the need for special non-commercial licences stems from political ideology rather than popular demand, since such licences differ only in the exclusion of commercial income – never an obligation for any local radio station.

Economic viability   It is characteristic of the local radio regimes under consideration that the economic viability of the stations has had a high priority with the regulators. This is brought out, of course, by the permission to carry advertising – a right the stations did not have to fight for, but were given from the outset. Also, the green light given to press ownership has a beneficial effect on the financing of local broadcasting. A further element of this policy is the relatively small number of licences issued. In contrast to Italy, France, Belgium, and the Scandinavian countries, where there are hundreds of radio stations, the authorities in West Germany, the UK, Finland and Switzerland have been less generous – or more protectionist – in their approach.

In a Finnish publication on electronic media the Ministry of Transport and Communications (1988) notes: 'There are no confirmed principles at the regulatory level for granting the licences. Instead, expediency is taken into consideration. Most of the applications have been refused.' As of mid-1989 there were forty local radio stations in operation and twenty-six new licences issued. In Switzerland thirty-seven stations have been licensed, in West Germany the number given is about ninety, and in the UK twenty-three incremental stations were issued with licences in 1989. This number is as mentioned expected to rise to 200–300 after the new broadcasting law has taken effect.

In all four countries frequency-sharing between licensees is the exception rather than the rule as in Scandinavia, presumably on the grounds that it requires a whole frequency to make a living. Beside sufficient air time for a sustained service, a coverage area large and populous enough to be attractive to advertisers is essential to the economic success of a station. In recognition of this, regulations concerning the delimitation of the local area are flexible. In Switzerland, where the most rigid rule applies (20 km is the stated limit), the wording of the decree has been changed from 'at most 20 km' in 1982 to 'as a rule 20 km' in 1987, implying that a political ideal has had to give way to the pressure for better commercial opportunities. In Finland, local stations cover on average 50 km, and in Germany and the UK there are no fixed limits. The range of the British incremental stations is about half the size of that of the ILR stations and will in future be decided on a case-by-case basis

Advertising is allowed, in Germany and the UK according to the same rules that govern other radio advertising (20 per cent of daily broadcasting time and nine minutes per hour), and in Finland 10 per cent of monthly broadcasting time. In Switzerland the current limit is forty minutes or 5⅓ per cent of daily broadcasting time – it is worth noting that this maximum has been raised several times since the first decree. Here, as in other areas of economic importance to the new broadcasters, the Swiss regulators have shown a preference for changing the rules rather than seeing them broken on a large scale.

Networking (the broadcasting of the same programme on several stations) is a well-known way of reducing expenses, thereby permitting the poorer stations a more substantial output than they could afford on their own. It is also a way of financing which goes against the independence and local separateness of its participants, and for that reason it was initially banned in many countries. In West Germany, Switzerland, Finland and the UK networking has been allowed from the beginning, or at least not banned. In the UK it is permitted only outside prime time, and in Finland only between three stations.

Press ownership The controversial issue of cross-media ownership, that is, the participation of the press in the ownership of local broadcast media, has been dealt with more or less restrictively, ranging from no barriers in Germany (except in certain states) and Finland to a fixed 20 per cent limit in the UK. In Switzerland the decree states that the licensee cannot have a dominant media position. This clause, like those restricting advertising time, has had to be adapted to the pressures of reality – by and large it has been disregarded.

As a result of these policies the press is heavily involved in local radio in Germany and in Finland. German publishers control about half the total number of local stations in the former West Germany and have a stake in most of the rest. Several newspapers are co-owners of a number of radio stations. Only about 20 per cent of the stations are entirely without press influence. In Finland, nineteen out of the thirty-three initial licences were given to publishing interests.

It is difficult to judge whether or not the prevailing cross-media ownership actually causes less variety of local information than independent stations would provide – a principal reason for rejecting such ownership. In view of the fact that local radios in general tend to broadcast an increasingly uniform fare of pop music and small talk in order to attract as large an audience as possible, it would seem that the commercial imperative is more important for programming decisions than ownership in itself.

With the involvement of the press, a tendency towards professionalization is inevitable (although amateur broadcasters play a major role here as everywhere else in small-scale radio), and the ensuing 'rules of the game' encompass in all four regimes a measure of public service obligations, particularly in the treatment of news: in Switzerland news must be true and pluralistic, in Germany important political and social views and groups must be fairly presented, in Finland local radio stations are obliged to sell air time to different ideological associations, municipalities and parishes in order to give voice to a variety of local interests. In the UK existing rules on the accuracy and impartiality of news have been carried over to the Broadcasting Act of November 1990.

The ineligibility of political parties and religious organizations as licensees emphasizes that the new stations are designed to fit into an existing pattern of broadcasting with its obligations to impartiality and its rejection of onesidedness. (This is in contrast to, among others, the Scandinavian countries, where the systems aim at pluralism through a large number of competing stations, each voicing their own opinions).

Little idealism   Though different in many respects, the local radio regimes in the four countries reviewed have as a common element a large measure of realism in the regulations, particularly as they concern financing. One consequence of this is that the stations earn vastly more money here than in more strictly regulated countries such as Norway and Denmark. In 1987 the Swiss stations had an advertising income of $27 million, the Finnish (1988) $34 million, and the West German (1988) $30 million. The income is not, of course, evenly distributed among all stations, and the comparatively generous flow of advertising income to the new broadcasters is no guarantee that the present trend of expansion can continue – or even that the existing level of activity can be kept up. But by giving a higher priority to economic viability than to political ideology, the regulators have set up systems that operate without chaos and frequent close-downs – and most likely also with little of the idealism which gave rise to local radio in the first place.

Patterns of local TV in Europe

Re-defining the concept

In the literature on 'local TV', the terms 'community TV', 'local TV' and 'regional TV' are often used indiscriminately. Most of the time the difference is indicated by means of the criterion of territory, 'regional' referring to a potential range which is larger than 'local'. But this soon becomes confusing when used in the European context: what is 'regional' in Belgium becomes 'local' in France. A more structural approach can classify some of the confusion surrounding the concepts in question. 'Local' TV differs from the large traditional TV stations: its typically regional programme supply, its limited broadcasting schedule (often just a few hours a week), its limited range, its interactive role trying to stimulate audience participation. Such local stations have evolved according to three scenarios: firstly, as a pilot or experimental station; secondly, as an illegal station which has eventually won official recognition; thirdly, as a station which continues to be illegal or which, although tolerated, finds itself in a juridical vacuum. As in the section on local radio, local TV does not refer here to the several regional stations set up by national PSB or national commercial stations (such as the 5 decentralized production centres set up by the BBC, the fifteen regional ITV companies, ARD's nine regional stations, TF1's network, RTL-TV, etc.).

Although the 'ideal' model of local TV is still a matter of debate, the available literature and the results of research projects do enable us to find a number of recurrent features. The present chapter will therefore use the 'idealistic' model as a starting point, and will subsequently outline a number of less 'exemplary' cases, in other words local TV systems which deviate from the 'ideal' model or do not bear any resemblance to it at all. By comparing the existing local TV systems to the model, or by pointing out the differences, an attempt will be made to survey recent developments in local TV in Europe.

The nearest approximation to the 'idealistic' model: the Netherlands, Belgium and Scandinavia

In an 'ideal' model, allowance will have to be made for a number of imperatives. The size of the region to be covered is crucial. The region has to have a certain socio-cultural profile within an administrative entity (a city, a county, etc.). The cost of one hour of television is so expensive that local TV stations with a very limited range are not viable. It is not practicable for every village to have its own local TV station, for both financial and organizational reasons. Some experts have concluded that local TV stations must have a catchment area of some 500,000–1,000,000 people.

Financing is another thorny question. If local TV is exclusively financed by advertising, it will turn into a mere commercial station: it will try to enlarge its coverage area and as such will deny its local characteristics; the programme supply will not remain local but it will be filled with commercial entertainment such as game shows, quiz shows, soap operas, etc. Besides, the market for local advertising seems not to be big enough to generate adequate financial resources. In France for example, the larger local TV stations are unable to attract a substantial amount of advertising. Making TV is very costly and one hour of local TV typically costs between 8,000 and 10,000 ECU. Therefore local TV has to fall back on other sources of funding: the authorities (both national and regional), support from participating associations, voluntary contributions, etc. This type of mixed funding, public and private, implies that the number of licensed local TV stations cannot be too large. Public authorities may not give financial support to several local stations in one single region and the local advertising market is not large enough.

Programming must be in tune with the region: local news, social and cultural information and entertainment, all at the local level. This imperative automatically entails the necessity to limit broadcasting time. If the station is required to fill a full-time schedule, it will fall back on purchased programmes; in the latter case, networking becomes an attractive proposition.

The means of transmission is not a crucial element in the ideal model. Needless to say, the most suitable form of transmission is the star-system cable network, in which segmentation is a useful way of delineating the region served. In view of the low cable density in a number of countries, the stations tend to resort to terrestrial transmission.

In applying the ideal model, the authorities obviously play a major regulating role. It is precisely in those countries where the ideal model can be said to have evolved that the authorities themselves took the initiative to start up pilot projects of local TV experiments.

The closest approximation to the ideal model is found in the local stations of the Netherlands and French-speaking Belgium.

In the Netherlands the first experiments were conducted in the period 1974–79. The authorities gave financial support, and research teams closely monitored the stations' evolution. The outcome was assessed to be positive, so that the experimental stage changed into an operational one and several local stations were granted official recognition. Of course, this implied that the stations had to find other means of finance: advertising was forbidden, and most stations turned to the local authorities and to sponsorship by industry and trade. In 1985, there were seventy local TV stations in the Netherlands; twenty of these local TV stations have fixed daily or weekly broadcasts; the other stations broadcast once a month.

In 1988 a new Media Act regulated local TV, pushing it even further towards the ideal model outlined above: one single local station per municipality; a continuing ban on advertising and continued reliance on local authorities, benefactors and voluntary contributions for subsidies. It goes without saying that, in view of the large number of local TV stations, funding continues to be the great weakness of local TV.

In French-speaking Belgium several pilot projects were launched as early as 1976. They were financed by the area's Department of Cultural Affairs. Over nine years, eleven projects were started. All these stations were examples of the 'ideal model': limited broadcasting time, a well-defined region, a small number of licences (one per province), regional interest programmes and a ban on advertising. The stations gradually became popular and they were given permanent status in 1985. As in the Netherlands, the end of the experimental stage meant that the subsidies granted by the Department of Cultural Affairs were phased out. Mixed financing, local authority subsidies along with advertising revenue, was authorized. The stations' status was to remain that of non-profit associations. Although the new 1987 'audiovisual decree' provides for the setting up of commercial local stations, there is a political consensus to continue protecting the eleven local stations now in existence. So far no licence has been granted for a commercial station.

In Flanders (Dutch-speaking Belgium) local TV was given the go-ahead in 1987. But there are so many gaps in the legislation that the road to deregulation and to the Italian model is wide open. Indeed, nothing is laid down on the size of the region covered, on broadcasting time and on the number of stations per region. The financial status too is left open, so that it is perfectly natural for the stations to resort to advertising.

The Flemish Media Council is boycotting the present system by refusing to issue licences for local TV stations (so far only four

licences have been granted): it is hoped that the Flemish government can thus be forced to adopt a more adequate media policy. Of
course, it is the politicians who will decide whether or not local TV
in Flanders will follow the 'ideal' example set by its French-speaking
compatriots.

In Denmark, too, local TV started as an experiment, with an
initial phase in 1973 and a second series of experiments in 1983. The
second series resulted in the institutionalization of some thirty local
stations. The starting point for all these experiments was the same
as in the Netherlands and in French-speaking Belgium, but funding
was a continuing worry. Local stations were run by a great variety of
social, cultural and religious associations and by trade unions and
were often funded by money-raising activities such as benefits,
parties and the like. In April 1989 the local stations were given
permission to insert advertising spots, although with a number of
restrictions. Is this the beginning of commercialization?

In Norway and Sweden local TV developed along the same
pattern. Advertising is forbidden and the local stations have to rely
on subscription fees or subsidies. Since October 1990 advertising
has been allowed in Norway. In Norway – as in Denmark – lack of
finance remains a major problem. In Sweden, business companies
as well as local newspapers are showing a growing interest. In
Sweden eighteen local TV stations are active, in Norway ten.

Clearly, these countries have adopted a coherent media policy
with regard to local TV. All the stations set up are very close to our
'ideal model'. It is certainly not a coincidence that it was the
authorities who took the initiative.

The idealistic model abandoned? France, Germany and the UK

France and West Germany began to be interested in local TV in the
1980s, Britain as early as 1972. The start-up of local stations went
together with the construction of new cable networks, particularly
in France and West Germany.

Moreover, the three countries concerned enjoyed well-developed
regional centres within the existing national broadcasting institutions. This structured decentralization is probably another reason
why local TV was not awaited with much impatience.

The Federal Republic of Germany set up its first local stations in
the 1980s mostly in cabled areas; Ludwigshafen, Munich, Dortmund and Berlin were the first cities to have a local TV station.
Funding was carried out in different ways: Dortmund and Berlin
could draw on television licence fees and were granted public funds;
Ludwigshafen and Munich, moreover, were allowed to resort to the

private sector. These experimental local TV projects disappeared and today open channels are organized by the respective Local Media Supervisory Body in, for instance, Berlin, Hamburg and Ludwigshafen.

In 1988, the different Länder granted broadcasting licences to the supranational stations RTL Plus and Sat-1 on condition that they offer, *inter alia*, local TV broadcasts; it is a development which greatly accelerated commercialization.

In France the first local stations emerged with the 'Plan cable' of 1982. Biarritz, which had an optical fibre cable network, was chosen as the site of a pilot project financed with public funds. Since the construction of the cable network was slow, and since the number of applicants for local stations steadily increased, France, like West Germany, decided to grant licences for terrestrial transmission.

Many applicants have submitted their candidature for a licence. Until now, only three stations have been licensed: Télé Toulouse (April 1988), Canal Europe Mont Blanc (February 1989) and Télé Lyon Métropole (February 1989). All three stations (even though they include regions with a population of 500,000–1,000,000) faced financial problems: advertising revenues were smaller than expected. Certainly they want to extend their respective range and attract more advertising revenues.

In France some twenty-eight 'occasional' local TV stations were authorized: they broadcast only in connection with certain events (cultural and rural events, during the tourism season, etc.). They are subsidized by local authorities and associations.

We find much the same story in the UK. A few cable networks gave rise to the first experiments: Greenwich, Swindon, Bristol, Wellingborough, Sheffield and Milton Keynes (1972–83). They were not successful, and the only station to survive is Swindon.

The Cable Act of 1984 provided scope for new local TV stations. The initiative was left to the cable companies, but they were slow to react, since the cost of local TV was steep and the revenues from television licence fees (restricted by law) bound to be inadequate. The Cable Act also provided for the setting up of local stations for ethnic minorities, and for open access channels. Again the shortage of financial resources barred the way to success. The new Broadcasting Act gives the green light to the distribution of local TV via microwave (in addition to cable distribution).

Considering the dominant trend of commercialization in the UK, it goes without saying that advertising is bound to become the major source of revenue for local stations.

One final observation is that local TV has so far remained insignificant in France, Germany and the UK. There is hardly any interest in it on the part of the authorities, the investors or the public.

The 'deregulated' model: Italy, Spain and Greece

In the two models discussed so far, the authorities assumed a regulatory function from the very beginning. By contrast, Greece, Italy and Spain lacked a legal framework, so that local TV had to fight for its existence, much like local radio in the Latin model. In Greece and Italy local TV recently received a legal framework.

The development in Italy is very well known. The first local stations operated illegally, until the monopoly of RAI was abolished and the Act of April 1975 allocated local TV a place on the cable network. The provisions laid down in the directives resemble the characteristics of the ideal model: limited broadcasting range, a maximum of 5 per cent of broadcasting time to be allocated to advertising, 50 per cent of broadcasting time for regional programmes. The 1975 law, however, was clearly out of touch with reality. Even at the end of 1974, Italy had as many as fifty-five local TV stations, several of which were transmitting over the air.

In July 1976, the Italian Supreme Court authorized terrestrial local TV, and this decision produced a boom in local TV: in 1976 there were 1,200 local terrestrial stations, most of them over the air. Their only sources of revenue were advertising and sponsorship. The large advertising managers ('regies') began to invade local TV and to set up networks. Berlusconi in particular, having launched Telemilano in 1974, actively took over and competed with local stations.

The end of the story is widely known: Berlusconi has incorporated the local stations into his three networks (Canal 5, Italia Uno and Rete Quattro). Recently a new law finally created a legal framework, but so far it is not clear whether the Berlusconi empire will be broken up. The surviving independent local stations are still fighting a huge battle for survival.

In Spain legislation provides only for the two PSB channels, the three commercial stations and the nine 'autonomous' regional stations. In 1980 a number of local stations were launched in Catalonia: despite being illegal most of them are supported and funded by the municipal authorities. Today their number stands at around one hundred stations. Their broadcasting time and their range (on the air) is limited, and their programmes have a regional slant. Most stations are on the air during weekends only. The most professional station is undoubtedly TV Sabadell, which broadcasts every day from 8 till 10.30 am.

The Catalonian example was followed by the Basques (seven stations) and in Galicia (three stations).

All these stations are non-profit associations and restrict their programmes to local and cultural information and entertainment.

It is striking to observe that once again, just as in the case of local radio, it is the municipal authorities which lend their support to local TV. The only difference is that, unlike local radio, local TV is still illegal.

In Greece, two cities set up illegal local TV stations in January 1989: TV 100 (Saloniki) and TV Plus (Piraeus). It is no coincidence that these two cities were also those starting up local radio stations, which were legalized in 1988. The staff of the local TV stations often work for the municipal radio stations as well. The situation in Greece is similar to that in Spain, in that it is the municipal authorities who took the initiative. The government has legalized local TV, at least as far as municipal TV is concerned.

Overall, then, local television in Western Europe is certainly less highly developed than local radio is, even though the regulatory regimes for local media in nearly all of the countries considered in this book make some kind of provision for local television, as is outlined in the next chapter.

References

Béaud, P. (1980) *Community media? Local radio and television and audiovisual animation experiments in Europe*, Strasbourg: 179.

Benhain, J.P., Bonvoisin, F. and Dubois, R. (1985) *Les radios locales privées*, Paris.

Bustamente, E. (1989) 'TV and public service in Spain: a difficult encounter', *Media, Culture and Society*, 11(1): 67–87

Collard, S. (1990) *Les télévisions communautaires et locales en communauté française en Belgique*, Guide des Médias, Radio & TV, Suppl., I and II.

Conseil Supérieur de l'Audiovisuel (1990) *Les télévisions locales en France*, Paris: 1–25.

Coriminas, M. (1990) *Models de ràdio dels paisos occidentals*. Barcelona: Univ. Aut. Barcelona.

De Bens, E. (1989) 'Kanttekeningen bij lokale televisie', *Communicatie*, 18 (4): 45–8.

Herroelen, P. (1982) *1, 2 . . . veel? Kroniek van 20 jaar Belgische Radio en Televisie*. Leuven: Acco.

Hollander, E. (1983) 'Kleinschalige massacommunicatie', *Massacommunicatie*, 3, :107–13.

Home Office News Release of 7 December (1989) *Broadcasting Bill Published*. London: HMSO.

Home Office (1990) *Community Radio: Guidance Note on the Licensing of Experimental Stations*. London: HMSO.

Jens, C. (1989) 'Privater Hörfunk – eine Verlegerdomäne', *Media Perspektiven*, 1/89.

Kiamaki, O. (1990) 'Télévisions locales en Grèce' in S. Collard, *Les télévisions communautaires*, op. cit., II, pp. 27–38.

Langre, A. (1990) 'De la décentralisation de la TV en R.F.A.' in S. Collard, *Les télévisions communautaires*, op. cit., I, pp. 28–39.

'Lokale omroep op de Nederlandse kabel' (1986) *Koepel 5*, XIII, 16.

Madsen, J. (ed.) *Nærradioen i Norden*, Aarhus: De samvirkende Lokalradioer i Aarhus.

Mahoux, P. (1989) 'Communauté française de Belgique', in *Les télévisions communautaires, locales et régionales dans la CE*, proceedings of a conference held 9–10 March, Namur, I, pp. 35 ff.

Manders, H. (1986) 'Reclame op de lokale omroep', *Massacommunicatie*, 2/3: 165–9.

Ministry of Transport and Communications (1988) *Electronic Mass Media in Finland*. Helsinki.

Montes Fernandez, F.J. (1989) 'La télévision privée, une réalité en Espagne', *Revue de l'UER*, 5/89: 32–5.

Moragas, M., De Mateo, C. and Prado, E. (1986) *Electronic Mass Media in Spain*. Barcelona: Univ. Aut. Barcelona.

Mulryan, P. (1988) *Radio. The story of independent local community and pirate radio*. Dublin: Borderline Publications.

Petersen, V. 'De lokale stationer' in *Pressens Aarbog*. Aarhus: Pressehistorisk Selskab.

Reyniers, A. (1986) 'L'Audiovisuel en Belgique francophone' in *Tendances et Perspectives*, Dossiers COMU, 7: 14–37.

Saxer, U. (1989) *Lokalradios in der Schweiz*. Zürich: Universität.

Tudesq, A.J. (1987) *Les mutations de la radio en Aquitaine*. Bordeaux.

Truetzschler, W. (1991) 'Broadcasting law and broadcasting policy in Ireland', *Irish Communications Review*, 1: 24–36.

12

Regulation of Media at the Local Level

Wolfgang Truetzschler and Denis McQuail

During the course of the 1980s, the majority of the seventeen countries of Western Europe introduced significant changes in the legal arrangements for local radio and television, in response to the technological and economic challenges sketched in Chapter 2. In a number of cases, it was local media developments which had spearheaded the pressures for change and undermined existing law. Even where this was not the case, the general changes in the media system required a fundamental re-formulation of regulations, especially those relating to ownership and financing. The purpose of this chapter is not to discuss and interpret change, but to provide basic information in summary and comparative form about the current (1991) state of local media regulations on several key points. In order to compile this information, a questionnaire was completed for all countries and relevant statutes and documents were examined.

The main scope of new legislation

Central in the new regulations in most countries are regulations governing private local broadcasters, which have appeared alongside the older public broadcasting authorities familiar to all countries before 1980. Only the United Kingdom and Finland had fully legalized commercial local broadcasting before this date, but even here the regulations have been extensively changed (as in the UK) or are under review again (in Finland), in the light of drastically changed circumstances and policies. The only exceptions towards allowing private local media operators other than the existing public monopoly of local media are Austria and Luxembourg (the latter always fully commercial), although both countries are planning to introduce appropriate legislation, partly in response to internal or cross-border unlicensed stations. The public service monopoly has been broken everywhere else and by 1991 all countries except Sweden allow the financing of local broadcasting from advertising.

The most recent pieces of major legislation affecting local media have been in the United Kingdom and in Italy. In the latter case, the law of August 1990 formally ended RAI's public service monopoly and largely legitimated the existing dual system of financing and control of national as well as local media.

All the laws and regulations referred to specify the licensing authority for local radio and the criteria of eligibility in the awarding of licences. They also have something to say about the procedures of accountability and review that apply to licence holders. All laws also provide rules concerning the financing and content of radio services, although in widely varying degrees of detail. Most of the laws, especially those in countries with a history of illegal or pirate radio, contain more stringent provisions for the prosecution of illegal radio operators. The question of ownership of local media by other media operators is addressed in some, but not all, of the national laws on local broadcasting.

Licensing arrangements

The actual granting of licences for local radio and the procedure for ensuring that licence holders adhere to the regulations are subject to control by either the government department or the minister responsible for broadcasting, or by a specially created central authority or commission (as with the British Radio Authority, the French CSA, or the Dutch Media Council), or by organs of local or municipal government. In most countries, licences are awarded for periods of between five and seven years, usually with an option of renewal for the same period of time. The various laws also make provision for the temporary suspension or withdrawal of licences in the case of non-compliance with the regulations.

The regulatory regimes for local radio in Europe recognize three basic kinds of local radio: public service broadcasting of the traditional kind; private commercial radio serving suitable media markets (such as a town, region or a demographic segment); and local community or access radio. Each type implies certain organizational features, which are not always easy to reconcile within the same framework. Thus private commercial radio may be obliged to broadcast a fixed quota of certain kinds of material (such as news and current affairs), the cost of which may endanger the financial viability and profitability of the operation. Similarly, local community radio may be debarred from taking advertising revenue, which may make this type of operation non-viable. Regulations for the different types of radio may also be influenced by other media interests (often the local press). For such reasons, the new local media regimes are rarely very coherent or ideally suited to achieving all their supposed objectives.

Eligibility

The eligibility criteria differ from country to country, and generally reflect the many differences of national circumstances and traditions. There are some common patterns, for instance the requirement that applicants are nationals of the country (or citizens of the EC, where this applies), and the requirement that applicants can demonstrate financial viability and competence to run the service which they are seeking to operate. Some countries are quite specific in debarring certain types of applicant, for instance political or religious organizations. Other countries specifically mention such groups as being eligible.

Content regulations

Variations in content regulations are considerable, both as to their actual contents and the degree of specificity. In general, the countries with a strong tradition of opposition to commercialism, as in Scandinavia, have the most detailed regulations concerning content, while those with a more commercial tradition such as Ireland, Greece or Finland, have the 'lightest' regulatory regimes. However, most countries have general and rather unspecific regulations concerning the upholding of public order and morality, balance, protection of minors, etc. There are also usually more detailed regulations about the proportions of certain kinds of programming, such as news, local content, provision for youth, access programming and certain kinds of cultural content. Particular attention is sometimes paid to the question of the national (or regional) language and culture.

Finance

The rules for financing are equally diverse. All countries, with the exception of Sweden, now allow advertising in some form, provided it does not exceed a certain percentage of programming time (up to a maximum of 20 per cent in some places, but less in others) and is broadcast according to the local codes of standards about content. In some cases, the networking of local stations, which helps financial viability, is explicitly forbidden or is restricted to certain kinds of programme content, such as news. There may also be rules stating the maximum number of local stations that are permitted to form a network. Other forms of permitted, or not permitted, sources of income are variously identified in laws, particularly in relation to sponsorship, which has proved one of the most difficult issues for legislation and effective supervision.

As was outlined in the previous chapter, local radio has not so far turned out to be a 'licence to print money' in most of Europe, although there are occasional success stories. In part this stems from the lack of economic realism and strict content controls embodied in many laws. This early negative experience had led to several trends which are reflected in the development of local media legislation. Increasingly, advertising is being admitted as a source of finance and the rules are being relaxed. The ownership of local media by the press is also on the increase, for similar reasons. Moreover, programming is becoming more music-dominated, at the expense of local content. Networking is also increasing throughout Europe, whatever the regulations say, another trend which does not augur well for the 'localness' of local radio.

The regulation of local television has developed less fully and explicitly than that for radio. Frequently, because it is distributed by cable, regulations are embodied in those governing cable television generally, without specific local rules. In some countries, there is still no local television, or it is being operated without legal control.

Appendix

AUSTRIA

1 *Main legal instrument and planned change, if any:* No local radio or TV other than the regional outlets of ORF (Broadcasting Act 1974).
2 *Type or name of licensing/regulatory body:* National government (ORF has the *de jure* monopoly, but *de facto* pirate radio from abroad).
3 *Types of local radio:* Public local radio only.
4 *Content regulations*: Standard PSB regulations.
5 *Networking:* Does not apply.
6 *Connections with press and/or other media:* Does not apply (but in practice agreement between ORF and the Association of Austrian publishers on the length of advertising periods.)
7 *Financing:* Licence fee and advertising (ORF).
8 *Local TV:* German-language local TV from Italy.
Note: There are some plans for the introduction of private local media which are likely to be realized in 1992.

BELGIUM

1 *Main legal instrument and planned change, if any:* Radio Comm. Act of 1979; Act of August 1981; Decrees of 1981/82.

Belgium (continued)

2 *Type or name of licensing/regulatory body:* Walloon and Flemish community legislatures (by decrees).
3 *Types of local radio:* Private non-commercial, private commercial (the majority). (More than 500 radio stations in total.)
4 *Content regulations:* Local programming; information and education programmes; no ties with political parties allowed.
5 *Networking:* Prohibited by law, but in practice networking of news and advertising.
6 *Connections with press and/or other media:* Extensive links with the press.
7 *Financing:* Advertising allowed since 1985 (limited to 20 per cent of programming time).
8 *Local TV:* Local commercial TV on cable systems only – regulated by Walloon and Flemish decrees.

Note: Regulations on local radio are not applied in practice.

DENMARK

1 *Main legal instrument and planned change, if any:* Local Broadcasting Act of 1981, amended 1990; Law on Danmarks Radio (DR).
2 *Type or name of licensing/regulatory body:* Central committee grants frequencies; local bodies give licences.
3 *Types of local radio:* Local area is the municipality (there are 275). Two types of radio: DR local radio stations, and independent local radio.
4 *Content regulations:* Connections with locality.
5 *Networking:* Forbidden.
6 *Connections with press and/or other media:* Newspapers can own local radio and TV.
7 *Financing:* Advertising, sponsorship, fund (not public) for poor stations (will be abolished in the course of 1991).
8 *Local TV:* Local TV allowed under same rules as radio.

FINLAND

1 *Main legal instrument and planned change, if any:* No specific law on private local radio, only guidelines on the awarding of licences; Finnish Broadcasting Corporation (YLE) local radio is governed by Radio Act.
2 *Type or name of licensing/regulatory body:* Ministry of Transport and Communications.
3 *Types of local radio:* 58 private commercial local radio stations, 7 non-commercial local stations. YLE has 1 local radio, but 27 regional radio stations.
4 *Content regulations:* Localness; prohibition of programmes with immoral or violent content; access programmes.
5 *Networking:* Networking of advertising; network programming is limited to 3 local radio stations.
6 *Connections with press and/or other media:* Newspapers own many local radio stations.

Finland (continued)

7 *Financing:* Advertising on commercial radio; municipal subsidies and other forms of finance (e.g. subscriptions) for non-commercial local radio.

8 *Local TV:* Local TV is governed by the Act on Cable Television 1987. There have been applications for local TV, but no licences have been awarded to date.

FRANCE

1 *Main legal instrument and planned change, if any:* Law on private local radio 1981; law on audiovisual communication 1981; law on freedom of communications 1986.

2 *Type or name of licensing/regulatory body:* Radio France and CSA (which allocates frequencies and licences).

3 *Types of local radio:* Two main types: PSB has 35 regional and 12 town stations; private commercial local radio. (Many local radios have not yet been legalized by CSA; in theory frequencies could be allocated to a possible 1800 radio stations.)

4 *Content regulations:* CSA requires (*inter alia*): public order and morality; honesty; sex equality; balance; right of reply; etc. 20 per cent of programming must be self-made programmes; French content is favoured.

5 *Networking:* Not forbidden.

6 *Connections with press and/or other media:* Multimedia concentration is not favoured; limits to connections with the press.

7 *Financing:* Some local radio licences permit advertising, others do not allow it. Some public subsidy.

8 *Local TV:* Permitted and has begun under a similar regime as that for local radio.

GERMANY

1 *Main legal instrument and planned change, if any:* Each Land makes its own law (e.g. Hamburg law of 1985). The five new Länder are in the process of drawing up relevant legislation.

2 *Type or name of licensing/regulatory body:* All Länder have their own licensing authority (e.g. 'Hamburgische Anstalt für Neue Medien').

3 *Types of local radio:* PSB local radio (rare); commercial Land network (only in some Länder); commercial local radio (only in some Länder); non-commercial local radio (rare – only one station in Baden-Württemberg).

4 *Content regulations:* Varies from Land to Land, but the regulations have little practical significance. (E.g. Hamburg requires localness, independence from political parties, churches, etc., limitations on press ownership.)

5 *Networking:* Possible in some Länder only (see 3.)

6 *Connections with press and/or other media:* Connections with the press allowed and there is a heavy involvement by the press in local radio. There are some legal limits on press ownership.

7 *Financing:* Advertising and sponsorship allowed under Länder rules. (E.g. Hamburg has a 20 per cent rule.)

8 *Local TV:* PSB local TV and commercial local TV in some city Länder (e.g. Hamburg).

GREECE

1 *Main legal instrument and planned change, if any:* Law 1730 of 1987; presidential decree 25 of 1988; Law 1866 of 1989; amendments to these laws and various ministerial decisions.
2 *Type or name of licensing/regulatory body:* National Radio and Television Council; Minister to the Prime Minister.
3 *Types of local radio:* Municipal, state and mainly private commercial local radio. There are some 1,000 local radio stations – all operating without licences, as the licensing procedure is not working.
4 *Content regulations:* Local programming; information, education and culture programmes; access and youth programmes.
5 *Networking:* Generally prohibited until 1991, but there was a limited amount.
6 *Connections with press and/or other media:* Several stations are owned by other media companies.
7 *Financing:* Mainly advertising finance under rules.
8 *Local TV:* Local TV is possible: there are some 30 stations – all without licences (see 3.); some have near national coverage by means of networking which was legalized in 1991.

IRELAND

1 *Main legal instrument and planned change, if any:* Radio and Television Act 1988; Broadcasting Act 1990.
2 *Type or name of licensing/regulatory body:* Minister for Communications awards licences on advice of the Independent Radio and Television Commission (IRTC).
3 *Types of local radio:* 23 commercial local radios of which 3 are community radios; 1 PSB local radio.
4 *Content regulations:* Balance; decency; fairness; objectivity; 20 per cent of programming time must be news and current affairs; respect for privacy; localness; 25 per cent ownership by political parties and churches allowed.
5 *Networking:* Requires permission by the IRTC – in practice networking of news.
6 *Connections with press and/or other media:* 25 per cent ownership of local radio by press allowed.
7 *Financing:* Licence fees and advertising on PSB; advertising finance on private commercial radio.
8 *Local TV:* Local TV on cable is possible, if licensed by the Minister for Communications – to date only on Cork cable.

ITALY

1 *Main legal instrument and planned change, if any:* Broadcasting Act 1990 (Law 223/90).
2 *Type or name of licensing/regulatory body:* Minister of PTT on advice of a regulatory authority.
3 *Types of local radio:* Local commercial radio; local community radio.

Italy (continued)
4   *Content regulations:* Public order and morality, etc.; 20 per cent of programming time must consist of news and other non-commercial programmes.
5   *Networking:* Not mentioned in the law, limited through rules on advertising.
6   *Connections with press and/or other media:* Limitations on cross-ownership in the law.
7   *Financing:* Advertising, subscriptions, subsidy.
8   *Local TV:* Law applies to local TV, licences have yet to be awarded. (Numerous stations prior to the enactment of the law.)

LUXEMBOURG

1   *Main legal instrument and planned change, if any:* Law on electronic media (Law 3396) will be passed by parliament during 1991. (This law will abolish the RTL monopoly.)
2   *Type or name of licensing/regulatory body:* A new independent authority will be established.
3   *Types of local radio:* The law envisages the licensing of up to 40 local radios and 4 regional networks.
4   *Content regulations:* No content regulations are planned.
5   *Networking:* Networking will be allowed in order to establish the regional networks.
6   *Connections with press and/or other media:* Individual shareholders, including press, will be limited to owning 25 per cent of the shares in local radio stations.
7   *Financing:* Advertising finance will be permitted.
8   *Local TV:* No local TV is planned.
Note: Currently there is no legislation concerning local radio, the table therefore summarizes the bill currently before parliament.

NETHERLANDS

1   *Main legal instrument and planned change, if any:* Media Act of 1988 and amendments.
2   *Type or name of licensing/regulatory body:* Commissariat for the Media (main national body for the media) awards licences on advice from local (municipal) body and the PTT (technical aspects).
3   *Types of local radio:* Only one legal type of municipal radio and only one per locality. (There are around 700 municipalities; 270 licences for local radio have been awarded to date.)
4   *Content regulations:* Local needs; diversity and balance; non-commercial; public access; programmes for minorities.
5   *Networking:* No networking.
6   *Connections with press and/or other media:* Press ownership is permitted.
7   *Financing:* Local means 'soft' sponsoring, entrance fee for commercial operators. Advertising finance was made legal during 1991.
8   *Local TV:* Local TV allowed under the same rules as local radio. 70 licences have been awarded to date, mainly to large city cable systems.
Note: More than 100 'pirate' radio stations are also operating in 1991.

NORWAY

1 *Main legal instrument and planned change, if any:* Local Broadcasting Act 1988, Advertising in Broadcasting Act 1990.
2 *Type or name of licensing/regulatory body:* Municipal councils; Local Broadcasting Council (national).
3 *Types of local radio:* Regional broadcasts by NRK (17 regions and a service in Lapland); local radio ('Nærradio') of two types: local organizational radio and local community radio.)
4 *Content regulations:* External regulation by legislation, internal regulation in accordance with ethical rules drawn up by the Association of Local Broadcasters in Norway.
5 *Networking:* Networking of news and advertising on approximately 100 local radio stations ('RadioNettverk').
6 *Connections with press and/or other media:* Press ownership is allowed, but the press was only (very) active in the early phases of local media operations.
7 *Financing:* Advertising mainly, but also radio bingo, etc. and subscriptions/donations.
8 *Local TV:* Local TV under similar rules to local radio. Only a few TV stations operated in 1990, but this will change, as advertising on local TV is allowed from 1991 onwards.

PORTUGAL

1 *Main legal instrument and planned change, if any:* Laws no. 8/88, 87/88, and 338/1988 of 1988.
2 *Type or name of licensing/regulatory body:* Institute of Communications of Portugal rules on technical aspects and issues the radio licences; the Social Communications Agency regulates programming.
3 *Types of local radio:* There are 315 local commercial radio stations and 2 regional commercial radios (North and South).
4 *Content regulations:* Local information and education programmes.
5 *Networking:* Not authorized by law.
6 *Connections with press and/or other media:* Both regional radios are connected with private companies of the communications sector.
7 *Financing:* Advertising mainly, under rules.
8 *Local TV:* There is no local TV.

SPAIN

1 *Main legal instrument and planned change, if any:* Law of Telecommunications 1987; Law on local public radio (municipal radio) 1991.
2 *Type or name of licensing/regulatory body:* National and regional bodies.
3 *Types of local radio:* Public (municipal) radio and private commercial radio.
4 *Content regulations:* There are no regulations.
5 *Networking:* Prohibited for public local radio.
6 *Connections with press and/or other media:* No restrictions on links to other media companies.
7 *Financing:* Advertising in private local radio, advertising and public funds in public local radio.

Spain (continued)

8   *Local TV:* Local TV is not regulated, but there are numerous instances of it.

SWEDEN

1   *Main legal instrument and planned change, if any:* Radio Act of 1966/1986; agreement between the State and Swedish Local Radio Company; Community Radio Act of 1982/6.
2   *Type or name of licensing/regulatory body:* Government licenses public local radio; Community Broadcasting Commission licenses public access radio.
3   *Types of local radio:* Public local radio (Swedish Local Radio Company); community (public access) radio.
4   *Content regulations:* Detailed set of content regulations including references to education, opinion formation, minority needs, and those of the handicapped. Public access by voluntary bodies on community radio.
5   *Networking:* Public local radio is allowed to network; community radio should not but may do so.
6   *Connections with press and/or other media:* Not allowed.
7   *Financing:* Licence fees for public radio – advertising not allowed. Any method of financing access radio is allowed, except advertising or direct sponsorship.
8   *Local TV:* Local TV is permitted on cable systems in accordance with the Cable Law of 1986. Advertising is not allowed. There are only a few cable systems with local programmes.

SWITZERLAND

1   *Main legal instrument and planned change, if any:* Statutory Instrument on Experimental Local Broadcasting of 1982 and amendments to it. A new law on Radio and Television is expected in 1992.
2   *Type or name of licensing/regulatory body:* Federal government.
3   *Types of local radio:* Private commercial local radio and community radio.
4   *Content regulations:* Programming should contribute towards the formation of public opinion and should enhance local culture.
5   *Networking:* In general prohibited, but some exceptions are allowed (e.g. networking of PSB news on local radio).
6   *Connections with press and/or other media:* Extensive links with the press.
7   *Financing:* Advertising and subsidy.
8   *Local TV:* There are 6 long-term trials of local TV and 35 short-term ones.

UNITED KINGDOM

1   *Main legal instrument and planned change, if any:* BBC charter to 1995 and Broadcasting Act of 1990.
2   *Type or name of licensing/regulatory body:* Currently BBC and Radio Authority.
3   *Types of local radio:* 47 BBC local radio stations and 79 independent local radio stations (ILR). (A further 30 ILR stations are planned for 1991 and another 30 ILR stations for 1992.)

United Kingdom (continued)

4 *Content regulations:* Similar content obligations to national PBS – impartiality, balance, etc. Future 'lighter' regulation likely.

5 *Networking:* Some networking of news and some other programmes outside prime time.

6 *Connections with press and/or other media:* Press ownership is limited to a maximum of 20 per cent.

7 *Financing:* Licence fee and advertising; sponsorship now allowed on ILR and INR (Independent National Radio) (planned for the early 1990s). No advertising on BBC.

8 *Local TV:* Little local TV except on cable systems. No special regulation required (responsibility of the Cable Authority).

This appendix was drawn up with the help of information provided by members of the Euromedia Research Group. The information on Portugal was provided by the Institute of Communications, Lisbon.

PART V

CONCLUSION

13

Wake up, Europe!

Karen Siune and Denis McQuail

Changing logics

Throughout this book, in chapter after chapter, we have presented
evidence about the causes, pace and effects of a significant change in
electronic media arrangements in Western Europe. It was very clear
at the start of the 1980s that change was on the way. Looking back
we can record a gradual acceleration of the pace of change until it is
hard to recognize the traditional broadcasting order of Europe,
which once seemed so stable and all-embracing a model and so
resistant to change. Its institutional strength and accepted legitimacy had much to do with the strength of a political and administrative logic which would not countenance a system which would not
be amenable to control and might not respect the delicate balance of
political forces in many European states. In many countries the old
system was usually agreeable to a broad coalition of forces which
included the political right as well as the left, and many cultural as
well as economic interests. For instance, the established national
commercial media were often not very anxious to have new
competitors and not very interested in expanding their activities at
home or abroad.

This somewhat cosy situation was undermined, first of all by
technology. Initially the new distribution technology served as an
instrument for undermining the regulations, as in Italy, or enabled
the various outbreaks of communications piracy. Very soon, pressure to change appeared in a more abstract form – that of the logic of
technology, for instance in the French drive for the 'informatization'
of society. The core element of this new logic was the presumption
that the new electronic media had an almost unlimited capacity to
overcome barriers of space, time and limited resources. If the
technology could enable low-cost two-way interactive communication over large distances and across frontiers, then this was the path

that should be taken. This way of thinking, reinforced by an industrial logic, according to which future national and European economic survival might depend on the maximum development of all high-cost technologies, played an important part in helping to undermine the old order of broadcasting. It found powerful advocates in Britain and Germany, as well as in France.

Both these logics (of technology and industry) were quite compatible with the political/administrative frame of mind and initially they seemed to imply little more than a new kind of *dirigisme* in media policy. This was represented in early British and French plans for promoting cable and videotex infrastructures. Gradually, however, it became clear that the new logics also challenged existing monopoly arrangements and that it would take more than logic, however compelling, to get the new systems off the ground. In other words, it would need money for investment and for consumption. Somewhere along the road in the 1980s, an economic logic took control in the only form that fitted the reality and the spirit of the times – the free market. The interactive triangular relationship between politics, economics and technology is now very clearly being driven by market forces. The brief period when technological logic predominated was important for its undermining effect on the old order, but it is market forces, more than anything else, which now determine what is thought worthwhile to pursue and which set the limits on what is possible in practice.

Internationalization

This shift in the balance of forces has been accompanied by a number of other related changes and it has found a variety of expressions. Amongst the other changes which have occurred, the most important is probably the increased significance, relative to the national or local levels, of the international level of media policy and commercial activity. The older order was not only governed by a political or administrative logic, it was very much a separate preserve of each nation-state. In general, the power of national regulators has been weakened, and transnational forces, in the form of European institutions and international media companies, have increased the scope of their activities and the amount of influence which they have on events. A gap has also opened up between the supranational process and localistic policy-making. It is the latter which nearly always has to give way, when the gap becomes too large.

In this potential clash between supranational forces and 'localistic' policy concerns, it is the smaller states, as we saw (Chapter 9), that are under most pressure and are the first to feel discomfort. Because of their vulnerability to larger and richer neighbours, they are more likely to experience a loss of national and cultural autonomy and they are weaker voices in the struggle to arrive at a European consensus on standards. They have also less to gain economically from the new market-driven logic of media policy, which it is hoped will deliver new opportunities to those countries with a larger home market and media production potential. In general, a rift has opened up between the interests of larger and smaller countries, exposing the potential damage which can be caused by the market and industrial logics given free reign. Within some countries, this subordination is parallelled by a pressure on local and community media to conform to market forces, which usually entails a loss of 'localness' and of autonomy. The widely felt pressures towards 'internationalization' have not yet resulted in a strong European media identity or institutional existence, even when the tendency of European-level policy has been to encourage this internationalizing process.

From politically inspired regulation to liberalizing re-regulation

In general, the two sets of actors which have played the principal role in the process of transnationalization – European policy-makers and multinational media concerns – have been operating according to much the same logic – that of market forces – despite their seemingly different goals and interests. In general, European-level regulation (especially the 'Television without Frontiers' Directive of October 1989) has had a liberalizing impact on national regulation and is designed to create a framework within which 'responsible' and lightly regulated commercial electronic broadcast media can operate more freely. What has often been referred to as 'deregulation' is more correctly a form of re-regulation according to the new logic which has been endorsed by most national governments as well as by the agencies of Europe. There are many new detailed rules also for the component elements of the media system in each country. The evidence of Chapter 12 on the re-writing of laws for local media provides an illustration of recent tendencies. In general, media laws have become more complex and in some respects more specific. As a result, there is likely to be a much greater role for lawyers and the courts in the future, partly as a result of the many new property rights and forms of ownership and control which have supplemented or replaced the older monopolistic structures.

The main issues of the moment still concern the balance between the public and the private sector and the relative importance of the market versus regulatory bodies in shaping the new order. Tied in with both is the question of what conditions can be imposed by regulators on the private sector and in what form. Sometimes these conditions are found in general legal requirements concerning standards of content and amount and kind of advertising; sometimes they are conditions built into contracts given to private franchise holders operating cable or satellite channels. We are still at an early stage in the process of empowering the expanded private electronic media sector, but there is cause for doubt (from experience elsewhere) about the effectiveness of regulation of private media on matters of social and cultural policy.

New commercialization

The concept of 'commercialization' refers to the process which is widely under way in Europe, having by now largely bypassed what seemed the firm defences of the public sector monopoly which held out longest in the far north of Europe. However, it is a vague term and has diverse manifestations. It can refer to 'privatization' or 'denationalization', as when public assets are sold into private hands (for instance the sale of TF1 in France to private owners); general relaxation of rules and regulations on private media operators; obliging public broadcasters to operate more efficiently and engage in commercial activities; changing the balance of media income from consumer payments or licence revenue towards advertising or sponsorship receipts; changes in media content from the more unprofitable cultural or educational content to more popular entertainment content. Evidence for all of these trends can be found in different places in this book and commercialization in any or all of these forms is an inevitable consequence of the market logic which has come to predominate.

Commercialization is not only diverse in its forms but it carries such a heavy normative weight that it is difficult to examine it objectively. For some actors in the media policy debate it stands for freedom of action and a guarantee of freedom of expression. For others it entails vulgarization and a dilution of traditional cultural values. It also implies an advantage for the political forces of the right, who are more likely to benefit from private, capitalist, forms of ownership and whose interests have usually been best served, according to most theorists, by commercial media. Central to the process of commercialization is a struggle for limited resources – in our case the resources of access to channels and the income from consumers and advertisers. This most visible form of struggle in national and local media markets is, however, probably less significant than the international struggle between multinational media firms and between nations or economic regions for future hardware and software markets, especially in the not so distant era of DBS and HDTV. Success or failure in these markets will have a larger impact than the struggles we have seen up to now.

The future for public broadcasting

At the present time, the issues named above and the theme of commercialization are still most clearly recognized in terms of a widely expressed policy question: what to do with public broadcasting and what future does it have? In the brave new world of market forces and of 'television without frontiers', public broadcasting of the traditional kind – national, non-commercial and monopolistic – does not seem clearly justified and is subject to major assaults in some countries and irritating sniping in others, from new as well as old enemies. It has been attacked on grounds of loss of legitimacy (under conditions of channel abundance), but most of all because it seems to stand in the way of further development of the many new technological, industrial and economic possibilities. These matters have been discussed in some detail above. There is no doubt that in Western Europe as a whole, the public sector of radio and television has declined markedly in relative terms during the 1980s and that the surrender of the public monopoly principle has opened the way for more sweeping changes in the future.

Some facts about the condition of public broadcasting are clear enough. One is that it has often proved surprisingly resilient in the face both of its apparently weakened logic and the increased competition which it has faced in many countries. Secondly, this resilience stems in part from the support of political forces which have not simply withered away under the glare of market logic and in part from skilful tactics employed by public broadcasters themselves to secure their own survival. With the considerable resources still left to them in many countries many public broadcasting organizations have sought to balance their cultural and social obligations with a determined effort to please their audiences. To some extent, they have re-defined their goals in order to give higher priority to pleasing the audience. One result has been a measure of success in retaining audience share and also popular support for continuing the status quo. Many critics have claimed that the resulting cultural 'dilution' and 'levelling down' have removed the rationale for having a public sector at all.

A third point which is reasonably clear is that there is little uniformity in the position of public broadcasting across the countries discussed. Each national case tends to reflect the relative strength of political forces and other vested interests. In Germany and Britain, the public sector has still suffered little in absolute terms and the same is true in several of the smaller, richer countries of Europe which have chosen to protect their cultural and political status quo. Elsewhere, the sector has been much weakened by commercial competition (as in France, Belgium, the Netherlands and Greece). This variability can be taken as a reminder that the politics of the media live on, despite the tendency of some to equate commercialization with depoliticization. Certainly resistance to commercialization is very much a political project, even if the process itself is usually only partly or indirectly politically motivated (as it has been in Britain and Germany, but much less so in Spain, France, Italy, the Netherlands and Scandinavia generally, where economic motives have been dominant).

An excessively narrow focus on the progress of commercialization and on the survival or adaptation of public service broadcasting may obscure the fact that larger themes are also at issue. Amongst these are the question of the vitality of national and regional cultures and of cultural identities in the wider European market, and also the question of national autonomy itself. These matters are often linked with the fate of public broadcasting, which has traditionally been allocated a cultural task in these respects. Nevertheless, these issues will remain on the agenda of media policy, whatever kind of new media regimes are introduced.

An additional matter easily lost sight of concerns one of the main original purposes of public broadcasting. The latter was not only meant to serve the ends of political control and technical efficiency. It was also intended to promote social equality, by ensuring universal provision and fairness of access to the new channels. Benefits as receivers and senders of information and culture should be widely and fairly distributed. It seems now to be widely assumed that liberalization, by promoting more choices in the media market place, has removed the need to have a strong policy directed at ensuring equality of access and a fair diversity of political and cultural content. We may, perhaps, conclude from the widespread acquiescence by political parties in the changes under way that negative effects for social equality have not yet been experienced by politicians at least.

The initial experience of change, for those audiences which have so far been affected, has probably also seemed quite positive, whatever the pessimists have argued. Very little of the old order provision has actually disappeared or changed for the worse. It has often been supplemented by more choice and, at worst, relegated to less favourable transmission hours. So far there has been little tangible loss to the consumer and there has been a gain in choice. Even so, the broader question of the extent and nature of the public interest in the means of public communication remains for consideration when the pattern which results from current developments becomes more clearly discernible. There is no reason for the interim stage of relative diversity to last indefinitely.

An example of the downgrading of public interest concerns in the old sense of the term can be found in relation to local media developments, which were charted in Chapters 11 and 12 of this book. It is hard to resist the conclusion that the hopes of the 1960s and 1970s for more democratic and participant media which would serve local communities have largely turned out to be dreams, punctured by commercial reality. The concepts seem to live on in some utopian clauses of legal documents, while the reality is very different. The mistake, if there was one, may have been to place too much faith in technology, whose advocates promoted the potential of local interactive cable as the basis for a vital urban community life, driven by shared local interests. There was also too much optimism about the social equality which would come with more prosperity. More and more it seems as if cable systems, linked to satellites and exploited commercially, are more likely to provide an even more effective instrument for centralizing tendencies, which also internationalize and divert from local culture and social needs. In general, the new media developments, highly responsive to the varying spending power of different groups of potential consumers, are likely to promote inequality rather than equality in local community life.

Charting the future

The current situation is still characterized by uncertainty, fragmentation and inconsistency of trends. This is hardly surprising in a time of experimentation with new technologies and new regulatory arrangements, not to mention the stop–go situations and divisions about more fundamental political and economic changes in Europe, East as well as West. It is time for Europe to wake up and realize what is happening. Nothing is completed, little can be planned, nothing is very certain. This applies to the wider processes of

European development as well as to media institutions, technology and markets. Despite the heralded convergence of media modes (Pool 1984) and the planned convergence of national media institutions into a common European model, neither has proceeded very far. The convergence of modes, which could theoretically lead to a single, simple and permissive regulatory regime for all media, has so far found little concrete expression on any scale. The unification of Europe, while continuing, is proceeding at a slow pace, and the media, because of their close ties to cultural, political and market differences, may be amongst the last institutions to be unified, other than within very sketchy parameters.

The media sector is still made up of a very wide array of different kinds of technology of delivery and of organizational and legal arrangements, and is becoming more rather than less fragmented. This state of affairs is a logical outcome of allowing market forces more freedom to operate. The technological form of delivery is only one factor in defining media markets, and it is not their sole main determinant. Nor are political factors, which have a declining impact on markets. European politicians have to be aware of the changing structures and decide whether or not they want to influence the developments. In the present climate, regulations are more likely to follow markets than to shape them, even if, in their liberalizing form, they may open new market opportunities.

This book has been a work of description and analysis, attempting to interpret trends and to generalize from the experience of different countries which are being subjected to much the same external political and economic forces. It is inevitably historical rather than predictive, although it gives some basis for short-term predictions. As usual, there is a high probability that tomorrow will be something like today and on this assumption we can expect a continuation of several of the main tendencies which have been described. Several of the more significant market opportunities in television and radio are still quite new or only just in prospect, with much room for undisturbed evolution in competition with the declining public sector.

This would seem to apply to: the new private television channels in Spain; multiply distributed private television in the enlarged Germany; the new terrestrial and satellite/cable developments in the UK; the commercial opportunities opening up in Scandinavia and the Benelux countries. The EC Directive is also relatively new and awaiting full implementation. In short, the scenario sketched in this book is likely to form the backdrop for enactment during the next five years or so, leaving aside the possibility of major social or political upheavals in Europe.

Any more detailed prediction of the future is impossible. On the other hand, we can remind readers that the logic of technology, which has played such an important role as a catalyst of change, though it may have been subordinated to the logic of the market for the time being, has not disappeared. The question of how the abundance of the new electronic media would be delivered, which seemed so important in the early 1980s, with predictions of a transnational/interactive communication revolution, has gradually moved out of focus. At least, it does not seem theoretically so interesting, although it still matters to investors in cable or satellite systems. The question has, in the event, been answered in a piecemeal and pragmatic fashion, according to local factors of demand and pricing.

For various not very mysterious reasons, consumer demand for new cable and satellite services has been modest and the two alternative modes have not really competed with each other in the same market place (though Britain will be the first case). As a result, we still do not know very much about the relative advantages and future potential of cable and satellite. Their impact so far, especially that of satellite, has been undramatic. It is at least probable that this question remains a key item on the agenda of future media politics, after the present round of changes has taken its full effect. In particular, we can expect renewed media policy debate and market adjustments in the later 1990s, when satellite distribution and high definition television will again be the centre of attention for European business and politicians.

Endnote: the wider Europe and the public interest

The wider context may then be different, depending on how the trend to European unification proceeds and also on how relations with neighbouring Eastern Europe develop. These countries already look west, not only for investment, aid and increased contacts, but probably also for some institutional models for the reform of their own media systems, in which major changes are bound to occur. The spectacle offered by much of Western Europe, as described in this book, is likely to be more confusing than helpful and, perhaps, not very encouraging to reformers. They will see market forces given more freedom and social purpose and cultural goals relegated to the background. Similar tendencies are occurring in Eastern Europe, although for quite different reasons. It is possible that the wrong lessons, or maybe no lessons at all, will be learnt.

The term 'public interest' has been used above to refer to the wider expectations, of national societies and local communities, of their means of public communication, especially in the service of participatory democracy. Often the term 'public interest' refers to benefits which cannot be identified with, or delivered by, market forces. Although ideas concerning the nature of public interest and how it should be realized belong to the political logic, which has been subordinated in recent years, the pursuit and defence of the public interest is no less relevant or necessary. As Melody (1990) argues in respect of telecommunications, the concept of public interest, with its key components of delivering efficiency and equality, needs to be re-defined and not simply abandoned as a result of technological change. The familiar ways of safeguarding the public interest in telecommunications, especially by way of public monopoly control, may no longer be appropriate. This also applies to television and radio, where we do not need to equate the idea of public interest with public service broadcasting or with public monopoly. We did not set out specifically to address the question of the public interest in this book but we think that our research can help inform debate on a topic which still lies at the core of media policy analysis.

References

Melody, W.H. (1990) 'Communication Policy in the Global Information Economy: Whither the Public Interest?' in M. Ferguson (ed.), *Public Communication: The New Imperatives. Future Directions for Media Research*. London: Sage.

Pool, I. de S. (1984) *Technologies of Freedom*. Harvard, Mass.: Belknapp Press.

Index